Degree Course Descriptions

edited by
John Mainstone and Ken Reynolds

Degree Course Descriptions

This 4th edition published in 2010 by Cambridge Occupational Analysts Ltd
Sparham, Norwich, NR9 5PR

Editorial and Publishing Team

Editors John Mainstone and Ken Reynolds
Design and typesetting Simon Foster and Paul Rankin

British Library Cataloguing in Publication Data
A catalogue record for this book is available from the British Library.

ISBN 978-1-906711-06-1

Typeset by Cambridge Occupational Analysts Ltd, Sparham, Norwich NR9 5PR
Printed and bound in Great Britain by Clays Ltd, Bungay, Suffolk NR35 1ED

Contents

Introduction

The illustrious author of one of the Degree Course Descriptions in this book offers the following advice to aspiring students of his subject:

Explore, enquire, experiment and enjoy!

These words apply just as much to every other subject covered. How do you find the right course in higher education? How do you know where to study? There is no single truth; no simple answer. There are over 50,000 potential courses in more than 300 universities and colleges. It is down to you to find the most suitable course to meet your personal needs.

The Degree Course Descriptions offered should prove a valuable resource as you research your higher education goals. The articles are written in most cases by leading university professors and lecturers, and have been selected to cover the major degree course fields. They are regularly updated and checked for accuracy. The intention is to give a broad overview of each subject area rather than to promote courses at any particular institution.

In addition to the Degree Course Descriptions, we offer a series of general articles on higher education and a selection of pieces covering specific issues:

General articles

- Applying online
- Budgeting
- Choosing a course
- Self-Select

Specific issues

- Applying for Art and Design Courses
- Gap Year considerations
- Medicine dissected
- Undergraduate study in the United States

Applying online

Original article by Jasper Selwyn, formerly Head of Careers, Marlborough College

Introduction

Applying for admission to higher education is very much an online process nowadays. The essential starting point for almost all provision in the United Kingdom is the Universities and Colleges Admissions Service (UCAS) website at: *www.ucas.com*

The equivalent for students in the Republic of Ireland is the Central Applications Office (CAO) website at: *www.cao.ie*

Either website will give you several options. From the UCAS home page, for example, clicking on 'Students' at the top of the page will open up several pages of detailed information on how to research appropriate courses and course providers, how to complete your application and how to submit it at the right time. You will almost certainly want to spend a lot of time in the 'Course Search' section, where you can select subjects from an alphabetical list and obtain details of all higher education institutions (HEIs) offering relevant courses. Clicking on the course title leads to a summary of Entry Requirements, and on to an Entry Profile giving more details about what the course requires. You can link directly to the HEI website from this screen.

HEI websites are all organised differently but generally include:

- News about the institution
- Descriptions of facilities
- Lists of courses, which may get as detailed as individual lecture notes if you go on digging
- Names of lecturers, with email addresses. Click on one and you can send an email straight away
- Information about accommodation, the surrounding area and so on

Having researched all the relevant information, you can apply online and subsequently track the progress of your application.

Working online allows you to proceed at your own pace, gradually making sense of a vast amount of information and extracting just what you need to meet your own requirements. The UCAS website alone has details of over 50,000 courses at 325 HEIs. By 30 June 2010, UCAS had processed for 2010 entry some 2,517,100 choices from 660,953 candidates. Demand for undergraduate places is growing every year, making it more important than ever that you present yourself as a strong, well-informed applicant.

Finding a focus

If you are struggling to decide which course and institution might suit you, you could start by making use of *Centigrade Online*.

Centigrade Online analyses your interests, study subjects and qualifications before inviting you to explore up to eight strongly matched course areas. Once you have answered the questionnaire, publishers COA will send you a detailed bound report with your best-matched selections. Centigrade costs £20 in the UK or £23 overseas for a full-colour printed personal report of approximately 48 pages.

Further information

Woody's Webwatch - an independent guide to essential websites for HE entry
www.woodyswebwatch.com
Centigrade Online
www.centigradeonline.co.uk
Unistats - an official site to help you compare subjects at different HEIs in the UK
www.unistats.com
Yougofurther - networking site where you can chat with other candidates
https://yougo.co.uk

Budgeting

How much will it cost you to be a student in higher education? The answer depends to a large extent on what you study, where you live and how extravagant a lifestyle you aspire to.

There are two major financial elements to consider when planning your studies in the UK: course tuition fees and living costs. Tuition fees can be extremely complex to calculate, depending on whether you have 'home' or 'overseas' status, where you live in the United Kingdom and where you intend to study. For example, an English student starting at an English university in 2010 will normally have to pay tuition fees of £3290 per year. A Scottish student starting a similar course in Scotland will pay nothing, while an overseas student in England will usually have to pay the full economic rate. You may be able to reduce the impact of tuition fees by obtaining a grant, scholarship or bursary. Most higher education institutions (HEIs) provide details of possible financial support via each course entry profile on the UCAS website. Failing any other form of support, you may be able to secure a loan to cover your tuition fees for the duration of your course.

As for living costs, we identify the key components and illustrate how you can plan to manage your finances when living as a student.

Accommodation

Unless you are lucky enough to be offered free accommodation at home, or with friends or relations, you will find that getting a roof over your head will make the greatest demands on your non-fee finances, usually taking away at least half and sometimes as much as three-quarters of your budget.

It is essential to find a suitable place to live, especially during the first twelve months. Everything else revolves around your feeling secure and comfortable- your attitude to student life, your ability to focus on studying successfully, your opportunities to make new friendships and so on. Will you, for example, be able to walk to your study centre or will you have to make a long and possibly expensive journey every day? Do you want to be surrounded by other students or do you crave peace and quiet?

Before you accept a place, contact the accommodation office at your chosen university or college to check out the service on offer. Is there official accommodation in a hall of residence? Will you get a priority place if you need to travel a long way to start your course? Are meals provided? Would you be expected to share a room? Can you inspect the accommodation before you sign any agreement? Does the accommodation office have a list of approved premises in the private sector?

Here are some key points to consider:

- *Cost*. Ask especially how many weeks you have to pay for. Is it term-time only (in which case you would have to go home or find somewhere else to live during the vacations) or do you have to take out a full ten- or twelve-month rental agreement?

- *Catering*. How many meals are supplied a day, if any? Are meals provided at weekends or Monday to Friday only? Do you have access to a kitchen to prepare your own meals?

- *Space*. How big are the rooms? Do you have to share? Is there an en-suite bathroom?

- *Transport and travel*. Will you be on-campus or many miles away? What sort of transport is available and how much does it cost?

- *Local services.* Would you have easy access to a bank, shops and leisure facilities?

- *Insurance.* Is there a comprehensive policy covering all students in a hall of residence? How secure are the doors and windows? Is crime a serious problem?

It goes without saying, of course, that London is far more expensive than anywhere else in the UK! Other pricey areas include south east England, Oxford and Cambridge. The cheapest part of the country for renting student accommodation is generally the north of England. A 2010 study by the website www.accommodationforstudents.com reports average student rent of £65.30 per week, ranging from £41.47 per week in Middlesbrough to £102.80 in London.

Food
Unless it's already included in your accommodation costs, food will be your second major expense. Unlike property rents, the cost of food is fairly similar all over the UK. London students tend, however, to spend more on food, perhaps because there are so many tempting restaurants and other places to eat!

Expect to spend around £50 each week making sure that you are reasonably well fed.

Going out
You may intend to devote all of your time to your studies but most students feel that socialising is an important part of their life at university or college. This is a serious lifestyle decision for each individual and it could cost you anything from nothing to over £100 per week, depending on how gregarious you are, whether you have a taste for expensive concerts or theatres and how determined you are generally to have a good time.

Books, photocopying and stationery
Books can be exceptionally expensive but you don't necessarily have to buy a new copy of every book mentioned by your tutors. Check to see how well stocked the library is in your subject area and find out whether there is a good second-hand bookshop. You will almost certainly have to photocopy some material and you will have to make sure that you have adequate supplies of paper.

You may need to allow around £6 a week to cover these items.

Computer and other equipment
You may already own a computer and decide to bring it with you. If not, you could easily spend £300 to £400 on a new machine! Do you really need it or does your university or college offer 24-hour IT facilities?

You may be required to purchase additional materials and equipment for some courses, especially in areas such as science and design.

Telephone
It seems that no student can live in the 21st century without a mobile phone! How much it costs depends entirely on how long you chat, but a typical student spends around £12 a week on phone bills. (That's about twice as much as they spend on books!)

Clothing
Even if you don't rush out every week to buy the latest fashions, you will need to allow a certain amount of money for new clothes. The average is around £15 per week but some students spend a great deal more.

Basics

You'll need to put some cash aside to wash your clothes and to keep yourself clean. You'll also have to pay for electricity and gas unless you are paying a fully inclusive charge in a hall of residence.

Travel

You may live on campus and walk everywhere but you could find yourself spending a small fortune if, say, you are living in a London suburb and have to commute every day to lectures in the centre of town.

It is generally not a good idea to drive your own car and we make no allowance for this in our calculations.

Plan your own budget!

Look at the figures in our rather modest student budget and then make your own projections about what it might cost you to be a student at your chosen university or college. We have left two columns blank for you to work out your own weekly and yearly expenses. Our calculations assume that you will need your accommodation for the full 52 weeks of the year but you may stay for, say, nine months or less and could make savings accordingly. You may want to repeat the exercise several times in order to get an idea of the real difference in costs between, say, London, Sunderland and Plymouth.

Item	Cost per week	Cost per year	Your weekly estimate	Your yearly estimate
Rent	£65	£3,380		
Food	£50	£2,600		
Electricity /Gas	£5	£260		
Clothes	£15	£780		
Telephone	£12	£624		
Basics - laundry and toiletries	£6	£312		
Travel	£5	£260		
Going out	£8	£416		
Books, equipment etc	£6	£312		
Total	**£172**	**£8,944**		

Remember that our figures don't allow for other expenditure such as insurance, TV licence, buying presents for friends and family, treating yourself to an occasional CD, DVD or other luxury or taking a weekend or more away from your studies from time to time.

Put everything together and you'll quickly see why you need to be budgeting for non-fee expenses of around £10,000 a year outside London and some £12,000 to £15,000 in London. Please let us know if your own calculations are very different from ours.

You can try to offset some of the expense by getting a job, working for up to 20 hours a week during term time and full-time during the vacations. Your university or college should be able to give you further information on employment options in the area. Depending on how many hours you work in total and how well you are paid, you may be able to cover a large amount of the living costs outlined in this article. The present recession will greatly reduce job vacancies, however.

Maintenance loans may be available to cover most of your living costs. These will have to be repaid after leaving your HEI once you start earning over £15,000 a year.

Be prepared!

The key message is to plan your finances carefully in advance. If you have thought about your budget and worked out how to cover the inevitable expense of eating and sleeping, you can focus on your studies without fretting too much about money.

Further information

The Daily Telegraph Guide to Student Money 2011 (formerly called Students' Money Matters): How to Manage Your Funds, Fees and Finances at University and College - Gwenda Thomas, Trotman, 2010

Financial Support for Higher Education Students
- downloadable from the website at: **www.direct.gov.uk/studentfinance**

Uniaid Student Calculator
- log on to: **www.studentcalculator.org.uk**

Explore the websites at:

www.student-support-saas.gov.uk (Scotland)

www.studentfinancewales.co.uk (Wales)

www.studentfinanceni.co.uk (Northern Ireland)

www.studentfinance.ie (Eire)

www.direct.gov.uk/studentfinance (Other EU countries)

www.ukcisa.org.uk (Non-EU international students)

Choosing a Higher Education Course in the UK

Original article by Jasper Selwyn, formerly Head of Careers, Marlborough College

Choosing a Higher Education Course:

You face a bewildering range of possibilities: over 50,000 different degree course options, covering 750 different subjects, at over 300 institutions in the UCAS scheme; courses with the same title can approach the subject in widely different ways; and you can only pick five to put on your form. You need to end up doing a course that motivates you and is suitable for your future career, at a place where you enjoy living. The entry requirements need to be within your reach. If you use an interests and ability questionnaire such as *Centigrade*, it will start the task for you by listing a range of different subject titles within some general areas which seem to match your interests, and identifying some specific courses. But you have to choose within that list, and you may want to move outside it. So how do you go about making your choice?

Three Ways to Choose Your Subject:

- **Forward from your school or college subjects:** If there is a subject you are enjoying and doing well at, you may wish to continue with it in Higher Education. But remember that the style of the course may be very different: in Modern Languages, for example, there could be more emphasis on studying literature. You may also be able to specialise in one area of a subject, such as Contemporary Literature, Economic History or Cell Biology.

- **Backwards from a career goal:** For the majority of careers, any Higher Education course is appropriate, and you are best advised to study something which will really interest you, so that you get a good qualification. For some, such as Law and Business, you can take a professional course at postgraduate level if you have not done the relevant first degree. You do not need any specific subject to become an accountant, a journalist or a marketing manager. Medicine and related careers, engineering, architecture, surveying, scientific research and translating are, however, examples of areas which do usually require a particular Higher Education course.

- **Leaping into the Unknown:** There are a vast number of subjects you can study in Higher Education which are not available at your school or college. If you have done *Centigrade* it may have come up with some, and it would be a pity to reject them just because you have not come across them before. Make sure that you find out as much as you can about them - sometimes what they actually involve turns out to be different from what you had assumed. Read the *Degree Course Descriptions* and do some background reading.

Types of Course:

- **Single Subject:** You may want to concentrate on the subject of your dreams, but often you will have the opportunity to do modules in other subjects as well, maybe unrelated to your main choice. Normally you will be expected to follow a broad course in the first year, but after that you will be allowed progressively to specialise. In the final year you are likely to complete a project on an area of your own choice.

- **Joint:** Many degree courses allow you to study two subjects. You may do both equally (X **and** Y), or you may spend more time on one of them (X **with** Y). You may be able to pick up a few modules in other subjects as well. The two main subjects may be formally linked (eg Business Studies with a Language) or they may be taught quite independently. A joint degree has the same number of modules in it as a single-subject one, so should not involve more hours, but having to switch continually between the disciplines may be intellectually challenging. You will not be able to explore a subject in as much depth if you are doing it as part of a joint course.

- **Combined:** There are some courses available which give great flexibility, allowing you to start with up to four subjects, and then discard some, and maybe take up new ones, as you move on. This is excellent if you have a wide range of interests, or feel you can't decide about a subject until you have tried it out. A combined course may also allow you to approach a particular theme from the viewpoints of different disciplines: for example Geography, Anthropology and Economics would all support an interest in International Development.

- **Sandwich:** Some people like to see how what they are learning relates to a career area, and employers value people with relevant work experience. A sandwich course builds in work placements alongside your study, so it normally lasts an extra year. A *thick* sandwich involves a full year of work, usually after the second year of study. A *thin* sandwich gives you several shorter periods of work (typically, three or four months each). Often your course tutors help you find a work placement, and almost always you are visited while working, and asked to write a report. You may well do a project in your final year based on a problem you have encountered in your work place. If you solve it, and save the company some money, obviously your prospects for a longer-term job after you graduate will be good!

- **Study Abroad:** The European Union operates a programme called Erasmus to encourage students to spend time in other European countries. Many courses (but not all) are linked to this programme, so that you can spend between four months and a year studying abroad. What you do counts toward your degree, you are given financial help if the cost of living in the other country is higher, and you will have tuition in the foreign language before you go. Some universities also have links with America, particularly for Engineering and Business courses, and of course American Studies. Many sandwich courses allow the option of a work placement abroad.

- **HND and Foundation Degree:** These courses are normally a year shorter than an honours degree, and the entrance requirements are lower. Students who do well can transfer easily onto a degree programme, and there are even some special one-year conversion programmes.

Choosing a Place:

It is important to start by deciding *what* you want to study, and with what kind of course structure. But you may find that the kind of course you want is available at a number of institutions, so you have to think about *where* to go. If you are going to spend three or four years of your life somewhere, it is important that you should enjoy being there.

- **Near or Far from Home?** For financial reasons you may need to live at home while you are studying, or you may want to be near enough to go home at weekends (although in practice university often takes over your social life, and you go home less and less often). You may want to break your ties with home completely, or just experience living in a different part of the country.

- **"Established" or Modern?** Some people like the idea of traditions and old buildings. But even at the oldest universities traditions may be dying out, and there are plenty of modern buildings. At a newer institution there may be more scope for starting new activities yourself.

- **Campus or Spread Out?** Most universities and colleges are on a self-contained campus, but a few (eg Bristol, Edinburgh) are spread over a wider area. Many have several separate campuses. Accommodation may be on the same campus as the teaching facilities, or it may be some distance away. You may appreciate the convenience of a self-contained campus, or you may find it claustrophobic.

- **City Centre or Semi-Rural?** If you are in the middle of a big city, then shops and entertainment are close by, but you have to put up with traffic and there may be security risks. Out-of-town campuses are peaceful and safe, and often students are more active at creating their own entertainment, but it is harder to escape and the architecture may get on your nerves.

- **A "Good" University:** A lot is said about the reputations of different institutions. League tables are published, sometimes based on rather doubtful criteria of excellence. Some employers express preferences, often favouring the university they went to themselves and others they have heard of. It is certainly true that standards vary from one place to another, and that some institutions develop a particular ethos (good or bad). But within the same institution there can be big differences between departments. It is important to visit the places which interest you most, and decide for yourself whether you like the department which is going to teach you. Ask about employment records, and talk to current students. Don't assume that higher A-level grade requirements mean a better course: they usually mean it is more popular, but that can be for a variety of reasons. Above all, remember that there is no such thing as a good course or a bad course, but only one which is good or bad for *you*.

Use a calendar of Open Days to plan visits to the places which interest you most. Refer to the UCAS Open Days booklet and take advantage of the Taster Course opportunities, which allow you to spend several days living the life of an undergraduate.

Self Select

One of the key features of higher education in the UK is freedom of choice. You are free to decide what you want to study and where you would like to pursue your studies.

The system works very well for most people but it can sometimes be difficult to know where to start. The choice is simply so great that narrowing things down to one course in one place appears overwhelming.

Given that there is so much emphasis on individual choice and decision-making, we suggest the term 'Self-select' as a handy way of remembering ten key factors in the process of researching ideas and information to help you find your way through the fantastically rich maze of opportunities in our higher education system.

We'll run through the headings briefly at first before taking each in turn to explore in more detail exactly what we mean.

- Subject
- Employment prospects
- Location
- Finance

- Status
- Entry requirements
- Living arrangements
- Entertainment
- Community
- Time

Subject

We start with this because we feel that it really must be the starting point for most people. Once you have decided on this top priority, other things begin to fall into place behind it.

Of course, it's easy for us simply to say 'choose your subject' but the reality is much tougher for you. With over 50,000 different programmes of study on offer at 325 institutions, you need to get down quickly to some hard thinking!

Here are some of the questions you should be asking yourself, together with our comments on the issues they raise:

Do I want to study a single subject or do I want to combine two or more subjects for my degree studies? If you are unsure, look for universities that offer a broad-based first year, allowing you to keep your options open while you find out what degree-level work is all about.

Do I want to continue with a subject I know from my school or college experience - English, Chemistry or French for example - or do I want to start something new at university - such as Medicine or European Law? An advantage of sticking with something you know is that you will already have a 'feel' for the subject and the confidence that comes from already having done well in it in recent exams. On the other hand, you may decide that you have gone far enough with that subject and are eager to seek stimulation in something entirely different.

Do I want to study a subject for its own sake - History, for example - because I like it or am I considering higher education purely as a route to obtaining a specific professional qualification? This is clearly related to the previous question and could be critical in helping you refine your choices. There is a world of difference between an academic degree in Biology and a vocational qualification in, say, Physiotherapy - even though the entry requirements may look broadly similar. The Physiotherapy course no doubt has a very focused employment record but this is only relevant if you are sure that you want to work as a physiotherapist!

Don't assume, by the way, that subjects with similar titles have the same content or are taught in the same way at different institutions. There are often considerable variations and it is up to you to find out what they are.

Employment prospects

You'll be investing a lot of time and money in your higher education and you need to be sure why you are considering it. If your top priority is to qualify for a graduate job, make certain that the course you choose has a good employment record. Some courses are 100 per cent vocational, which is perfect if you are similarly 100 per cent committed to the relevant career path - Dentistry if you want to practise as a dentist, Veterinary Science if you aspire to become a vet - but of limited value if you are not. Some courses appear to offer virtually nothing in terms of related graduate employment but could give you the opportunity to delve deeply into a subject - Philosophy perhaps or Anthropology - that seriously engages your intellect.

Always ask for details of the destinations of previous graduates for any course you are considering. At the same time, you can find out if any periods of work experience are included as part of the course.

There is particular emphasis in the UK now on teaching employability skills - communication, presentation, team work, problem solving and information technology - as part of any undergraduate course and you should, once again, enquire about how these skills are delivered on the courses you are considering.

Motivation is a key element here. By all means, if you really know what you want, go for the course that will get you a professional qualification in the shortest possible time. But don't make the mistake of forcing yourself to endure the drudgery of a subject you dislike simply because you hope it will be good for you at some later stage in your life!

Location

Many students are drawn to the obvious appeal of London but you should be warned that London and the south east of England can be exceptionally expensive and suitable accommodation may be difficult to find.

It is worth taking some time to explore the geography of the entire United Kingdom and to experience the joy of discovering that there really is life outside London (although many native Londoners do not appear to be aware of this!).

You can decide whether to base yourself in a big city centre, in a quiet country setting or beside the sea. You may have particular reasons for choosing an industrial, cultural, agricultural or commercial environment.

If you follow our advice of selecting a subject first, then location may be determined by the number of institutions offering relevant courses. English, for example, can be studied almost anywhere but a specialised course in, say, Meteorology, African Studies or Naval Architecture would immediately restrict your options in terms of location.

Finance

How much will your studies cost and how are you going to pay? You need to establish the total cost of tuition fees and your own living expenses. You might also want to find out if there are ways of meeting some of the costs through grants and bursaries or by working part-time while you are a student.

You then need to add the cost of accommodation, food, travel and whatever luxuries you permit yourself. It is hard to generalise about personal living costs because some people have more expensive tastes than others but it would be difficult to survive as a student anywhere in the UK for less than £10,000 a year...and you may need considerably more than that. You should add another £5-6,000 a year if you are heading for London. These figures are based on what you might need for roughly nine months rather than a full calendar year.

It is absolutely essential that you calculate - long before you even think of applying - the total financial implications of your higher education needs. It is equally essential to be clear about how you plan to meet the cost.

Status

All degree-awarding institutions in the UK must meet stringent quality criteria but it is evident that some universities are much more prestigious than others.

If you are an ambitious high achiever and set your sights on the best of everything, you will doubtless want to seek out the most highly rated places in the land. There are various league tables, both official and unofficial, ranking universities by such criteria as research, teaching quality and employment record, and they mostly feature similar groupings of institutions near the top.

Oxford, Cambridge, Imperial, London School of Economics, University College London, Durham, Edinburgh, Glasgow, St Andrews, Bath, Bristol, Nottingham, Warwick and York, for example, would be part of almost any top twenty UK universities.

It goes without saying, of course, that these are among the most difficult places to get into and you will need impressive qualifications to gain a place.

If, on the other hand, your achievements to date are more modest, you can still gain a very valuable university education but you would be well advised to avoid the most prestigious institutions and start your search rather lower in the league tables.

You may find, in any case, that Status is a less important factor than Subject and Location as described earlier in this article.

Entry requirements

You will often find the entry standard expressed in terms of UCAS tariff points based on grades achieved in GCE Advanced level (A level), Scottish Higher/Advanced Higher, International Baccalaureate, Irish Leaving Certificate or other equivalent examinations.

Each A grade at A level, for example, is worth 120 UCAS points (140 points for A*) and you will find that the standard Cambridge offer for 2011 entry, to quote one of the most prestigious examples, is A*AA or 380 points. By contrast, each E grade is worth only 40 points.

The UCAS tariff is currently under review but there will be no changes to the existing system before the 2012 entry cycle at the earliest.

The number of points needed beyond the elite institutions usually goes down roughly in line with the university's perceived status! This means that, as stated above under Status, you need to match your examination performance to date with the published entry standard of the institutions you are considering.

If you have pursued a pre-university course other than A level, Higher/Advanced Higher or equivalent, you can get detailed advice from the admissions office of your preferred university regarding the acceptability of your qualifications.

If your first language is not English, you may also have to take a test to demonstrate that you have sufficient language proficiency to complete a degree level course. Alternatively, you may take an English course before starting your degree.

Living arrangements

This is another issue that can vary according to your own personal circumstances.

The cheapest deal is almost always to stay with family or friends during your studies but this is rarely possible and may not be desirable because of the ways in which it could restrict your social life.

Finding the right place to live is almost as important as choosing the right course. If you get it wrong, it can have a seriously detrimental effect not only on your studies but also on your attitude to student life generally, making new friendships and even having the motivation to continue.

Evenings and weekends, for example, can be long and lonely if you're cut off from friends and fellow students.

Your chosen universities or colleges should each have an accommodation office to help with your living arrangements. Use their services to the full, asking especially about such things as:

- **Cost** - not just the weekly rent but whether you have to pay for 52 weeks a year or just the number of weeks per term

- **Number of rooms** - whether you have your own room or have to share with somebody else

- **Food** - does the rent include all meals (full board), some meals (half board) or no meals?

- **Facilities** - is there an en-suite bathroom, a fully-equipped kitchen, a television and so on? Is the cost of heating and electricity included in the rent?

- **Location** - is the accommodation within walking distance of your study centre or will you need to travel by bus or train? If so, how long does it take and how much does it cost?

- **Shops** - are there enough in the immediate area to meet your needs?

Entertainment

It is important to establish the right life-work balance to suit your lifestyle and perhaps your cultural or religious expectations.

Whatever your personal priorities might be, most people agree that too much work can be just as bad for you as a surfeit of late-night parties. You may be shocked or delighted to discover just how much of student life revolves around drinking alcohol in bars and generally 'having a good time.'

Even if you don't wish to join in with the overall socialising, you may still want to visit the theatre, go to concerts, join a sports club or take advantage of other facilities on offer.

You will find that almost all UK universities boast an impressive range of things to do when you're not actually studying. Entertainment ought not to be right at the top of your priority list but the provision of facilities for leisure and recreation might just tip the scales one way or another if you are still undecided after considering issues such as Subject, Location and Living arrangements.

Community

You'll be living and working in the midst of a large student community and you may find it important to check out information on some of the following questions:

- Does the university recruit many other students from my part of the world?

- How many students are in the same age-range as me?

- Is there a religious community of people of the same faith as me?

- Is there access and support for people with disabilities?

- Is single-sex accommodation available?

- Who can I talk to if I feel lonely or have difficulty settling in?

Time

How long are you prepared to spend on your higher education? Most full-time degrees last three years but there are foundation degrees and higher diplomas that can be completed in two years.

Sandwich degrees - which incorporate some time spent in industry, commerce or a clinical environment - usually last four years, while subjects such as Medicine and Veterinary Science require at least five years.

You may prefer a part-time course or one based on distance learning. These could offer advantages in terms of saving on accommodation costs or avoiding debt by working to earn enough to cover your immediate needs but you may find that your learning is spread over a considerably longer period of time.

If you enjoy your studies so much that you choose to stay on for a postgraduate course, you may be looking at several further years before you are in a position to earn some serious income. There is currently no standard time allocation for the purpose of acquiring undergraduate and postgraduate qualifications but most European countries are now working towards a common programme, often referred to as 3-5-8.

This means that you could expect to take at least three years to obtain a first or Bachelor level degree; you could then take another two years to pursue a Master level qualification and a further three to obtain a Doctorate. There are many variations on this theme, and it may not apply in your particular circumstances, but the 3-5-8 pattern should give you a broad feel for the shape of higher education provision not only in the UK but also across Europe.

One attraction of having broadly comparable Bachelor-Master-Doctor qualifications that transcend national boundaries is that it can enable you to travel widely, selecting different locations for different levels.

Have you thought about how long you will be away from home? Have you considered how often you might want to return to visit family and friends? Do you know how much travel costs will add to your financial calculations?

Further information

The essential starting point for almost all higher education provision in the United Kingdom is the Universities and Colleges Admissions Service (UCAS) website at: www.ucas.com

The equivalent for students in the Republic of Ireland is the Central Applications Office (CAO) website at: www.cao.ie

Suggested reading

Heap 2011: University Degree Course Offers (formerly Degree Course Offers)
- Brian Heap, Trotman, 2010

The Daily Telegraph Guide to UK Universities 2010 (formerly The Student Book)
- Klaus Boehm and Jenny Lees-Spalding, Trotman, 2009

*The Daily Telegraph Guide to Student Money 2011 (formerly Students' Money Matters):
How to Manage Your Funds, Fees and Finances at University and College*
- Gwenda Thomas, Trotman, 2010

Applying for Art and Design Courses

Original article by Tony Charlton - Professional Development Officer, UCAS

Have you ever imagined yourself working as a website designer, an animator or a packaging designer; or as a sport and fitness equipment designer, a magazine photographer, film set designer or a fashion illustrator? The key to success in these and literally thousands of other jobs is that career advancement is increasingly dependent on gaining a degree, foundation degree or higher national diploma (HND).

In choosing any career, it is vital to separate fact from fiction. With art and design, some students (and their parents) have misgivings about its suitability due to a lack of first-hand experience and an over-reliance on misleading media reporting. The true picture, however, is much rosier. The creative industries are a significant contributor to the economic wealth of the UK and employ more than 1 million people. The influence of artists and designers is so all-pervasive that it would be hard to imagine our world devoid of their creative inputs. If you doubt this, just take a moment and look around you, at items in your home, place of work, study or leisure environment. Consider, for example, furniture in your home, the 'white goods' in the kitchen (ie cooker, fridge etc), soft furnishings such as carpets and curtains, the adverts on your TV, your weekend mountain bike or, on a personal note, the clothes and shoes that you are wearing today. In all likelihood, the vast majority will have been designed by art and design graduates.

The sort of person you need to be

An ability for sustained effort and a willingness to work, on occasion, in a non 9 to 5 environment are both important. It is vital to realise that the art and design job market is extremely competitive and that a high level of commitment is needed. Increasingly, work opportunities are offered on a short-term contract or self-employed basis and, to secure work, you must be prepared to market yourself. The importance of self-promotion, for even the most gifted students, is recognised by most colleges and universities and forms part of supporting studies.

How important is drawing ability?

The ability to express yourself through the medium of drawing is still viewed as essential for most art and design courses. Do not be beguiled into thinking, as some school pupils sometimes do, that drawing is somehow yesterday's skill and that a computer can 'do it all'. It can't, and your progress in art and design will be severely limited, if not totally jeopardized, unless your portfolio contains sound evidence of competent drawing skills.

Study options

Art and design has expanded to embrace an enormous range of study opportunities at degree level. Choices vary from 'Fashion Merchandising' to 'Digital Imaging', and from 'Calligraphy and Bookbinding' to 'Museum and Exhibition Design'. In total, there are over 70 specialisations on the art and design subject menu. This means, in reality, that a significant number of schools are hampered in offering the full spectrum of art and design possibilities through lack of specialist resources.

Do I need to take an Art Foundation course?

In England, Wales and Northern Ireland, a significant number of students who take A levels choose, before applying for degree level studies, to take a one-year art foundation course. Usually this is done at a college or university near the student's home and, in reality, most students live at home whilst taking their art foundation course. For application purposes, apply direct to your chosen course and not through UCAS. In Scotland, the first year of a four-year degree has a similar purpose.

Choosing the right course

With more art and design courses in the UK than in any other country in Europe, a snap decision could prove costly. Instead, take time to research your options fully and, whenever possible, try to make a personal visit. Before doing so, you will find it useful to visit a UCAS *Design Your Future Fair*. Taking place annually in London and Manchester, and exclusively for UCAS art and design applicants, the Fairs are a golden opportunity to meet staff and students from all major art colleges and university art departments. With a token admission charge of £2, it is not surprising that over 15,000 art students attend the Fairs each year. When making subsequent visits, remember to check the studio and workshop facilities very carefully (this is of course where you will spend most of your time as an art and design student).

Making a UCAS art and design application

The Universities and Colleges Admissions Service (UCAS) annually handles applications from more than half a million people for places at UK colleges and universities. Of these, just under 40,000 students apply for one or more art and design courses.

Applications for studio-based art and design courses should reach UCAS between early September and either *15 January* or *24 March 2011*. (The only exception is Fine Art at the Ruskin School of Fine Art, University of Oxford, which requires applicants to apply by 15 October, 2010).

The deadline applicable to each course is clearly given in UCAS Course Search and is also embedded into the 2011 Apply software.

As a new feature, online notification of interviews, including the date, is available for applicants through Track.

May I apply for courses with both dates?

Yes, this is perfectly acceptable. You may make up to five choices overall, with any combination of dates permissible.

Do I have to express any preference in my choices?

No, art and design applications now follow standard UCAS procedures in being considered on a simultaneous basis. You therefore should not express a preference for a particular college or university in your personal statement (unless, of course, you are applying as a single choice applicant).

Suggested reading

Getting into Art and Design Courses 2011
- James Burnett, Trotman, 2010

Progression to Art and Design 2011 Entry
- UCAS, GTI/UCAS, 2010

Further information

Universities and Colleges Admissions Service
www.ucas.com

Institute of Designers in Ireland
www.idi-design.com/students/courses.html

Gap Year Considerations

Organisations in the business of setting up gap year activities are very skilled at promoting the idea that a year out between school or college and higher education and a job can offer you, as one website puts it: "an EXCITING, CHALLENGING and VALUABLE opportunity, be it in the UK or OVERSEAS. It can and probably will ENRICH YOUR LIFE FOREVER, aside from broadening your view of the world and those around you."

The gap year is portrayed as a light at the end of the tunnel; a vision of freedom after exams; a break from academic goals and pressures. Get set, trills the enticing publicity, for the adventure of a lifetime; the chance to 'find yourself' as you battle in the heat and dust against poverty, famine and injustice; the opportunity to live your dreams and make the world a better place.

All of this undoubtedly turns out to be true each year for some among the 200,000 or so young people from Britain who decide to bite the bullet, pack their rucksack and head for the hills. Yet a very different overall picture emerges from a three-year study of the habits and experiences of gap year participants published by Lucy Huxley, a sociologist at Manchester Metropolitan University.

Lucy's report - *Seeing the World: an Examination of Backpacking as Global Youth Culture* - claims that most gap year travellers rarely interact with local people, learn nothing about the countries they visit, hang out only with fellow backpacking Brits and stay in constant contact with home via mobile phones and the internet. Rather than exploring the tropical rainforest or learning an obscure language, they are more likely to be downloading the latest plot twists in Eastenders or checking the scores in the Premier League.

The findings led one newspaper columnist to write that adventure and education are no longer part of the gap year. "It's about pretence," she maintains, "the pretence of independence. The advent of the e-mail has made that pretence increasingly difficult to uphold, but we do it anyway."

Her rather harsh conclusion is that: "gap years have forfeited any claim to be an essential part of the maturing process. For middle-class British students, the best that can be said is that a gap year begins, very gently, to wean them away from the culture of the risk assessment exercise and the health and safety checklist that has cosseted them all their lives so far. Though insured to the last strand of designer-straightened hair, gap-year students must, I hope, take at least a smidgen more responsibility for themselves than they did in their school sixth form."

Perhaps surprisingly, Lucy Huxley herself is more positive about the benefits of a gap year, saying that the students she interviewed felt the experience had been worthwhile and had given them new confidence.

"They are getting a sense of confidence and maturity. It's a cliché about finding yourself," she says, "but that still seems to be apparent and they are certainly getting something from it. They enjoyed it and got something out of it."

Personal Development and Work Experience Guide

If you feel that a gap year would benefit you, spend some time exploring the COA *Personal Development and Work Experience Guide*. The sheer number of gap year agencies can be bewildering, so we have grouped them under headings to help you become aware of the range of opportunities available and decide what sort of gap year activity best meets your needs.

Internet links are provided for all the organisations listed. The websites will provide detailed information on the type of experience offered, the likely demands on your character and abilities, and the potential benefits for you and/or the community involved.

You can spend your time in the UK or overseas; you may be paid or you may have to pay a considerable sum in order to participate; you may choose a course of study or you may go on an expedition. The choice is yours.

Medicine Dissected

how medical degrees vary from one university to another

Medical courses in the UK can be said to fall into three different categories: traditional, integrated and problem-based. The main differences between them lie in the way they organise 'pre-clinical' and 'clinical' teaching, although we should stress that the 'clinical' element - based in hospitals or in primary care with teaching carried out by clinicians leading small groups - is ultimately similar for all three types of course. It is also true that the categories are not rigid and that there is some overlap between, for example, integrated and problem-based courses. What is vital is that you research the full range of courses on offer, talking to practitioners and advisers, reading prospectuses and checking out websites, before you draw up a shortlist for your application. In the process of doing this, you should find that the categories we mention here will help you identify courses that correspond to your preferred personal learning style. Different types of people suit different types of course and only you can decide which one might suit you best. Wherever you study medicine, you should end up with a broadly similar qualification - but it is wise to pick a university where you perceive that you will have the best chance to flourish both academically and socially.

- *Traditional, or subject-based*, courses are now something of a rarity in the new world of medical education, being limited to venerable establishments such as Oxford, Cambridge and St Andrews. There is a clear pre-clinical/clinical divide and the pre-clinical years are taught very rigidly in subjects. In some of these institutions, you may have to apply again for a clinical place and this could be somewhere very different from your original location. Some Oxbridge students, for example, finish their clinical years in London, while St Andrews medics migrate to Manchester. This type of course tends to appeal to exceptionally academically able, scientifically minded applicants, although there is the potential risk of losing motivation due to the complete lack of patient contact in the pre-clinical years. Also, students can sometimes feel a little unprepared and isolated when they take their first steps into hospital in the clinical years. This type of course offers considerable scope to complete research (such as a Masters or PhD) without overly disrupting your degree. In summary, traditional courses are well worth considering if you are highly confident about your long-term motivation and like the idea of taking a science degree before embarking on your clinical studies.

- *Integrated, or systems based*, courses are run at the majority of UK medical schools, such as Birmingham and Leeds. Devised under the recommendation of the General Medical Council (GMC), these courses may be said to occupy a mid-way position between traditional styles and problem-based learning. A key feature is that they generally claim to have patient contact from day one, although this varies in amount from place to place and may be limited in the first year to local community visits. Patient contact increases as the years progress, with what could still be seen as a sort of division between pre-clinical and clinical years. Many students, it should be said, are happy with relatively limited contact with patients in year one as they feel that at this point they do not have sufficient clinical knowledge to approach patients on the wards. Teaching is based on body systems such as the digestive system, learning the anatomy, physiology, pharmacology and biochemistry of the relevant system, and supplementing clinical knowledge. There is also an emphasis on communication skills and understanding the local community. Teaching is a mixture of lectures, tutorials, self directed learning and hospital work in later years. Integrated courses tend to appeal across the board to all types of aspiring doctors.

- *Problem-based learning (PBL)* is a new, dynamic style of course, pioneered by medical schools such as Liverpool and Manchester. Taught with a patient orientated approach from day one, students are heavily involved in clinical scenarios even in the first year. This type of course, with its emphasis on self directed learning, can require a great deal of self motivation, especially for students expecting to be spoon-fed large doses of information. Teaching generally revolves around small, tutor-led groups, with computer work, practical sessions and a large amount of time for personal study. As to whether this type of course offers a better way of teaching medicine than the others mentioned above, the jury is still out. Indeed, some of the new schools have yet to produce their first doctors. Medical schools offering this type of course include the new ones such as East Anglia, Hull and York, Keele and Peninsula, together with Barts and the London (Queen Mary), Glasgow, Liverpool, Manchester and Sheffield.

Four other factors to consider

As is clear from our brief analysis of different types of course, not all medical degrees are taught in the same way. The GMC also accepts that there is simply not enough time in the day to teach medical students everything they need to know. It has therefore identified a 'core' curriculum, which all medical schools must follow, supplemented by *student-selected components* (SSCs). Given that SSCs can form as much as 25-30% of the course at some universities, you should check carefully what might be available at any medical school you are considering. SSCs generally reflect the way in which medical teaching is currently developing, with a diverse range of projects, which not only give you the opportunity to study areas of interest in some depth but also equip you with the skills to source information for yourself.

Another feature to look out for is *Intercalating*, the opportunity to incorporate a degree (BSc or BA) into your medical course. It takes one year, which is often completed after your second or third year. At some medical schools it is compulsory (most of the 6 year courses), some offer it as an option to all students and at some places it is only offered to the most academically able students. The degrees can range from the more traditional science topics such as biochemistry, anatomy or physiology to more unusual subjects such as medical law, ethics, journalism and even history of medicine. There are many reasons why you might intercalate: to extend your knowledge of a particular subject or to gain more experience in carrying out research or laboratory work. The main downside is the extra time and money it takes, adding a year to an already long degree, and carrying implications for what might already be a precarious bank balance! If you have no interest in research, there might be little point in applying to a medical school where intercalating is compulsory; conversely, if you seriously want to intercalate, it may be risky to apply to a school that offers intercalation only to, say, the top 10% of the year group.

Thirdly, an *elective* could give you the opportunity to practise medicine anywhere you want in the world for two months during your clinical years. Electives range from running outreach clinics in developing countries to accompanying flying doctors in Australia. Most medical students see their elective as a wonderful opportunity to visit some exotic destination before they qualify, although you can opt to stay at home if you wish.

Finally, there was a time when all medical schools undertook full body *dissection*, although many now use videos and computers for their anatomy teaching. Some teach from prosections only (parts of the body dissected by a professional anatomy teacher), while some still do full body dissection. Because it is very practical, dissection is often a welcome break from lectures and most students get a lot out of it. It also helps to make clear the differences in the human body between different individuals. If you want to become a surgeon, dissection would be really useful and you should look for courses where this is a strong feature.

Exploring medicine courses

A group of medical students at Leeds University has created a very useful website to help future candidates. Visit it at: **www.wanttobeadoctor.co.uk**

Another option is to visit the website at: **www.medschoolsonline.co.uk** and explore the options available. You can even register to join in debates about various issues related to studying medicine.

For the most reliable, up-to-date, official information, visit the General Medical Council website at: **www.gmc-uk.org** and click on Education.

Undergraduate Study in the United States

Original article adapted from material supplied by the Fulbright Commission and the Institute of International Education

Statistics in **Open Doors: Report on International Educational Exchange**, published annually by America's Institute of International Education, indicate that, in the academic year 2008/09, there were 8,701 students from the United Kingdom studying in the United States (up 4% from the previous year). Some 50% of this total were studying at undergraduate level. The United Kingdom is the 15th-leading country of origin for students in the United States and has remained for many years in the list of top 15 senders.

While international students have always been welcome in the United States, the events of 9/11 led to a total review of national security, which had the effect of discouraging many legitimate would-be students.

Students are subject to the same law as other temporary visitors, who must convince a consular officer they intend to return to their home country after they finish their course of study. You must also show that you are able to pay for your education, either from family funds or from grants or other sources, and that you truly intend to pursue a course of study.

All US embassies and consulates worldwide follow a uniform policy about who may be excused from a visa interview. There are few exceptions, and this procedure applies to all non-immigrant visa applicants, not just to students. Although visa interviews are brief, they are an important step in ensuring security and integrity in visa issuance. All visa applicants must provide a biometric identifier that can be encrypted on the visas that are issued.

The best starting point for information on study options in the US is the Educational Advisory Service (EAS), which has offices both in the United Kingdom and the Republic of Ireland. EAS receives a grant from the US Government to provide free, objective information on all aspects of US education.

Courses and course providers

American degrees are based on a Liberal Arts philosophy, which requires that students take a wide variety of courses in the arts and sciences before concentrating on one academic area so that they gain a well-rounded education. The American Bachelor degree consists of:

- a major, which is a concentrated field of study
- general education courses in a wide range of subjects
- supporting courses for the major
- electives, which are a student's free choice

A degree is designed to be completed in four years, although there is no fixed timescale. Instead, a degree is awarded after a student has completed a required amount of coursework, expressed in terms known as credits/units or semester hours. Usually a student will need to accumulate approximately 110 to 130 credits in order to graduate, with each course on average earning 3-4 credits. Continuous assessment is a feature and each course (class) per term is graded and then converted into a numeric equivalent called a Grade Point Average on a scale of 0 - 4.0 which indicates how well a student is performing. Colleges and universities both award undergraduate degrees and colleges are in no way inferior to universities. Indeed, the terms 'colleges' and 'universities' tend to be used interchangeably. You should note that medicine, dentistry, veterinary science and law are not subjects studied at undergraduate level

in the United States.

Each institution has its own application deadlines and procedures, although nearly 300 American colleges and universities subscribe to a Common Application Form in order to simplify the undergraduate applications process.

Qualifications needed

American colleges expect you to hold secondary school qualifications that would admit you to higher education in your own country. Colleges expect students to have English, mathematics, a language, a science subject and one other subject, plus an aptitude test. This is most often the Scholastic Aptitude Test (SAT).

When to apply

Ideally, begin the process 12-18 months in advance. Application forms for the autumn or fall term (beginning August or September) are available in August of the previous year. Each university has its own deadline, which may be as early as November. Allow six months for processing the application. Some universities accept students for January admission.

Remember: the later you apply, the narrower your choice will be.

Funding

Funding opportunities are available from US universities for international students, but you should note that full funding is rare unless you have academic, athletic or artistic talent. You can approach the university you plan to attend to ask about potential scholarship options. This should be done prior to actually submitting your application, so that you will know what scholarships you might be eligible for.

Cost is clearly a major consideration. International students must prove that they have sufficient funding to cover all costs for at least the first year in order to receive a student visa. Tuition fees may run anywhere from $2,500 to approximately $35,000 per academic year (nine months). In addition, books and other supplies have to be purchased and living expenses met. You will need to include transportation between the US and home, health insurance and personal expenses. Your family will be expected to contribute as much as they can afford towards the cost of your education.

Five steps to success

1. Obtain information about institutions offering the subject you want to pursue. You will probably need to spend some online for this, conducting your research through search engines such as Peterson's *www.petersons.com/educationusa*, College Board *www.collegeboard.com*, US News *http://colleges.usnews.rankingsandreviews.com/college* or The Princeton Review *www.princetonreview.com*. There are excellent colleges all over the US, some of which you may never have heard of before.

2. Write to the Director of Undergraduate Admissions at each of the colleges you are interested in for an application form and a catalog (prospectus). Contact more than one institution: at this stage, you are writing for information/application form, and you should write to 12 - 15 colleges. When you decide which institutions to target, your letter of application should include the following information: name, age, address and nationality, the qualifications you will hold by the time you begin your studies, proposed major (if undecided it's OK), when you want to begin the course and finally how you plan to finance your education.

The letter should be prepared carefully and legibly. Always give your name in exactly the same way on the application and in all correspondence.

3. Register to take the SAT and ask the Educational Testing Service to forward your scores to the institutions to which you are applying. For online sample questions and preparation materials, visit the SAT Preparation Centre at *www.collegeboard.com/student/testing/sat/prep_one/prep_one.html*. The SAT Reasoning Test is a measure of the critical thinking skills you will need for academic success in college. The SAT assesses how well you analyse and solve problems-skills you learned in school that you will need in college. The SAT has three scores, each on the scale of 200 to 800, and will include writing (W 200-800), mathematics (M 200-800), and critical reading (CR 200-800). The total testing time for the SAT is 3 hours and 45 minutes. Most institutions will require the SAT in addition to school qualifications. Some may also require SAT 2, to measure your knowledge in specific subjects. If English is not your native language, you will also be required to register for the TOEFL (Test of English as a Foreign Language) and you should again ask the Educational Testing Service to forward your scores to the institutions to which you are applying.

4. Read carefully through all the application forms you receive and complete carefully. Incomplete information will cause delay. After you have selected the colleges to which you would like to apply, complete and return the applications forms direct to each college before their individual deadline dates. There is no limit to the number of colleges you can apply to; however, most students apply to between three and eight to keep costs down. An application fee is required with each application form. Submit the appropriate amount in US currency with your application. Most institutions will not process your application without the fee. The information accompanying the application forms will give you the college's deadline for admission, required tests, required documents (such as school records), possible essay questions and the application fee (non-refundable, ranging from $30 to $90 per university) for processing the application. There is no clearing house in US higher education. Colleges usually notify their applicants between April and June. Note the deadlines by which you have to reply if you are accepted. If you are accepted by more that one institution, write to the one you decide to accept (pay a deposit if required) and also write to those whose offers you wish to decline.

5. Once accepted by a college, you will receive a letter of admission and the form you require to apply for a visa: the Certificate of Eligibility for Non-Immigrant F-1 Status. Remember that the Certificate of Eligibility (I-20 or IAP-66) cannot be issued until you have been admitted, your level of English proficiency has been determined and your funding has been established as a sufficient amount to meet the institution's expenses. A Certificate of Eligibility is valid only for study in the institution which issued it - and only for the dates stated.

The key to submitting a competitive application is to allow plenty of time to complete all the steps of the process, especially concentrating on essays and personal statements.

Suggested reading

The Official SAT Study Guide
- College Board, 2009

Uni in the USA: the UK Guide to US Universities
- Stephen Baldock, Alice Fishburn and Anthony Nemecek, Lucas Publications, 2005

Further information

To find out more, you may find it useful to attend one of the *Undergraduate Study* seminars held in London. You can register online at the EAS website but you should note that places are filled very quickly. The annual *College Day Fair*, also held in London, gives you the chance to meet around 100 US university representatives. Apart from the EAS offices in London and Dublin, there are six regional and six secondary information centres around the UK.

US Educational Advisory Service
The Fulbright Commission
62 Doughty Street
London WC1N_2JZ
Fax: 020 7404 6834
Email: programmes@fulbright.co.uk

US Educational Advisory Service
www.fulbright.co.uk/study-in-the-us

Open Doors
http://opendoors.iienetwork.org

Education USA
http://educationusa.state.gov

Common Application Form
www.commonapp.org

EAS in Ireland
http://dublin.usembassy.gov/ireland/undergrad_study.html

Office of Public Affairs
Educational Advisory Service
US Embassy
42 Elgin Road
Dublin 4
Tel: 353 1 668 8777 ext. 2106
Fax: 353 1 668 9184
Email: edudublin@state.gov

Degree Course Descriptions

The following pages contain the *Degree Course Descriptions*, carefully selected to give a flavour of each major course area.

The articles are written in most cases by professors and lecturers at leading UK universities. These people know the courses from the inside and understand the difficulties facing students who are about to make choices that could have a lasting influence on their future.

Each *Degree Course Description* contains:

· an introductory overview of the course area

· details of a typical course structure

· information on potential career opportunities

· suggestions for further reading

· website links to sources of more detailed information

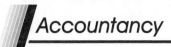
Accountancy

Original article by Ken Pratt, University of Stirling

Introduction

Few organisations survive or prosper without financial information for planning, decision-making and control. Accountants are the skilled professionals who provide and verify this information. Accounting has been described as 'the language of business' and the ability of managers to communicate and co-ordinate their activities depends in part on their ability to understand and use that language. Accountants liaise with managers in all functions, which makes the work endlessly varied and provides a broad experience of the workings of the organisation. This breadth of experience makes them valuable to many different organisations and opens up a wide choice of careers. These include financial and management accounting, auditing, taxation, consultancy and financial services. Accountants may also choose to work in organisations or industries which particularly interest them or match their career goals including, for example, international oil companies, high-street retailers, health care, sports organisations, local and national government and charities.

Degree Courses

To pursue a successful career in accountancy you are likely to need both a university degree and a recognised professional accountancy qualification. Your university degree could be in almost any subject: it does not have to be in accountancy or a related discipline. A degree in a subject other than accountancy is commonly referred to in an accountancy context as a 'non-relevant degree' but this is perhaps an unfortunate and misleading term. Some employers are very keen to recruit applicants with non-relevant degrees, say for example in engineering, computer science, mathematics or languages, because these can bring additional skills which will be very useful in the work they will do. Most employers are pleased to recruit able students no matter what their degree subject, arguing that graduates in, for example, philosophy or anthropology or English literature bring variety and a wider education to their workforce.

There are also good reasons for choosing to do a university degree in accountancy. It is an indication that you are clear about your intended career and it allows you to study the subject in much greater breadth and depth than is possible in study for professional examinations, where study is often completed in short intensive blocks or in the limited time available outside the demands of busy and sometimes long working days. A university honours degree provides not only practical technical competence but also a thorough grounding in the theoretical and conceptual context of accountancy, not to mention powers of inquiry. Graduates with a recognised degree in accountancy who go on to pursue a professional qualification will be required to take fewer professional examinations than those with a non-relevant degree. A number of trends, such as the almost universal use of computers, wider concepts of financial accountability and greater regulation, have increased the level of knowledge required by accountants and make studying for an accountancy degree a desirable first step for would-be accountants.

As is the case with most subjects, there is considerable variation between the courses at different universities. At some, there is a greater emphasis on the use of computers; at some, certain aspects (taxation for example) are a compulsory part of the course, whilst at others the aspect is an option.

Expect degree courses to include a basic core of accounting, finance, taxation and business law. Another likely part of the core is operations research, which employs mathematical methods to assist in making decisions. You will often find that accountancy courses are combined with other subjects that have a clear connection with accountancy. Economics, marketing, computing and management science fall into this category. Many universities offer degrees in accountancy with a modern language. These combined degrees often enable students to work in areas other than accountancy when they obtain their degree. There are many alternatives in degrees involving accountancy and also finance. This makes it even more important than usual to study university prospectuses carefully and to find out which option suits you.

The major companies and professional firms normally expect applicants to graduate with a good Honours degree. An Honours degree in England is normally completed within three years. In Scotland, however, it is often necessary to stay on for a fourth year.

Career Opportunities
There are very many openings in the accountancy profession, in industry, government and commerce for well-qualified graduates.

Related Degrees
International Accounting, Accounting for Management, Business Accounting

Suggested Reading
Accountancy Explained
- Christopher Nobes, Penguin Books, 1990

Accountancy Uncovered
- Jenny Keaveney, Trotman, 2010

Further Information
Association of Chartered Certified Accountants (ACCA)
www.acca.co.uk

Chartered Institute of Management Accountants (CIMA)
www.cimaglobal.com

Chartered Institute of Public Finance and Accountancy (CIPFA)
www.cipfa.org.uk

Institute of Chartered Accountants in England and Wales
www.icaew.com

Institute of Chartered Accountants in Ireland
www.icai.ie

Institute of Chartered Accountants of Scotland
www.icas.org.uk

Institute of Certified Public Accountants in Ireland
www.cpaireland.ie

Acting

Original article by Malcolm Griffiths, Nottingham Trent University

Introduction

The image of the successful actor or actress projected by the media and magazines is one of often far-fetched glamour. Real success can mean being able to afford to choose between work in theatre, films or television or to remain with a company over a number of years developing a particular form of theatre. The majority of performers, however, face a harsher reality where stretches of unemployment are broken by the occasional television engagement, promotional video or short repertory season. A career in acting requires a special toughness and determination in addition to real talent. If you succeed, it will be very rewarding. Should you fail, nobody else will shed a tear.

Degree Courses

Please note that this article is primarily about courses at drama schools - usually but not always at degree level - designed to offer vocational training for aspiring actors. See the separate article on Drama for more academic degrees exploring the history and development of drama and analysis of texts.

Drama schools are a comparatively recent phenomenon and have largely replaced the actor's traditional apprenticeship on the job with opportunities for developing skills, learning techniques, making mistakes and acquiring self-confidence before trying to survive in a highly competitive market. Although there will always be room for people with irrepressible natural talent, the importance of drama schools in nurturing ability and improving standards is now recognised. Schools are acutely aware that a professional actor needs to be adaptable to all kinds of theatre - compelling a pub audience in cabaret, projecting the nuances of a character's psyche in a large auditorium, devising a show with disabled children etc. Each school will try to prepare students to meet the exceptional range of responses and skills required, but each will have evolved its particular philosophy and style. It is here that care needs to be taken in selecting a course. All drama schools provide tuition in voice, movement and acting but how these three fundamentals are taught will differ widely. Movement teaching, for example, can vary from exercises drawn from gymnastics or acrobatics to precise schooling in dance. One school may place great emphasis on a highly individualistic approach focusing on students' technical and expressive proficiency and on the production of play texts in order to give the student the experience to develop as a flexible and disciplined instrument of interpretation. Another will stress the essential collaborative aspect of theatre and develop work from a basis of group improvisation in order to increase students' creative responsiveness and social awareness. No drama school would claim to be able to turn you into a great actor but it can help you further your ambition by providing a thorough grounding, expertise and time.

Before deciding which course to apply to, you should consider what facilities the school has and how much work is done on radio, television and film as these will become a crucial source of your future livelihood. Also find out whether the school employs visiting professionals for projects or productions and whether it covers both past and contemporary theatre forms.

In addition to drama schools there are a number of performing and creative arts courses, which offer opportunities for more experimental approaches to performance in conjunction with, for example, dance, music and visual arts studies. These courses do not claim to provide the kind of training found at drama schools but to encourage students to create their own performance events and to learn through both practice and the wider debate on the arts.

Related Degrees

Performing Arts, Performance and Live Arts, Theatre (Acting)

Suggested Reading

Performing Arts Uncovered
- Dee Pilgrim, Trotman, 2007

Being an Actor
- Simon Callow, Vintage, 2004

Year of the King
- Antony Sher, Nick Hern Books, 2004

The Making of the Professional Actor
- Adrian Cairns, Peter Owen, 1996

Other People's Shoes
- Harriet Walter, Nick Hern Books, 2003

So You Want To Be An Actor?
- Timothy West and Prunella Scales, Nick Hern Books, 2005

Actor's Guide to Auditions and Interviews
- Margo Annett, Methuen Drama, 2004

The Complete About Acting
- Peter Barkworth, Methuen Drama, 2001

Voice and the Actor
- Cicely Berry and Peter Brook, Harrap, 2000

So You Want to Be a Film or TV Actor?
- Lisa Rondinelli Albert, Enslow Publishers, 2008

So You Want to Be a Film and TV Actor
- Anthony Brown, Infinity, 2009

How to be a Working Actor
- Mari Lyn Henry and Lynne Rogers, Backstage Books, 2008

An Actor's Guide to Getting Work
- Simon Dunmore, Methuen Drama, 2004

Further Information

Conference of Drama Schools
www.drama.ac.uk

British Actors' Equity Association
www.equity.org.uk

National Council for Drama Training
www.ncdt.co.uk

National Association for Youth Drama in Ireland
www.youthdrama.ie

Aeronautical Engineering

Original article by Professor Donald McLean, University of Southampton

Introduction

Aeronautical engineering is not easy to describe in just a few words because it is a very big subject embracing a large number of specialised technical disciplines. Each of those disciplines can become a lifetime study for some of us, yet to be any good at aeronautical engineering means that you must have some understanding of all of them. You must learn about the physical principles involved when anything flies, or when it moves through space where there is no real atmosphere. You have to learn the techniques needed to analyse and design aerospace vehicles for specific tasks.

It is that very variety and the corresponding great complexity of these vehicles that gives aeronautical engineering its special grand dimension: as an engineering subject it calls forth the greatest imagination and enthusiasm from everyone who works in it. The kind of vehicles you may be lucky enough to deal with can range from those which operate in the earth's atmosphere to those which go beyond it. There are the single- and twin-engined general aviation aircraft, which don't fly very fast, very far or very high, but which are the most common aircraft type in the world; commercial jet transports fly millions of people daily in safety and comfort over millions of miles at affordable cost; and the different types of military aircraft must have a performance which is evidently a function of the intended mission. Although each of these aircraft types has its special problems, because each operates in a different speed regime, and although research is carried out continuously on them in industrial design offices, university laboratories and military research establishments, each type is linked by a common core of technical specialisations and disciplines which are used as the basic subjects of any British aeronautical degree.

Degree Courses

Typically, degrees have a first year devoted to subjects like mathematics, mechanics, computing, elasticity, thermodynamics, fluid mechanics, properties of materials and basic electricity, which are common to all engineering subjects. In the second year all the specific aeronautical subjects, like aerodynamics, aircraft structures, propulsion, system dynamics and stability and control, which every aeronautical engineer should know something of, are dealt with. The final year is usually devoted to optional subjects and a project, which are chosen by the student to help the individual specialise in his or her chosen branch of aeronautical engineering.

When we study how and why the shape of an aircraft can be arranged so that the required forces and moments are produced satisfactorily by the airflow, we are concerned with aerodynamics. From aerodynamics, for example, we learn why high-speed aircraft must have swept wings. To study aerodynamics effectively means that you have to be able to have access to a wind tunnel in which a model aircraft or an airfoil can be tested to obtain good measurements to apply to a real aircraft. For a good understanding of aeronautical engineering, a knowledge of aerodynamics is indispensable, and familiarity with wind tunnel techniques is most helpful in learning about aerodynamics. So, try to study where there are plenty of wind tunnels. But be warned: such facilities are expensive, so they are heavily used for laboratory classes, projects, and even for staff research.

Of course, when an aerospace vehicle is moving around it has to be structurally sound: its frame and surface must be strong enough to withstand the stresses which result from the very great forces to which a vehicle is subject whenever it is manoeuvred, or whenever it meets atmospheric turbulence. Even spacecraft orbiting outside the earth's atmosphere can be subjected to torque disturbances caused by gravity gradients and solar pressure. Thus, the study of the behaviour of materials, the stresses and strains within that material, the study of vibration, and the deflection and twisting of the structural elements, are referred to as structural analysis. It is an important subject for every aeronautical engineer and it is taught in every aeronautical engineering course. Equally important is the study of how a vehicle is accelerated: propulsion. Every engine is governed by the laws of thermodynamics and every course will give a brief introduction to propulsion, including reciprocating petrol engines and their associated propellers, the turbojet, the ramjet and, perhaps, the rocket motor. Some courses have specialised option subjects in propulsion, which are particularly useful if you want to work with aircraft or spacecraft engines.

Aircraft and spacecraft carry a considerable amount of systems equipment for auxiliary power, heat exchanging, life support, fire extinguishing, communication, navigation, and flight control, not to mention the wide variety of weapons systems fitted to military aircraft. Some of these systems are described by the term avionics, a compound word from aviation electronics. How such systems work, and how aerospace vehicles depend upon them, are usually covered in degree courses but there are also specialist courses in avionics systems or aerospace systems engineering. The core subjects of an aerospace systems course are likely to include mathematics, computation, communication theory, electromagnetism, system dynamics, signal analysis, power and actuator systems, as well as aerodynamics, propulsion and structural design.

Avionics systems courses involve the five principal areas of modern aeronautical engineering: aerodynamics and structures, propulsion, communication and guidance, flight control systems and information systems. If you understand that a little more than half the cost of a modern military aircraft (and sometimes as much as a third of the cost of a commercial passenger aircraft) is spent on such systems, you will be able to appreciate how important such new courses are going to be in helping provide industry with the well-educated aeronautical engineers it needs to respond to the great challenges of aerospace in the future.

Career Opportunities

Pilot, aircraft design engineer, aerodynamicist, avionics design engineer, communication engineer, aircraft systems engineer, propulsion engineer, electrical power system engineer, hydraulic system engineer, safety systems engineer and maintenance engineer. There are opportunities in these specialisations with aircraft manufacturers, avionic and aircraft systems manufacturers, Airbus, the Armed Services, government research organisations, the Civil Aviation Authority and the National Air Traffic Services. The opportunities are worldwide.

Related Degrees

Avionic Systems, Space Technology, Aero Mechanical Engineering, Aerospace Technology, Aerospace Manufacturing Engineering

Suggested Reading

Fundamentals of Flight
- R. Shevell, Prentice Hall, 1989
What Makes Airplanes Fly?
- P. P. Wegener, Springer-Verlag, New York, 1998

Further Information

Aerospace Defence Security
www.sbac.co.uk
Civil Aviation Authority
www.caa.co.uk
Royal Aeronautical Society
www.raes.org.uk
UK Space Agency
www.ukspaceagency.bis.gov.uk
Engineers Ireland
www.engineersireland.ie

Agriculture and related courses

Original article by Professor W Holmes, Wye College, University of London, now Imperial College Wye

Introduction

The study of natural resources and their management to provide food, fibre, wood and other materials is of major importance throughout the world. The current emphasis on the environment makes it even more important that the physical, biological and economic principles underlying the production of crops, trees, and animals, and their interactions with the environment, are well understood.

Agriculture, horticulture, forestry and related subjects studied at degree level deal with these subjects in a very effective way. General courses give a broad training. There are also specialist courses in sciences (agricultural botany, agricultural biochemistry, agricultural zoology, animal science, horticultural science, wood science); courses emphasising economics (such as agricultural economics, agricultural business management, agricultural and food marketing); environmental courses (agriculture and environmental science, forestry and natural resources, terrestrial ecology) and in agricultural engineering.

Before you start, you must have a genuine interest in the subject. You might have grown up on a farm but this is certainly not essential. The subject may appeal because you like growing plants or working with animals. Alternatively, you may wish to apply your skills and interests in biology, chemistry, economics, geology, mathematics or physics to the real life situation. Or you may just like the countryside and country pursuits. Whatever your motivation, evidence of a keen interest and that you have read something about the subject, and preferably worked in it, will help to impress the selectors; a vague sentimental interest in nature and the open air is not likely to be enough.

For most courses, it is recommended that you spend at least one year after school gaining practical experience on a farm, a horticultural holding or an agricultural research station before you start. Even farmers' sons and daughters are encouraged to gain experience away from home. Many employers consider such experience to be essential. As an alternative, some courses provide for the student to take a sandwich year to gain his or her practical experience in the middle rather than before the course begins.

Degree Courses

Courses in the UK normally last three or four years, in addition to the practical year, with a progression from basic studies in the first year to more applied studies in the later years. For example, a course in *agriculture* will probably include the study of biology, biochemistry and economics together with introductory aspects of agriculture and statistics and computing in the first year. Soil science, crop production, animal production, farm mechanisation and farm management would be second-year courses. Advanced aspects of crop and animal production and of farm management, together with selections from more specialist topics (eg animal breeding, marketing, plant pathology or intensive horticultural cropping) might occupy the final years. In addition, most final year courses include a project, in which the student pursues a particular interest in some detail and submits a report or dissertation as part of the final examination.

Courses in *horticulture, plant science* and *agricultural botany* concentrate on plants. The horticultural courses include production and amenity horticulture, economics, management and marketing as well as the sciences of plant nutrition, plant physiology and plant pathology. Courses in plant science and agricultural botany are more science oriented: they omit management and use the additional time for experimental techniques and frequently for the conduct of small-scale investigations.

Similarly, courses in *animal science* and *agricultural zoology* provide for more detailed study of the anatomy, physiology, biochemistry, and genetics of farm animals and of the parasites and insects of agricultural importance but omit some of the more practical aspects of animal husbandry and management. Since some of the work is conducted with smaller organisms, practical laboratory projects may be included.

Courses in *agricultural economics* are intended primarily for planners or consultants rather than for farm or estate managers, whose needs are usually met by courses in agriculture, agricultural business management or horticulture. These courses therefore start from a base of economics, mathematics and statistics and progress to advanced economics, agrarian development, agricultural policy, economic statistics, management and marketing with relatively brief reference to agricultural technology. Courses in *agricultural business management* and *land economy* depend more heavily on economics, management techniques and legal aspects and they give less emphasis to scientific subjects.

Career Opportunities

A good degree gained opens a remarkable variety of career opportunities. Some graduates are soon running their own businesses in farming or horticulture; many are managing businesses for larger organisations, estates or conservation agencies. A further large proportion is involved in advisory work with national or international organisations or with commercial companies. Education, research and government posts at home or overseas also provide many opportunities.

Related Degrees

Agronomy, Organic Agriculture, Crop Science, Agricultural Science, Agriculture of the Environment, Agricultural Technology, Agricultural Biochemistry, Organic Agricultural Food and Marketing.

Suggested Reading

Agriculture and the Citizen
- Colin Spedding, Springer, 1996

So shall we reap
- Colin Tudge, Penguin, 2004

Farmers Weekly magazine

Further Information

Farmers Weekly Interactive
www.fwi.co.uk

Department for Environment, Food and Rural Affairs
www.defra.gov.uk

Grow Careers
http://www.growcareers.info

Lantra
www.lantra.co.uk

Irish Agriculture and Food Development Authority
www.teagasc.ie

American Studies

Original article by Mike Nicholson, University of Essex

Introduction

Students pick American Studies for a combination of reasons:

- North America, particularly the USA, has a pivotal influence in modern society. The USA is the last remaining superpower and the cultural impact of America on the world stage continues to grow.

- Courses provide an opportunity to study America at first-hand, with students spending anything from a term or semester up to a full academic year abroad.

- The historical, literary and cultural development of the North American nations has been influenced by a variety of differing sources - settlement of the country by immigrant populations from Africa, Central Eastern and Western Europe, the Pacific Rim and Asia, Central and South America as well as the presence of a Native American population has contributed to create a diverse and broad tapestry of ideas, beliefs and values.

On the UCAS application form, the personal statement is your main opportunity to develop your case for admission to an American Studies degree. Evidence of a genuine interest in topics related to North America will be beneficial to an applicant. Travel in North America is also a positive sign. Candidates who link their American Studies degree to long-term career aspirations will also strengthen their case for admission.

Degree Courses

Whilst courses differ considerably, there are some general rules of thumb on course content.

Most American Studies degrees have a core content that involves the study of North American or US literature, history and/or politics. Above and beyond this, specific institutions can provide additional specialisms e.g. American Studies and Criminology at **Essex**; American Studies and Law at **Keele** and **Sussex**; American Studies and Sport and Exercise Psychology at **Canterbury Christ Church University** ; American Literature with Creative Writing at **University of East Anglia** in Norwich.

The first year in most degree schemes encourages a broad study pattern covering several topics, to give students the opportunity to get a feel for the diversity and range of the degree scheme.

Specialisms usually start in the second year. In most cases, students will have an upper limit of three areas e.g. American history, literature and film.

In most degrees the coursework completed in North America will count towards your overall degree result.

Many courses will require completion of a project - the fieldwork is expected to be done whilst a student is engaged on their study period abroad.

Note where a University or College has exchange partners - and if possible do some research on the American institutions.

You also need to know what you will have to pay for e.g. some exchange students going to America will pay for a room at their own UK university which their exchange partner will occupy for the duration of their study. In other cases, exchange students pay for their accommodation at their US institution.

The increasing cost of undergraduate study will inevitably impact on American Studies students. America can be an expensive place to live and study.

Look at the specialisms that differentiate departments - if you know that you want to study American literature then look to an institution with a strength in that field.

Career Opportunities

Many opportunities are available for well-qualified graduates, eg in banking, finance, export, commerce, government, management and so on.

Related Degrees

Comparative American Studies, English and United States Literature, United States and Latin American Studies, North American Studies, American and Canadian Studies, Hispanic Studies (Latin America)

Suggested Reading

Penguin History of the United States of America
- Hugh Brogan, Penguin, 2001

A New Introduction to American Studies
- Christopher Bigsby and Howard Temperley, Longman, 2005

Get set for American Studies
- Edward Ashbee, Edinburgh University Press, 2004

Further Information

American Literature links at Keele:
www.keele.ac.uk/depts/as/Literature/amlit.html

British Association for American Studies
www.baas.ac.uk

Irish Association for American Studies
www.americanstudiesinireland.materdei.ie

Anatomy

Original article by Professor Anthony Firth, St Mary's Hospital Medical School, London (now part of Imperial College School of Medicine)

Introduction

The anatomical approach is to explore the structure of living organisms as a way of getting at how they work. Anatomists tend to think in terms of shapes and relationships in space as the most striking and exciting aspects of living things - their imagination tends to be visual and spatial rather than abstract.

The earliest anatomists relied on dissection of dead organisms ('dissection' is another word meaning 'cutting apart') as their main method of study, and dissection of the dead bodies of people or of domestic animals still forms the core of many anatomy courses in medical, dental or veterinary science.

Whether or not students of biology, outside the health sciences, come across anatomy as a formal subject in their courses, they use the methods of structural study which typify the anatomical approach to biology. These now range from naked-eye observations during dissection to high-resolution microscopic examination of cells and their components. The first effective use of the electron microscope on biological materials in the 1950s both emphasised the power of the visual approach and also underlined its limitations. With these instruments it is possible to reveal the organisation not only of cell interiors but also of the large molecules such as DNA and proteins which characterise living tissue, but until quite recently this ability to see fine structural detail has been offset by the maddening difficulty of finding out anything precise about the chemical nature of the structures so revealed.

Over the last generation, and particularly in the last ten years, biologists have learned to characterise the molecular composition of microscopic structures by a range of methods which allow the presence of specific molecules to be revealed by light or electron microscopy. This hybrid science of histochemistry is an extraordinarily powerful tool, for it has allowed specific chemical information to be obtained with all the precision about structure and spatial relationships which characterises microscopic science. At first this could only be exploited for a fairly limited number of biologically interesting chemicals which were sufficiently distinctive for them to be stainable by chemical reactions which failed to stain other substances: starch and neutral fats are good examples. The most interesting molecules of living systems, the nucleic acids and proteins, could be identified as classes but it seemed impossible to label selectively a single species of protein or a single gene in a chromosome. Something could be done with those proteins which happened to be catalysts, the enzymes, as they could often be manipulated to yield a visible and insoluble reaction product which could be recognised by light or electron microscopy. Enzyme histochemistry has been with us for about thirty years and grows in subtlety and usefulness every year; it can show us not only where enzymes are within a cell, but also which reactions they can catalyse and even how fast they can do it.

Degree Courses

For students entering biology these are exciting times. Those training for medicine and allied professions meet both the traditional and the new anatomy. They study the human body by dissecting the dead, by examining pictures generated by an ever-growing range of non-invasive imaging methods such as x-radiographs, computerised tomography, ultrasound and magnetic resonance imaging. They explore living anatomy by examining their own bodies and those of other students. They study the mature and the developing body by microscopic means, which increasingly depend on the chemically specific and functionally informative methods of histochemistry. For all biologists, form and function are becoming unified by new methods in microscopy. Whether we work on the unfolding of the genetic programme of development, the functional organisation of the brain, the subtly disordered biology of cancer cells, or the means by which amoeba achieves the extraordinarily complex task of crawling across a piece of glass, our approach leans heavily on the central insight of anatomy: that form is the visible aspect of invisible functions and so can serve as a road to understanding them.

Career Opportunities

Anatomical science provides an ideal training for those students wishing to pursue a research or other career based on the biomedical sciences. Typical employers offering laboratory-based careers are the universities, government establishments, the National Health Service and the pharmaceutical and food industries.

Anatomy also provides an excellent basis for careers in education, biomedical information services and scientific management. Graduates can register for higher degrees (PhD, MSc), or take further training for a career in, say, physiotherapy or osteopathy; in exceptional cases they may gain admission to medical, dental or veterinary programmes.

Related Degrees

Anatomical Science.

Suggested Reading

Molecular Biology of the Cell
- Bruce Alberts Ed, Garland, 2008

Atlas of Human Anatomy
- Frank Netter, Saunders, 2006

Further Information

Anatomical Society of Great Britain and Ireland
www.anatsoc.org.uk

Gray's Anatomy Online
www.bartleby.com/107

Royal Society for Public Health
www.rsph.org.uk

National Health Service Careers
www.nhscareers.nhs.uk

Anthropology

Original article by Professor Adam Kuper, Brunel University

Introduction

Anthropologists have a romantic image. They are pictured camping in an Amazonian rain forest, or sailing on a frail barque between two little Pacific islands. But few people have much idea what anthropologists are really up to, and they are surprised to discover that we may also do field studies rather closer to home, in Greek islands, Irish villages or even Midlands factories.

Anthropology is about the evolution, unity and diversity of the human species. One branch of anthropology, physical anthropology, is concerned largely with the biological evolution of human beings. Archaeologists drive deep shafts back in time, reconstructing cultural processes in the distant past. Social or cultural anthropologists study contemporary human communities, charting their customs and practices and attempting to explain them.

The central experience of social anthropologists is always fieldwork. Devoting one or two years to any study in the field, the researcher participates as far as possible in the life of the people, speaking their language and forging bonds of friendship and trust. This sometimes trying, often inspiring, always important experience of immersion in a strange way of life is then translated into a formal analysis either of the community or, more usually today, of an aspect of its life. (But a number of anthropologists do slip the academic restrictions and produce lively impressionistic and personal accounts of their experience, such as Nigel Barley's humorous reminiscences of fieldwork in West Africa and Indonesia.)

Fieldwork - ethnography - is only one aspect of the anthropologist's work. The challenge to field-workers is not only to make sense of their observations, but to relate what they have seen to studies made of similar institutions elsewhere. The ultimate goal is to further our understanding of social and cultural processes at large. Social anthropology is therefore a comparative social science. It has particularly close ties with history and sociology, though there are also fecund links with other disciplines. It can often be studied in association with another subject, sometimes in the traditional company of physical anthropology and archaeology, but otherwise together with ancient history, linguistics, African or Asian languages, psychology or sociology, or in more and more new combinations.

Degree Courses

At a typical university, the first two years of study of anthropology would be devoted to outlining the variety of cultures and customs which are to be found in the societies around the world, and to introducing the students to the main philosophers of society, such as Durkheim, Weber and Marx. These are at a more advanced level in the second than the first year. During each year, teaching would cover five main areas: (i) the study of family and kinship systems in human societies, (ii) the study of economic life in human societies, (iii) the study of political life, (iv) the study of systems of religion and ideology, and (v) the study of language in society. A major question running through all these sections is whether the findings of economists, political scientists and others on western industrial society are going to be relevant to the study of tribal and peasant communities in the Third World.

Among topics covered at the Honours level would be 'nationalism and ethnicity', 'sex roles in human society', 'communication in human and animal society', 'representation and narrative' and 'linguistic anthropology'.

Career Opportunities

First year students are sometimes shocked by their sudden exposure to the variety of ways in which people think it proper and sensible to order their lives, but this is itself a profoundly educational experience and the discipline provides rich insights into other cultures. Students are also given a training in social science approaches and techniques, which often provides a basis for further independent academic development or opens the way to careers in the media, market research, social work, teaching or, in some cases, to the adventure of anthropological research.

Applied anthropology is a growing field. Government departments or development agencies are the usual employers, but in the USA more than half of professional anthropologists are employed by the private sector. Anthropologists advise on problems of development abroad and are often to be found on teams of planners associated with development projects. Others have come to specialise in community relations at home, particularly in multi-cultural environments and they may contribute to policy-making in fields as diverse as medical or educational services and town planning.

For some anthropologists, the ultimate justification of their studies is a moral one. Levi-Strauss has suggested that the study of anthropology offers two advantages: first it encourages us to take a level-headed and unbiased view of customs and ways of life remote from our own; second, it dissuades us from taking for granted the 'rightness' or 'naturalness' of our own customs.

Related Degrees

Social Anthropology

Suggested Reading

Anthropology and Anthropologists: The Modern British School
- A Kuper, Routledge, 1996

Small Places, Large Issues
- T Hylland Erikson, Pluto Press, 2010

The Innocent Anthropologist
- Nigel Barley, Waveland, 2000

Encyclopedia of Social and Cultural Anthropology
- Alan Barnard (Ed), Routledge, 2002

Anthropology Today
- International journal published by the Royal Anthropological Institute

Further Information

Royal Anthropological Institute
www.therai.org.uk

Anthropological Association of Ireland
www.anthropologyireland.org

Aquaculture

Original article written with help from the University of Stirling

Introduction

In recent years there has been great progress in the cultivation of organisms and plants that live and grow in water based environments. Whilst we tend to associate cultivation of organisms in water with fish farming, aquaculture or aquatic agriculture is concerned with the culture or artificial development of many aquatic organisms. These include not only fish but also molluscs such as mussels and oysters, crustaceans like prawns and shrimps as well as crocodiles, turtles and algae.

Degree Courses

It is important to look very carefully at the different courses under an aquatic heading as their content is quite varied. A course in aquaculture will include courses in cell biology, physiology, ecology and evolution, molecular biology and genetics, followed by a varied programme including a core subject 'aquatic science' in which you will learn about aquatic environments and the management of living aquatic resources, as well as aquaculture and marine biology. The problems of disease and reproduction associated with this form of culture will also be studied as well as nutrition and biotechnology in aquaculture. You will then be able to choose optional courses such as freshwater science and ecotoxicology before carrying out a project over 12 to 14 weeks.

During the first year and a half (Semesters 1 to 3) at Stirling, for example, you take core modules in Oceanography, Introduction to Aquatic Environments, Cell Biology and Physiology, Ecology and Evolution, Genetics, Practical Skills in the Natural Sciences, People and Environment, Global Environmental Issues, and Earth Science. Honours students continue in Semesters 4 to 8 with core modules in Managing Aquatic Resources, Coastal Marine Biology, Biodiversity, Biosphere, Aquaculture, Pelagic and Benthic Processes, Aquaculture Field Course, Aquaculture Assignments and a final year Aquaculture Project. Optional modules can be selected from those available in: Fish Development, Fish Nutrition, Aquatic Diseases, River Ecology and Management, Animal Physiology, Ecology, and Environmental Sciences. Overseas projects are encouraged and past final-year projects have been located throughout Europe, North and South America, the Indian subcontinent, Asia, Oceania and Australasia.

The degree shares a common foundation with programmes in Freshwater Science and Marine Biology. Because of this, the option to take a degree in Freshwater Science or Marine Biology is retained until the end of third year, and the option to take a degree in another Biological Science is retained until the end of second year.

Career Opportunities

Graduates in Aquaculture are well equipped to enter the expanding field of Aquaculture or to follow any other career in which there is a need for scientifically trained personnel. Graduates can expect to seek employment in government and private laboratories, including environmental protection agencies and consultancy organisations.

A second degree (PhD or MSc) may often be required for more senior research posts or for senior management in the industry. Many graduates do therefore go on to pursue further study. Alternatively, a wide range of more general biological posts is available, including those in ecotoxicology and environmental impact assessment. A degree in Aquaculture can also be used to gain entry to careers outside science, such as those in management and finance, computing, and the leisure and tourism industry.

Related Degrees

Aquatic Sciences, Aquaculture & Fisheries Management, Aquatic & Fisheries Management, Freshwater Science, Applied Marine Biology, Aquatic BioScience, Aquatic Zoology, Coastal and Aquatic Science, Fisheries and Aquaculture, Marine and Freshwater Biology.

Suggested Reading

An Introduction to Marine Ecology
- R S K Barnes and R N Hughes, Wiley, 1999

Aquaculture: the Ecological Issues
- John Davenport et al, Wiley, 2003

Further Information

Institute of Aquaculture
www.aquaculture.stir.ac.uk

Centre for Fisheries, Environment and Aquaculture Science
www.cefas.co.uk

Aquaculture Development Centre, Ireland
www.aquaculture.ie

Archaeology

Original article by Dr S W Hillson, Institute of Archaeology

Introduction

Lost cities, great ancient works of art in gold and precious stones, the sumptuous tombs of forgotten kings. If you study archaeology, you can certainly learn about such exciting and exotic things, but most archaeologists spend most of their time dealing with much more mundane objects such as broken pottery and bones - the accumulated waste of ordinary households, farms and towns. What keeps us fascinated is the light that archaeology can shed on everyday life in ancient communities, rather than the lives and works of the great and powerful. This is one of the major differences between archaeology and history. Written history is mostly about rulers and the nobility, military and religious life. Archaeology is based on physical remains rather than records and the great bulk of the material which survives from the past represents the common people. Most ancient objects, even those which may seem to us to be ugly, poorly made or badly damaged, have a story locked up in them. There is a real thrill in taking a small, broken fragment out of the ground and bringing its story out with careful detective work. If you want to find out how people live, a good way is to look in their household refuse, and much of archaeology is tied up with the recovery and sophisticated analysis of ancient domestic rubbish.

Archaeology is an unusually broad subject, bridging the arts and the sciences. It ranges throughout the world, wherever people have lived, and extends from the earliest artefacts made by our extinct relatives some two and a half million years ago, through the period of historical records, including the industrial revolution and up to the present day. The basic approach is scientific, because objects must be excavated and studied in as methodical and objective a manner as possible, but there is also room for the artistic appreciation of beautiful artefacts and for interpretations, which involve history, philosophy and sociology. An expanding field is 'science-based archaeology'; applying techniques which originated in the more traditional sciences. Physics is used to date objects and to locate buried sites. Chemistry helps to discover ancient methods of manufacture and trade routes. Biology is applied in the study of health, hygiene and diet in ancient communities. With all these different strands to archaeology, it can be difficult to define the core of the subject.

Although not a course requirement, it is a good idea for those thinking of embarking upon a degree course in archaeology to join an archaeology society, take part in a dig or other fieldwork or do voluntary work in a museum.

Degree Courses

If you apply to study archaeology, you will find a bewildering range of degree courses and options. Some courses are highly specialised, such as classical archaeology, medieval archaeology, Egyptology, Near Eastern archaeology and archaeological conservation (the restoration and preservation of artefacts). These are really for people who already know the area of archaeology in which they would like to concentrate. The majority of people are less sure and apply for general archaeology courses, but the coverage of these also varies considerably. The subject is so wide that very few institutions have the staff to cover the full range, or even a substantial part of it. Look very carefully at what options are available before you apply. The majority of courses deal with the archaeology of Europe, Mediterranean and Middle Eastern countries. It is much harder to find course options on the archaeology of Africa, eastern Asia and Australasia, and the Americas. Some departments specialise in prehistory, whilst others concentrate on the classical or medieval periods. Relatively few institutions have specialist options in the various science-based archaeology subjects but some departments concentrate on them and several BSc degrees in archaeology are offered. Because of all these variations, it is a good idea to visit archaeology departments in good time before you apply. Most departments will be very pleased to arrange this.

Despite the rather exotic nature of the material, much of an archaeology course follows the traditional pattern of classes but one of the distinctive features of the subject is practical work. You are likely to do a lot of fieldwork because it is the basis of all archaeology. Fieldwork is one of the main attractions for most professional archaeologists and students, ranging from a regional field survey to full excavation of a particular site. Depending on the course, you may travel widely with your fieldwork. There may also be a lot of practical work in the drawing office and laboratory. You could be identifying and piecing together shards of pottery, learning to interpret aerial photographs, practising drawing site plans, learning to sort and identify animal bone fragments, or using a microscope to identify pollen grains. Archaeological conservation involves a specialised training with a great deal of laboratory work, learning various treatments and restoration techniques. Most students enjoy handling ancient objects very much. The fieldwork and practical content of courses varies, and it is well worth finding out what facilities are available in a particular department and how much hands-on experience of artefacts and other remains there is.

Career Opportunities

There are many archaeology graduates but fewer than 5,000 professional archaeologists employed in the UK. The main areas of work for archaeologists are in commercial archaeology units, museums, providing planning and development control advice through local authorities or specialist consultants. Many also work for the national heritage agencies (English Heritage, Historic Scotland and Cadw) or conservation charities, of which the National Trust is probably the biggest employer. A number of archaeologists continue with academic research after graduation and some of these go on to teach in colleges and university departments. Some archaeologists are self-employed and many of these work as specialist consultants in their particular field, such as pottery or bone analysis. Most archaeology graduates enter the general graduate market, taking up commercial, financial, managerial and teaching careers (eg history, ancient history or classical studies).

Related Degrees

Archaeological Science, Environmental Archaeology, Classical Archaeology, Archaeological Conservation

Suggested Reading

Archaeology: An Introduction
- Kevin Greene and Tom Moore, Routledge, 2010

Archaeology: Theories, Methods and Practice
- Colin Renfrew and Paul Bahn, Thames and Hudson, 2008

British Archaeology
- bi-monthly journal published by the CBA: www.britarch.ac.uk/ba

Sampling in Archaeology
- Clive Orton, Cambridge University Press, 2009

Further Information

Council for British Archaeology
www.britarch.ac.uk

Institute of Archaeologists of Ireland
http://iai.ie/index.html

Architecture

Adapted, with permission, from material supplied by the Royal Institute of British Architects (RIBA)

Introduction

At the forefront of designing the built environment that surrounds us in the 21st Century, architects are professional experts in the field of building design and construction, using their unique creative skills to advise on the design and construction of new buildings, the reuse of existing buildings and the nature of the spaces surrounding buildings in our towns and cities.

Society looks to architects to define new ways of living and working, to develop innovative ways of using existing buildings and creating new ones. We need architects' understanding of the complex process of design and construction to build socially and ecologically sustainable cities and communities. Architects can be extremely influential as well as being admired for their imagination and creative skills.

Architects design by drawing. This is their chief means of communication though they need to be able to speak and write well too. You will be taught how to do the necessary technical drawing; this is not a subject you need to study beforehand but you should enjoy drawing. At interview, most schools of architecture will want to see a portfolio of drawings and sketches but it is not essential to take Art as an examination subject.

Degree Courses

Training to become an architect takes a minimum of seven years, but only five of those are spent at a school of architecture. The **first three years** are normally spent working towards a degree at your chosen school, where the object will be to develop your sensitivity to people, places and technology in order to help you understand the ways in which buildings and their surroundings are affected by social, cultural and material factors. You will be taught the practice of design.

The **fourth year** is normally spent working in an architect's office under the general direction of your school of architecture. Some students also travel during this year or work in parts of the building industry.

You then return to a school of architecture for **two further years** to obtain a diploma or higher degree; this does not have to be at the same school where you took your first degree.

After the **seventh year**, which is again spent working in an office, you take a professional practice examination. If you pass, you can become a full member of the Royal Institute of British Architects (while studying you can become a student member). The title 'architect' is protected in the UK by law and you must register with the Architects Registration Board before you can start to practise professionally.

Much of the time in architecture school is spent on projects rooted in building design. By the time you reach the final year, you will also have touched on many related subjects such as urban design, town planning, landscaping and interior design. One day a week is generally spent at lectures or seminars which cover the history and theory of architecture, all aspects of building construction and technology, computer systems, professional practice and many other topics.

All RIBA validated courses are designed to ensure that students achieve the required standard in the core areas of study. Some courses also offer specialist areas of study or have developed strengths in particular areas, for example: technology, environmental design, history or theory. As a prospective student, you should research course options carefully in order to establish what best suits you.

There are also architectural studies courses designed for those who wish to study architecture as a non-vocational subject. Such courses do not give exemption from RIBA professional examinations but can be of interest if you wish to enter related areas such as conservation, planning or landscape architecture.

Career Opportunities

These can fluctuate with the economic climate and with demand for new housing, hospitals, factories, schools etc. Most architects work in private practice but may also work for building, civil engineering or other organisations in constant need of architectural design work.

Related Degrees

Interior Architecture, Architectural Engineering, Naval Architecture

Suggested Reading

Eco-tech: Sustainable Architecture and High Technology
- Catherine Slessor, Thames and Hudson, 2001

Architecture Today and Tomorrow
- Charlotte and Peter Fiell, Taschen, 1999

Architecture Now V.6
- Philip Jodidio, Taschen, 2009

Mastering Architecture
- Leon von Schaik, Wiley, 2005

Further Information

Architects Registration Board
www.arb.org.uk

Royal Institute of British Architects
www.architecture.com

Royal Incorporation of Architects in Scotland
www.rias.org.uk

Royal Society of Ulster Architects
www.rsua.org.uk

Royal Institute of the Architects of Ireland
www.riai.ie

Art and Design

Original article by Norwich University College of the Arts

Introduction

Art and Design can appear a bewilderingly complex subject. A vast range of courses at various levels prepares the student for a lifetime of professional practice and by far the best way to ensure compatibility is to undertake a preparatory diagnostic course prior to application for higher-level study. In England, Wales and Northern Ireland, full-time courses of one or two years' duration usually fulfil this important function, though some are available part-time. They include: Foundation studies in Art and Design and Access to Art and Design. Some specialist National Diploma courses are also offered at Further Education level. In Scotland, the first year of a four-year degree has a similar purpose.

Degree Courses

At Higher Education (Bachelor of Arts, Foundation Degree and Higher National Diploma) level there is a vast menu of specialist courses and broad-based programmes from which to choose. Many Graphic, Textiles, Fashion and 3-Dimensional Design courses arrange work experience in the industry, as well as business and professional studies to prepare for the world of work.

Fine Art courses are primarily aimed at supporting the student in the development of individual creative practice within contemporary and historical contexts. They may have a structured initial phase where skills are taught and many contain specialisms like painting, sculpture, printmaking and time-based media.

Graphic Design and **Visual Communication** courses prepare graduates for a range of professional opportunities as advertising designers, publishing designers, illustrators, animators, photographers and many other commercial disciplines. Some courses have a common first year, when students are able to experience the disciplines before specialisation, others specialise from day one.

Animation, Illustration and **Photography** are also offered as degree courses in their own right.

Film and **Video** courses prepare students for careers in film, broadcasting and independent production. Some concentrate on producing students with specialist knowledge and experience of production team roles such as camera, editing, or production design, while others take a more broad-based approach.

Textiles and **Surface Pattern** courses may emphasise commercial design, individual creative development, or craft practice, though these aspects frequently overlap. There may be a further specialism into printed or woven textiles, or specific applications of textile design, like textiles for fashion. Like other degree programmes, there may a broad introductory phase followed by an opportunity to specialise.

Fashion Design courses are sometimes allied to textile courses, though some are independent. They prepare the student for the highly competitive commercial world of fashion design and usually provide an intensive training in all aspects of the business.

Many offer options in Marketing and may include foreign languages. Students undertake work placements and must be prepared to work to deadlines. Like other degree programmes, there may be a broad introductory phase followed by an opportunity to specialise in areas like knitwear, swimwear or millinery.

Three-Dimensional Design courses include product, automotive, furniture, model-making, ceramics and jewellery design. These courses usually contain strong technical elements. A basic ability in mathematics may be required. 3-D design courses prepare graduates to take up positions in the design industry and all will have a strong industrial or craft profile.

Broad Based courses are available with titles like Visual Studies, or Art and Design. These courses suit those who have made an informed decision to undertake a high level of broad based or comparative study. Such courses can prepare graduates for specialised study at post-graduate level, careers allied to art and design like teaching, or suit those driven by each new concept they encounter.

Additional Specialist courses may combine disciplines to a specific end (as conservation courses do) or allow for the study of historical and contemporary practices (History of Art and/or Design) or may be highly specialised, such as wildlife illustration.

Career Opportunities

Getting established as an artist or designer can be difficult - but increasingly industry and commerce need artists to design their products and literature. Teaching can also provide a stable career. It helps to have talent and determination and to lay out your plans in advance of graduation.

Suggested Reading

To find out how to apply to art and design courses, see the introductory article *Applying for Art and Design Courses* on page xix of this book.

The Art of Looking Sideways
- Alan Fletcher, Phaidon Press, 2001

Design : a concise history
- Thomas Hauffe, Laurence King, 1998

Modern Art: Impressionism to Post-Modernism
- David Britt, Thames and Hudson, 2007

How to Be a Graphic Designer, Without Losing Your Soul
- Adrian Shaughnessy, Princeton Architectural Press, 2010

Further Information

Arts Council England
www.artscouncil.org.uk

Artists Information Company
www.a-n.co.uk

Your Creative Future
www.yourcreativefuture.org.uk

National Society for Education in Art and Design
www.nsead.org

Creative Scotland
www.creativescotland.com

Arts Council of Ireland
www.artscouncil.ie

Astronomy/Astrophysics

Original article by Dr George Lafferty, Department of Physics and Astronomy, University of Manchester

Professor Chris Kinchen, University of Hertfordshire

Introduction

Astronomy and Astrophysics mainly involve the application of known physical laws to distant regions of the Universe, which cannot be accessed directly by man-made apparatus and in which the physical conditions can only be inferred from the electromagnetic radiation emitted. This radiation may be visible light, detectable by optical telescopes; or radio waves detected by giant radio-telescopes; or it may take the form of more energetic radiation, such as gamma rays. Courses in Astronomy and Astrophysics include study of the sun and the solar system, the stars and the galaxy, distant galaxies and quasars and the beginning of the universe in the Big Bang. Training in mathematics, physics, information technology and computing would be involved.

Universities that offer the subject either have their own or have close connections with other observatories, and an important part of courses involves work in these observatories. Obviously, time spent in observatories will usually be when it is dark and relatively cloudless, and courses have to be flexible so that laboratory work takes the place of observatory work when it is cloudy.

Degree Courses

Astronomy is a branch of physics and most astronomers of today took their first degree in physics, mathematics or a combination of physics and astrophysics.

You can, if you are keenly interested, choose a course with a strong astronomy content, but a pure physics course will give you a firm basis for the postgraduate studies which are a pre-requisite for entry to a research career in astronomy. Only a minority of those graduating in astronomy, or physics with astronomy options, will spend their whole lives working in astronomy, but the training in scientific, mathematical and computing techniques, in either field, forms a sound foundation for many different careers. It is vital for aspiring astronomers to study prospectuses to be able to make an informed choice from the varying courses with an astronomical content offered by different universities.

The course structure is very flexible at many universities, with physics and astronomy degree programmes frequently sharing a common first year. The range of modules available in the first year is designed to stimulate your interest in physics, whilst giving you a sound foundation upon which to build in later years. Modules might include Atoms, Nuclei and Matter, Cosmos, and Astrophysical Concepts. It is often the end of the first year before you have to decide whether to continue with your original degree choice or choose another within the range of physics and astronomy degrees.

In the second and third years, you would take a selection of advanced modules that would allow you to practise and consolidate new skills by applying them to a wide range of astrophysical problems. In the final year, you could concentrate specifically on, say, astrophysics, spending half your time completing taught modules and half working on a major astrophysics project.

Career Opportunities

Very few careers are available in the astronomy or astrophysics fields - but the training you receive can open up careers in satellite technology, physics research, industry and in many branches of technology, as well as in finance, banking, industry, management and so on.

Related Degrees

Planetary Science, Geophysics/Planetary Physics, Space/Astrophysics

Suggested Reading

Penguin Dictionary of Astronomy
- Jacqueline Mitton, Penguin, 1998

The Elegant Universe: Superstrings, Hidden Dimensions and the Quest for the Ultimate Theory
- Brian Greene, Vintage, 2005

The Fabric of the Cosmos: Space, Time and the Texture of Reality
- Brian Greene, Penguin Books, 2005

So you want to become an astronomer
- Leaflet written by Cardiff Astronomical Society, downloadable from the website at:
www.nmm.ac.uk/upload/pdf/So_you_want_to_become_an_astronmer.pdf

Further Information

Royal Astronomical Society
www.ras.org.uk

British Astronomical Association
www.britastro.org

Royal Observatory Greenwich
www.nmm.ac.uk/places/royal-observatory

Royal Observatory Edinburgh
www.roe.ac.uk

Institute of Physics
www.iop.org

Students for the Exploration and Development of Space
www.uk.seds.org

Astronomy Ireland
www.astronomy.ie

Audiology

Original article by Ken Reynolds, specialist writer on careers and higher education

Introduction

Audiology is the field of clinical science and technology that is concerned with hearing and balance. As a healthcare profession, it also involves the assessment, management and therapeutic rehabilitation of people with hearing and balance problems and associated disorders. This includes patients of all ages, from newborn babies and children through to working adults and the elderly.

Your role as an audiologist would be to recommend and provide appropriate assessment, rehabilitation and management for people referred to you, applying a scientific approach in a caring and patient-focused way.

Degree Courses

The minimum standard for practice in the UK is the four-year BSc degree, currently available at ten different universities: Aston, Bristol, De Montfort, Leeds, Manchester, Queen Margaret Edinburgh, Southampton, Sunderland, Swansea and University College London. Alternatively, there are postgraduate MSc courses available as a top-up for science graduates in other subjects.

The first two years of the BSc are spent at university, where you would learn about the science behind the tests and treatments used in hospitals and acquire the knowledge needed to work with patients in a therapeutic relationship. The third year is spent in an audiology setting, learning how to carry out some of the procedures a qualified audiologist performs and learning how audiology services work in the NHS. This year is primarily a full-time salaried supervised clinical practice placement, working under the guidance of a qualified audiologist. You would be taking part in a national training scheme and would have to record regular competency assessments in a logbook. The final year involves returning to university to learn about more advanced aspects of audiology and to complete a dissertation.

Aspects of the course include the anatomy and physiology of the ear and the physics of sound and hearing aids, as well as the diagnostic and rehabilitative techniques used by an audiologist and how these may best be used in effective patient care. For the latter, you could expect to learn about relevant topics within health psychology, speech sciences, disability studies, counselling skills and research methods.

Students on MSc and postgraduate diploma programmes need to acquire assessed clinical experience as part of their studies or through part-time employment.

You should note that the training route set out here may change as a result of the 'Modernising Scientific Careers' programme currently being developed by the Department of Health.

Career Opportunities

Once qualified, most audiologists work in a hospital, assessing and treating patients, and may reach consultant level. Some audiologists work in a university, where their job is primarily concerned with teaching and research.

NHS audiologists work closely with ENT consultants, health visitors and speech and language therapists to provide the appropriate assessment and intervention for children and adults of all ages. They may also work with a range of other professionals to address the needs of groups with special requirements such as children and adults with learning difficulties.

Audiology is a rapidly developing field, and the need for audiological services is well documented. A national study of hearing shows that approximately 16% of the population have a significant hearing loss, indicating that working in this field is an important area of the NHS. Developments such as the provision of digital hearing aid technology and universal newborn hearing screening mean that employment prospects remain very bright. There are also opportunities available in the private sector.

With experience, many audiologists develop a special interest and expertise in one area of audiology, such as paediatrics or balance.

Related Degrees

Human Communication (Speech and Language Therapy)

Suggested Reading

Introduction to Audiology
- Frederick N. Martin and John Greer Clark, Pearson, 2009

Handbook of Clinical Audiology
- Jack Katz, Lippincott Williams and Wilkins, 2009

Further Information

British Academy of Audiology
www.baaudiology.org

NHS Careers
www.nhscareers.nhs.uk

Irish Society of Audiology
www.irishsocietyofaudiology.ie

Biochemistry

Original article by Dr Louise Banton, Lancaster University, with additional material supplied by the Biochemical Society

Introduction

Biochemists study the most basic of life processes. For example, identifying the ways in which DNA is transferred between cells and can be manipulated. This has led to the development of new technologies such as Molecular Biology and Genetic Engineering. The resulting recombinant DNA technology has formed the basis of modern biotechnology (e.g. production of human insulin), medical developments (e.g. prenatal diagnosis and genetic counselling) and forensic science (e.g. DNA fingerprinting).

DNA directs the production of proteins. These have diverse functions, such as catalysing biological reactions (enzymes), carrying oxygen round the body (haemoglobin), protecting us from infection (antibodies) and holding us together (collagen). Using both simple and high-technology methods, biochemists work out how these proteins function. Biochemists also develop methods for making use of proteins, such as enzymes in biotechnology and antibodies in hormone analysis.

With knowledge of the basic molecular mechanisms, biochemists study how life processes are integrated to allow individual cells to function and interact to form complex organisms. They work with all sorts of organisms, from viruses and bacteria to plants and man.

Degree Courses

At a typical university, the biochemistry degree will be made up of modules, which enable you to construct the most suitable course of study for your degree.

The emphasis of the subject will be medical and will include courses in immunology, blood biochemistry and genetic diseases. Later in the course, you will undertake projects, in which you may collaborate with a local industry or school; you will also be able to specialise in areas that interest you, such as biomedicine, immunology, genetics and microbiology.

The modules in all courses are likely to include genetics, the molecular design of life, introduction to the cell, nervous systems, biomedical physiology, protein structure, enzymes metabolism, bio-energenetics, physiology, blood biochemistry, glycobiology, immunology, enzymes, biotechnology and cell signalling. There will be modules in organic, physical and inorganic chemistry, together with an introduction to spectroscopic theory and techniques.

University courses vary and it is very important that you look at a range of prospectuses and visit as many universities as possible. Many universities offer sandwich courses, which give the opportunity to spend a year working in industry. Because biochemistry is a research-based discipline, many graduates continue into postgraduate training.

Career Opportunities

There are many areas of everyday life in which biochemists are employed.

Industry - Pharmaceutical, food, brewing, biotechnology and agrochemical companies.

Medicine - Hospitals, public health laboratories, medical research institutes, and the pharmaceutical industry.

Education - All levels of education offer prospects for biochemists.

Away from Science - Biochemists can be employed in sales and marketing, finance, journalism and patent work.

Related Degrees

Molecular Biosciences, Applied Biochemistry, Medical Biochemistry, Molecular Medicine, Biochemistry with Industrial Placement, Nutritional Biochemistry, Biochemical Engineering, Biomedicine, Agricultural Biochemistry, Biochemistry with Biotechnology

Suggested Reading

Schaum's Easy Outline of Biochemistry
- Philip W. Kuchel, Schaum, 2002

Biochemistry: International Edition
- Lubert Stryer et al, W H Freeman, 2006

Molecular Biology of the Cell
- Bruce Alberts et al, Garland, 2008

Further Information

Association for Clinical Biochemistry
www.acb.org.uk

Society of Biology
www.societyofbiology.org

Royal Society of Chemistry
www.rsc.org

Bioindustry Association
www.bioindustry.org

Biochemical Society
www.biochemistry.org

Biotechnology and Biological Sciences Research Council
www.bbsrc.ac.uk

Institute of Biology of Ireland
www.ibioli.net

Biotechnology Ireland
www.biotechnologyireland.com

Biology

Original article by Professor N Maclean, Southampton University

Introduction

Biology, the study of life and living things, occupies a unique position in the spectrum of human interest and knowledge. Although undoubtedly a science, it has much in common with the arts, partly because nature appeals to our aesthetic as well as our rational senses, and also because we ourselves are part of nature. For this reason many people who would not otherwise choose to study science finally settle on biology. On the other hand, with the rapid growth of molecular biology over the last decade, some who would previously have chosen to study physical sciences are now considering biology as a possible and challenging alternative. Many departments now offer a choice of degree options in eg biology, botany, zoology, cell biology and applied biology, the choice of degree title depending on courses chosen for study.

Thus, if you find yourself subscribing to any of the following categories then it may mean that biology should be your prime choice of subject. (1) Your interests straddle the two cultures of science and arts, (2) you are very keen on natural history, birds, plants, insects or whatever, (3) your greatest passion is conservation of the planet and its natural resources, (4) you are not at all keen about natural history or conservation, but you are intrigued by problems of living systems and how they work, (5) you are interested in medicine but don't want to become a 'doctor'.

Degree Courses

Biology is often taken to represent 'soft' science rather than 'hard' science, that is a science where the number of variables in any one situation may be so great that the construction of an equation or formula is impossible. Although with the recent growth of molecular biology and biotechnology this is much less true than it once was, it is still sufficiently true to mean that biology may appeal to those with limited expertise in the physical sciences. But do not be beguiled into thinking that the softer science indicates a softer option. The ability to analyse and understand complex situations such as arise, for example, in evolutionary genetics, requires a sharp mind as well as considerable breadth of knowledge.

The central core in most departments would consist of cell biology, genetics, ecology, and the form and function of living organisms; students will often be encouraged or compelled to study computation and statistics on the one hand and biochemistry and physiology on the other. From this basic groundwork will stem a range of optional specialisations in, for example, parasitology, taxonomy, evolution, cell and molecular biology, developmental biology, immunology, applied ecology, animal behaviour and advanced courses in genetics or comparative physiology. Of course many departments have their own special areas of research expertise, but these are reflected more in higher degree course structures than in undergraduate ones. When you visit a department as a prospective student, you should enquire about the areas in which the research strengths of the department lie. They may not coincide at all with the topic in which you would want to specialise.

Many of the key questions facing mankind now and in the future are essentially biological. How can we control our own population, avoid war, cure disease, conserve nature? To my mind one of the most exciting things about being a student of biology is that one learns so much more about oneself. You learn to understand your own anatomy, physiology, behaviour and evolution, and you also come to see yourself in the context of nature, as one amongst many other species, as a member of an evolved and evolving population of organisms, interacting at all times and all levels with the other diverse organisms with which we share the planet. Whether you are managing staff in Marks and Spencer or running field trials of agricultural crops, there is much to be gained from the bracing sense of perspective, both evolutionary and ecological, shared by those who have learned to think deeply about biology.

Career Opportunities

Some biology graduates enter research or continue with further academic or professional training, but the majority find employment in finance, administration and operational management, marketing/buying, medical and technical sales, computer programming, environmental health, laboratory work, technical journalism etc. Biology graduates are attractive to employers because they are normally well trained in communication skills, numeracy, scientific method and how to best deal with complex problems in management.

Related Degrees

Human Biology, Biotechnology, Tropical Disease Biology, Forensic Biology, Applied Biology, Medical Biology, Animal Biology, Computational Biology, Behavioural Biology, Biology with Overseas Study, Food Biology, Palaeobiology, Cancer Biology, Biophysics, Cell Biology, Developmental Biology

Suggested Reading

Life: The Science of Biology
- David Sadava et al, W.H. Freeman, 2009

The Selfish Gene
- R Dawkins, Oxford University Press (revised edition) 2006

Wonderful Life: Burgess Shale and the Nature of History
- Stephen Jay Gould, Vintage, 2000

The Language of the Genes
- Steve Jones, Flamingo, 2000

Biology (Pie)
- Neil A. Campbell et al, Pearson Education, 2005

Further Information

Society of Biology
www.societyofbiology.org

Biotechnology and Biological Sciences Research Council
www.bbsrc.ac.uk

Institute of Biology of Ireland
www.ibioli.net

Biomedical Science

Original article by Dr Christopher Smith, GKT School of Biomedical Sciences, King's College, London

Introduction

Different universities tend to use the term biomedical science in very different ways: some centre on the teaching of topics such as haematology and transfusion science, medical microbiology, pathology and clinical biochemistry. The Institute of Biomedical Sciences has approved these programmes with the aim of graduate entry into hospital and other diagnostic organisations as laboratory scientists. Other universities, mainly those with associated medical schools, have a different objective. They offer combinations of the science subjects that form the basis of biomedical research, such as physiology, pharmacology, molecular biology, anatomy, genetics, developmental science and neuroscience. The first biomedical science degree of this kind was a response to the increasing trend of joint-subject degrees such as physiology and pharmacology, recognising that - especially at research level - there is an important and essential integration between the traditional disciplines. A study of pain would nowadays be hard to fund with neuroscientists alone; a combined molecular pharmacological and developmental approach would be more likely to succeed.

Degree Courses

It is of course impossible to study at an advanced level all the subjects mentioned above. Most universities offer an integrated first year, usually with the emphasis on the base subjects of physiology, pharmacology, cell biology and molecular biology. In the second and third years, increasingly you will be asked to specialise. At some universities this may be by formal transfer to a specialist programme such as neuroscience. In other cases you will be required to make your own choice of individual units so that you can either develop a detailed knowledge of your chosen area, such as cardiovascular science, or follow a traditional specialist degree. Finally you might choose a wide range of topics including some outside biomedical science such as languages, management, environmental science or philosophy. This last pattern would be appropriate for jobs such as the management of science, science journalism or teaching. One factor to note is that the larger the size of the biomedical department, the larger the range of course units that can be offered. Larger schools, however, also have larger class sizes (rising up to 500 in first year courses): you must choose the style and options that suit your personal needs.

Career Opportunities

Biomedical science could well become established as a prime route to the rapidly growing field of graduate-entry medicine. Medical schools feel happier with graduates who have proved their ability for advanced study and also had time to develop their interest in medicine through extended work in the healthcare system. Please note that 'transfer' to medicine is not offered: you would apply to several medical schools at the beginning of your third year via UCAS. Most medical schools do not specify the exact degree programmes required but biomedical science at a university with a medical school clearly is a very good start. Biomedical science also offers you entry, depending on your chosen specialisations, to the bioscience careers detailed elsewhere in these Degree Course Descriptions, including biochemistry, physiology and molecular biology. Finally you should not forget that close to 50% of graduates move into the general job market, including management, the Civil Service, the Armed Forces and finance. It is for you to consider this range of careers and what type of biomedical science programme will best help your aims.

To work as a biomedical laboratory scientist, you would need to register with the Health Professions Council.

Related Degrees

Clinical Sciences, Clinical Physiology, Biomedical Materials Science, Life Sciences, Medicine, Pharmacology, Genetics, Pharmacy, Molecular Biology, Neuroscience, Haematology, Medical Microbiology, Chemical Biochemistry.

Suggested Reading

Biomedical Sciences Explained
- Series of books designed specifically to meet the needs of undergraduates studying biomedical sciences. Each volume covers a key topic, such as Clinical Biochemistry, Haematology, Cellular Pathology, Transfusion Science. C J Pallister, Series Editor, Hodder Arnold

Essentials of Human Anatomy and Physiology
- Elaine N. Marieb, Pearson, 2008

Biology of Disease
-Nessar Ahmed et al, Taylor and Francis, 2006

Further Information

Institute of Biomedical Science
www.ibms.org

Health Professions Council
www.hpc-uk.org

Wellcome Trust
www.wellcome.ac.uk

British Pharmacological Society
www.bps.ac.uk

Physiological Society
www.physoc.org

Royal Society
http://royalsociety.org

Academy of Medical Laboratory Science, Ireland
www.amls.ie

Biotechnology

Original article by Dr J H Parish, Leeds University

Introduction

Biotechnology is concerned with the application of the biological sciences to manufacturing. Some of the processes themselves (especially those concerned with the food and drink industries) are thousands of years old but the analysis of the processes by the application of scientific method and the use of scientific enquiry to expand the variety of biological products, are relatively recent. Biotechnologists are employed by breweries in order to optimise the performance of their companies by applying such subjects as fermentation technology and the molecular genetics of yeast to the brewing process.

Degree Courses

There are four major academic foundations of biotechnology:

Biochemistry emphasises a certain unity among living organisms. Organisms have energy-yielding metabolisms whereby substrates are converted to products and energy is trapped by the synthesis of Adenosine Triphosphate (ATP). This invariably involves oxidation/reduction (in our species reduced substrates such as cream cakes and fish and chips are oxidised to carbon dioxide and water) but the variety in different forms of life is considerable. All organisms use enzyme catalysts to convert substrates to the chemicals required for growth by processes that involve expenditure of ATP.

Genetic engineering Classical genetics is limited by the 'breeding barrier' (you can cross barley and rye, horses and donkeys, but not diverse species - such as carrots and elephants). There are techniques for introducing genes (i.e. a piece of DNA) from one organism into cells of a totally unrelated host. The hosts are commonly microbes but can be animal or plant cells.

Cell culture Bacteria, yeasts and moulds have been the organisms used in industrial fermentations. To these can now be added cells of animals and plants; specialised examples of these are used to produce vaccines, antibodies and natural products. Photosynthetic microbes suggest an alternative for the large scale fixation of CO_2.

Fermentation engineering and reactor design are specialised engineering subjects and biotechnology presents engineers with problems concerned with sterilisation, stirring, heat exchange and downstream processing of large volumes of aqueous materials.

The following examples are necessarily incomplete. Genetic engineering allows the construction of micro-organisms and animal and plant cells in culture that contain cloned genes from a variety of sources. Further manipulation allows the expression of these genes. We can construct a bacterial or fungal strain that will produce proteins of animal origin and which is of established value. Examples are chymosin (an enzyme used in cheese manufacture obtained otherwise from calves) and several human proteins of medical importance. The benefits of using fermentation technology vary between the economic, humanitarian and medically desirable. The implications of the ability to introduce and express foreign genes into cells are rather different. If these cells are used to generate whole plants or if their genetic information is introduced into embryonic animals we obtain 'transgenic' higher organisms. A transgenic plant might have properties of resistance to pests, diseases or herbicides. Transgenic animals might be used to generate recombinant proteins in their milk. The ability to manipulate DNA in the laboratory provides a method for altering or improving the performance of a protein for specific purposes. Such activities are referred to as 'protein engineering'. One example of protein engineering is the modification of the enzyme present in biological washing powders to allow it to perform better in washing machines. More important for the human race is the modification of proteins for medical use. The science of molecular biology has generated a technological revolution. Just as organic chemistry generated novel chemicals, such as dyestuffs and plastics, molecular biology has entered a synthetic or creative phase that is leading to a domination of parts of the fermentation, pharmaceutical and agricultural industries.

Career Opportunities

A biotechnology degree can lead to careers in the NHS, the Medical Research Council and the food and pharmacology industries, where the techniques involved are at the forefront of many new technical developments, eg in using enzyme systems in yeasts or bacteria to produce useful substances such as penicillin, antibodies (needed to fight specific diseases), foodstuffs, proteins, enzymes, carbohydrates or alcoholic drinks.

Related Degrees

Environmental Biotechnology, Medical Biotechnology, Biotechnology with a year in Europe

Suggested Reading

Environmental Biotechnology
- Alan Scragg, OUP, 2005

Biotechnology (Studies in Biology)
- John Smith, CUP, 2008

Biotechnology for Beginners
- Reinhard Renneberg, Academic Press, 2007

Further Information

BioIndustry Association
www.bioindustry.org

Biotechnology and Biological Sciences Research Council
www.bbsrc.ac.uk

Biotechnology Ireland
www.biotechnologyireland.com

Botany

Original article by Dr Julie Hawkins, University of Reading

Introduction

Botany encompasses all aspects of plant biology, from molecular biology to ecosystems, from the smallest green unicellular organisms to the tallest forest trees. In a world which is likely to become increasingly dependent on threatened plant resources for food security and even for maintaining the composition of the air we breathe, the subject is bound to assume ever greater importance in future years.

As you read this article, botanists are busy collecting and describing the plants of the rainforest, designing conservation strategies for urban nature reserves, examining peat cores to determine the effects of past climate change, cross-pollinating crop plants to breed new drought resistant varieties, managing museum collections, using electron microscopes and automated DNA sequencing for cutting-edge research into fundamental processes, extracting and investigating the useful chemicals that plants produce, advising customs officers trying to stop the illegal export of rare plants, reconstructing fossil plants, determining the extent of gene flow between GM crop plants and their wild relatives, optimising greenhouse conditions for ornamental plants, identifying plant fragments as part of forensic investigations to determine the scene of a crime, participating in ethnobotanic surveys to record how tribal peoples use local plants, and studying the genetics of plant metabolism. Botanists are certainly never short of challenges!

Degree Courses

As a botany undergraduate, you should find that your degree programme includes most or all of the elements listed below. Each of these elements impinges on and assists in understanding and interpreting the others. **Plant Ecology** is the study of the interactions of plants with each other, with other organisms and with their physical environment. The theory of evolution is the foundation of modern biological science; studies in **Plant Evolution** would include plant adaptation, the origins of land plants and of flowering plants as well as **Palaeobotany** - the study of fossil plants. **Plant Systematics** is the biodiversity science of naming and description, classification and documentation of plants. **Economic Botany** describes the study of past and present use of plants and plant products, from hunter gatherer societies, through Neolithic farming to contemporary initiatives to conserve plant genetic resources. **Plant Genetics** includes a range of pure and applied topics such as biotechnology and plant breeding, population genetics, genomics and cytology. **Plant Biochemistry** the study of metabolic pathways and the use of techniques such as nuclear magnetic resonance and X-ray crystallography to study protein structures, also includes **Phytochemistry**, the study of the defence and attractant chemicals. **Plant Geography** - often using Geographical Information Systems (GIS) - is the study of the distribution of plants, and explains the current distribution of plants in terms of evolutionary history, geological and climatic history and plant dispersal mechanisms. **Plant Morphology and Anatomy** is the study of the diverse and constant features of plant structures, such as fruits, flowers, shoots and roots. **Plant Development and Physiology** includes the study of transitions such as breaking of seed dormancy or flowering. The determination of the genetic basis of these transitions has become an important area of research. **Plant Conservation Biology** is the applied science which incorporates genetics (population genetics), vegetation survey and Environmental Impact Assessment, and applied ecology.

Universities with schools of soil science, zoology, meteorology, agriculture or geography would usually offer modules in these subjects to botany undergraduates.

Career Opportunities

Botanists are employed by botanic gardens and museums in Britain and overseas, by showcase educational attractions, such as the Eden Project, by conservation organisations such as Natural England, in public sector research (e.g. by universities and research centres such as the John Innes Centre in Norwich) and in the private sector. Industries and organisations related to horticulture, including the Royal Horticultural Society, are important employers. Botanists are also employed by international projects to reduce hunger and poverty, improve human nutrition and health, and protect the environment, such as those of the Consultative Group on International Agricultural Research (CGIAR). Many graduate botanists continue with further academic study before taking up a job with one of these employers. Other botany graduates use their degrees to enter other professions such as teaching, finance, administration, environmental health or science publishing.

Related Degrees

Plant Science, Environmental Biology, Conservation Biology, Soil Science

Suggested Reading

Botany: an introduction to Plant Biology
- James Mauseth, Jones and Bartlett, 2008

Biology of Plants
- Peter Raven et al, W H Freeman, 2005

Plant Physiology: international edition
- Lincoln Taiz and Eduardo Zeiger, Sinauer Associates, 2010

Further Information

Royal Horticultural Society
www.rhs.org.uk

Natural England
www.naturalengland.org.uk

John Innes Centre
www.jic.ac.uk

Internet Directory for Botany
www.botany.net/IDB/botany.html

Royal Botanic Garden Edinburgh
www.rbge.org.uk

UNEP World Conservation Monitoring Centre
www.unep-wcmc.org

Consultative Group on International Agricultural Research
www.cgiar.org

Royal Botanic Gardens Kew
www.kew.org

Botany Department at the Natural History Museum
www.nhm.ac.uk/botany

Eden Project
www.edenproject.com

Royal Horticultural Society of Ireland
www.rhsi.ie

Building, Surveying and Construction

Original article by K Hutchinson, Department of Construction Management & Engineering, University of Reading, Martin Simons, School of the Built Environment, Coventry University and John Pearson, Department of Quantity Surveying, University of Northumbria at Newcastle.

Introduction

Imagine a building such as a new sports stadium: it must be planned, designed, engineered, constructed and maintained. A host of skills are involved ranging from the selection of the most appropriate material through to ensuring that the structure is totally safe when there are extremes of temperature.

Degree Courses

Universities offer a wide variety of modular and linear degree courses in the areas of Building, Surveying and Construction but certain aspects are common to all.

Building Construction and Management is likely to appeal to students who see their future in planning, executing and managing the construction of building and civil engineering projects. Courses give a deeper understanding of the entire construction process, from the brief given to an architect through all the design and planning stages to the completion of the project on site. In addition, students follow courses in management, economics and law related to construction. Final year students usually undertake a major project that integrates all aspects of the course.

Building Environmental Engineering Design and Management covers all the environmental services (air conditioning, ventilation, heating, lighting, sound) and utility services (electrical power, communications, fire protection, water, lifts) which usually make a building function. Courses include: mathematics, thermal engineering, electrical engineering and building technology management. Some are continued with the addition of environmental engineering, lighting and acoustic utility and space engineering, computer aided design and human factors.

Building Surveying deals with the technological and managerial aspects of construction in relation to existing buildings. It is a base for careers in built facilities management including maintenance, refurbishment and rehabilitation of buildings. Building surveyors require creative design ability and technical and managerial competence.

A modular course in **Building Surveying**, at a typical university, has a common theme in Construction and Design. Level 1 deals with the domestic construction, developing at Level 3 into highly specialised systems and modular building components. Level 1 aims to lay the foundations with modules such as building mechanics, building materials, environmental studies, economics, information technology, building law and town and country planning. Level 2 builds upon these foundations with construction and design taken into the commercial and industrial property areas. Aspects of the specialist nature of building surveying are developed in property studies, planning and property development, and management principles. Practical skills, such as building and land surveying, are practised in the field course. At Level 2, a project brings these together to explain the integrated nature of the construction industry and the people and services which have an input into it. After a voluntary year of professional training, the major themes of Level 3 construction and design are aspects of innovative construction.

Quantity Surveying provides a sound foundation in the basic principles of quantity surveying practice and gives an intellectual challenge which equips students with the main problem-solving techniques needed in modern construction management. The course at one typical university has a total of 36 units spread over three years. Sandwich students spend a period of 12 months in industry in which students work in private practice, for a local authority, in a commercial setting or in a construction company. Examples of units include measurement and appraisal, building technology, economics of the built environment, computing for the built environment, introduction to law for the built environment, town and country planning, civil engineering technology and measurement, applied economics and cost studies.

Construction Management Engineering and Surveying courses are for students who aspire to senior management positions in the general area of building, construction and management. Courses have been designed to open up a comprehensive range of options for practice in the construction industry as project managers, cost managers or property managers.

Career Opportunities

The majority of graduates in these disciplines enter the construction industry. Few enter research, design, development and financial fields. The demand for construction managers depends to a great extent on the state of the building trade and it must be said that the picture in 2010 is not entirely encouraging, as the housing market tries to recover from the severe downturn of 2009. Forecasts suggest, however, that demand for homes and industrial, office, retail and leisure facilities will gradually pick up again. The task of building the London 2012 Olympics has created a large number of jobs in the building industry, with specialist construction knowledge in particularly high demand.

Related Degrees

Building Services Engineering, Construction Management, Construction Engineering, Building Surveying Management, Quantity Surveying Management, Architectural Technology, Building Conservation, Building/Environmental Service Engineering, Estate Surveying and Evaluation, Fire Safety

Suggested Reading

Building - Penguin Dictionary of
- John Scott and James Maclean, Penguin, 2004

Working in Construction and the Built Environment
- VT Lifeskills, 2007

Real Life Guide: Construction
- Dee Pilgrim, Trotman, 2007

Building Construction Handbook
- Roy Chudley and Roger Greeno, Butterworth-Heinemann, 2010

The Housebuilder's Bible: An Insider's Guide to the Construction Jungle
- Mark Brinkley, Ovolo, 2009

Further Information

Chartered Institute of Building
www.ciob.org.uk
Royal Institution of Chartered Surveyors
www.rics.org
Construction Skills
www.cskills.org
Association of Building Engineers
www.abe.org.uk
Society of Chartered Surveyors, Ireland
www.scs.ie
Construction Industry Federation, Ireland
www.cif.ie

Chemical Engineering

Original article adapted with permission from material supplied by the Institution of Chemical Engineers (IChemE)

Introduction

Chemical engineering is distinguished from other forms of engineering by its foundation in molecular behaviour. This is most obviously the case in the design of chemical reactors but is also very important in the prediction of the equilibrium behaviour of multiphase systems. It is the need for an awareness of molecular behaviour that is the key for an understanding of operations in most chemical processes.

Degree courses are available at 23 universities in the UK and Ireland, with the great majority fully accredited by the IChemE. Most departments of chemical engineering offer courses leading to the award of a Bachelor of Engineering (BEng) and a Master of Engineering (MEng). Some departments offer sandwich courses in which students spend a year in industry and others may offer such a year if so requested.

In recent years there has been a significant increase in the number of courses in which chemical engineering is combined with related areas such as food engineering, environmental engineering and minerals engineering. Courses are available with a significant process management content, with European studies and with studies in North America.

Degree Courses

Courses obviously have a significant chemistry content. However, if you are thinking of studying chemical engineering, it is important to be aware that the emphasis of the course is on engineering. In common with other engineering disciplines, mathematics and physics play a key role. Usually the chemical engineering content of a course is interwoven into all three or four years of study and is taught from the outset.

The first topics that are encountered are often thermodynamics and process analysis, which are right at the heart of chemical engineering and not only enable entire processes to be analysed in terms of material and energy utilisation but, equally importantly, open the door to the assessment of processes against fundamental thermodynamic measures. Once an appreciation of processes as a whole has been gained, attention becomes focused on the operations and plant items that constitute a process. This inevitably involves a study of the ways of bringing about the required chemical and physical changes that underlie chemical engineering processes. However, the story does not stop there as the products of these changes may have to be separated and purified, they may have to be heated or cooled and some may have to be recycled to undergo further changes. All of these topics are supplemented by teaching in areas such as information technology, including computer-aided process engineering, plant and equipment design, materials, safety, risk analysis, environmental compatibility, managerial economics and management studies.

In a typical degree course in chemical engineering you could be introduced to the study of process engineering and also build on your knowledge of chemistry, mathematics and microbiology. You would learn about instrumentation and control, fermentation, separation and also, as has been mentioned, thermodynamics.

Later, you would extend the work involved in the first year but also study chemical and biochemical engineering, reaction engineering, transport phenomena and various aspects of processes (including control, economics and development). You would begin to deal with the vital topics of design and safety and may be offered courses in other types of engineering so that you can better understand the problems faced by other engineers (e.g. electrical and electronic engineers).

The **later years** of the course are likely to give you the chance to pursue your particular interests by giving you some choice of modules. At this stage, some courses offer industrial placements. The culmination of a course in chemical engineering is usually the design project in which students work together in small groups on the preliminary design of a complete process plant.

Chemical engineers work with engineers from other disciplines. They have to work with civil engineers for the foundations, access roads and supporting structures, with electrical engineers for power and with mechanical engineers for the design of various items of equipment.

Career Opportunities

The chemical engineering profession is traditionally viewed as the domain of the petrochemical, oil and gas and pharmaceutical industries, but these days chemical engineers can be found in such diverse fields as food technology, water, mining and environmental protection. With the rise in media focus on processed foods, the lack of clean drinking water in poor areas and the need for more environmentally friendly fuels, chemical engineers developing solutions to these problems can enjoy a new status as the harbingers of change. The expansion of these industries has also ensured a growth in the need for chemical engineers worldwide.

Related Degrees

Chemical and Process Engineering, Environmental Chemical Engineering, Chemical Engineering with Study Abroad, Fire Science, Brewing and Distilling

Suggested Reading

Perry's Chemical Engineers' Handbook
- Robert Perry Ed, McGraw-Hill Education, 2007

Chemical Engineering: Introductory Aspects
- Robert Field, Macmillan, 1988

Further Information

Institution of Chemical Engineers (UK and Ireland)
http://cms.icheme.org

Engineering Council UK
www.engc.org.uk

European Federation of Chemical Engineering
www.efce.info

Engineers Ireland
www.engineersireland.ie

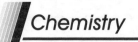

Chemistry

Original article by Professor Paul H Walton, Department of Chemistry, University of York

With contributions by the School of Chemistry, University of Hull.

Introduction

There were major changes a few years ago in the structure of Chemistry degree courses, the most fundamental of which was the introduction of four-year courses in England, Northern Ireland and Wales (most - but not all - entitled MChem or MSci) alongside the traditional BSc or occasionally BA courses. Don't be confused by the M in MChem: these are first degree courses, not postgraduate courses, with the same honours classifications (first, upper second, etc) as traditional BSc courses. One reason for this has been the dual award GCSE Science, which has had the effect of lowering the level at which degree courses begin in England, Northern Ireland and Wales.

Degree Courses

The choice between BSc and MChem is an important one, but at most universities the two degree programmes are similar or even identical for the first two years, so that you may well be able to switch from MChem to BSc as late as the end of year 2. Don't think simply in terms of "MChem for the best and BSc for the rest": ask yourself whether what universities are offering you in the extra MChem year will (a) be interesting and challenging and (b) help you in your likely career after graduation.

Look carefully at what the additional year can offer. Usually it will provide you with another year of study at the same university, and most of the year will probably be devoted to a long research project, but you should also be given the chance to specialise in advanced aspects of chemistry which suit your own interests.

There is also, however, the prospect of spending part or all of the extra year studying chemistry at a university in another country so that you may develop language skills (and a vocabulary which includes scientific terms) likely to be extremely useful in career terms. Whatever the timing of your period of study abroad, it is important that the chemistry taught should fit in with what you do in the UK, and that you should not miss out on important features of the entirely home-based courses (for example project work). Another option offered by several universities is the chance to spend part or all of the extra year in paid industrial training (see below).

Most universities now claim to offer modular chemistry degree courses, although the freedom you have to select your own modules and the range from which you can choose varies enormously.

Many chemistry departments, through their industrial contacts, can help you in finding work, which not only brings in money but also gives you useful experience. With the advent of the four-year MChem courses, your chances of obtaining a paid placement, which counts towards your degree, are much greater. The chemical industry also encourages students to choose chemistry as their degree subject by offering sponsorship.

Two final pieces of advice: Firstly, "If in doubt, ask!" There really is no excuse for failing to get the information you need. Secondly "See for yourself". All chemistry departments will arrange for you to visit them after they have received your application through UCAS: many will also be happy to see you individually or on Open Days. Make sure that you are happy with the surroundings in which you will be living and working and with the facilities which will be available to you!

Career Opportunities

There are generally good prospects of employment for chemists, although all of industry was affected by the economic downturn in 2009. As a graduating chemical scientist, you could choose to work in a field vital to the future, such as addressing climate change, providing energy, securing food and water or developing new technologies in healthcare, communication and security. Should you decide that you want to continue with postgraduate study, it is sometimes possible to get your research funded by your company once you start. Depending on the type of career you choose to pursue, you could find yourself working in a chemical production plant, a laboratory or an office.

Chemistry graduates also work in professions such as financial services, where their proven skills - not only data analysis and numeracy but an understanding of the physical world and providing robust intellectual challenge - are highly valued and well rewarded.

Related Degrees

Applied Chemistry, Chemistry with Management, Chemistry with Study Abroad, Biological Chemistry, Colour Chemistry, Analytical Chemistry, Forensic Science Chemistry, Chemistry with Industrial Experience, Chemistry in North America, Geochemistry, Computational Chemistry, Environmental Chemistry, Medicinal Chemistry, Industrial/Technical Chemistry, Pharmaceutical Chemistry, Chemistry with Materials, Chemical Physics, Biomolecular Chemistry, Polymer Science, Materials Chemistry

Suggested Reading

Chemistry
- Penguin Dictionary of - D W A Sharp Ed, Penguin, 2004

Chemistry: Molecules, Matter and Change
- Peter Atkins and Loretta Jones Eds, W H Freeman, 2000

Degrees in Chemistry and the Chemical Sciences
- Royal Society of Chemistry, downloadable from the RSC website at:
www.rsc.org/Images/Degrees_In_Chemistry-The_Essential_Guide_tcm18-10333.pdf

Further Information

Royal Society of Chemistry
www.rsc.org

Chemical Industries Association
www.cia.org.uk

Institute of Chemistry of Ireland
www.chemistryireland.org

Civil Engineering

Original article by John Oliphant, Heriot-Watt University, Edinburgh

Introduction

As a civil engineer, you could be involved in seeing projects through from design stage to construction and completion. Your projects might include the development and construction of bridges, tunnels, roads, railways, dams, pipelines and major buildings. At times, you might be in your office, working on designs at a computer or ensuring that your clients are kept up to date; at other times, you could be on site, leading teams, solving problems and literally being 'hands-on'.

Your first step is to study civil engineering at university to honours degree level (MEng or BEng) on a course recognised or accredited by the Institution of Civil Engineers (ICE). Having passed your course, your next important step is a professional qualification, which you can earn once you start working. This will define you as a true professional, capable of practising in most countries of the world.

There are three main types of professional qualification awarded by ICE. You can recognise who has these qualifications by letters (designations) after a name (e.g CEng MICE):

- An engineering technician (Eng Tech TMICE) applies proven techniques and procedures to solve engineering problems. They act as supervisors with technical responsibility

- An incorporated engineer (IEng MICE) is a professional engineer who promotes today's technology and applies and manages its use within the broad field of civil engineering

- A chartered engineer (CEng MICE) is an innovator who can lead teams of engineers and technicians developing solutions to civil engineering problems.

Degree Courses

The differences between courses at different universities can only be appreciated by reading prospectuses, and then visiting selected civil engineering departments. You must note clearly the strengths of each institution and its courses.

Some facts to find out are:

- What options are open to you later in the course?

- Does the course enable you to study for a time at a university abroad? This is of considerable importance to potential civil engineers, where firms are increasingly international.

- If you have the chance to study abroad, what arrangements are made for you to become competent in the appropriate foreign language?

- What does each university claim to be its strengths?

- Does the course involve any industrial experience, and if so how much?

- Is the course modular or is it linear?

Career Opportunities

Civil engineers can take advantage of work opportunities in both the private and public sectors, often changing jobs to gain more professional experience. They tend to specialise in areas such as roads and bridges, oil and gas rigs and pipelines, power stations, docks and harbours or public health and sewerage. There are courses run by the Institution of Civil Engineers for on-going professional development. UK civil engineering qualifications are internationally recognised and there are many opportunities to work on projects abroad. You could eventually become a director or partner in a civil engineering firm. Alternatively, you could become a university lecturer or set up as a consultant.

Civil engineering projects were severely affected by the economic downturn in 2009. However, the industry is slowly picking up again in 2010.

Related Degrees

Structural Engineering, Construction Engineering, Architectural Engineering, Civil and Coastal Engineering, Civil Engineering Surveying, Civil and Environmental Engineering, Civil and Structural Engineering, Offshore Engineering, Civil Engineering with Industrial Experience, Civil Engineering with Overseas Study

Suggested Reading

The new science of strong materials: or why you don't fall through the floor
- J E Gordon, Princeton University Press, 2008

Structures: or Why Things Don't Fall Down
- J E Gordon, Penguin Science, 2009

Introduction to Architectural Technology
- Pete Silver and Will McLean, Laurence King, 2008

Further Information

Engineering Council UK
www.engc.org.uk

Institution of Civil Engineers
www.ice.org.uk

Institution of Structural Engineers
www.istructe.org

Engineers Ireland
www.engineersireland.ie

Institution of Structural Engineers Republic of Ireland Branch
www.istructe.ie

Classics and Classical Studies

Original article by Dr Oswyn Murray, Balliol College, Oxford

Introduction

Classics is the study of the cultures of Greece and Rome. It was the original course in 'humanities' and is still a central arts discipline at most major UK universities. Its long tradition raises two questions: firstly, what is the justification of the classics in the modern world, and secondly, what are its strengths and weaknesses, both now and for the future?

The justification of classics lies in the nature of the Western cultural tradition. The essential characteristic of our culture, what the sociologist Max Weber called its 'formal rationality', is a creation of the Greeks. It was transmitted to the whole of Europe through the Roman Empire, and diffused through the rest of the world by the colonial expansion of Europe after the Renaissance, to become the basis of the first world civilisation. The Greeks were the first to separate clearly the three great functions of social civilisation - politics, religion and culture. In all essential aspects they set out the major branches of human investigation: biology, physics, medicine and mathematics in science; metaphysics, ethics, politics and logic in philosophy; sociology, psychology and anthropology in the social sciences; sculpture, pottery, architecture and the concept of representation in the arts; tragedy, comedy, epic, personal lyric, pastoral, history, biography and the divide between truth and fiction in literature. The Romans took over many of these artistic and intellectual pursuits from the Greeks but adapted them to the needs of their own younger and very different society. They made many original contributions, which remain central to our own culture, for instance legal science and public administration. In addition, many of the languages spoken on the continent of Europe are direct descendants of Latin. Of course many of these activities have transcended their beginnings, but the study of their classical origins reveals the interconnection between such different subjects and so the fundamental nature of the Western mind.

Degree Courses

For obvious reasons, therefore, the Western world has always looked back to the Greco-Roman past as an ideal and often sought to restore it in the present. One recurrent phenomenon in our culture is the creative importance of the renaissance or rebirth. The renewal of classical influences has marked every major new departure in culture from the fourth century AD to at least the nineteenth century. We cannot of course know the future. We may wonder if the chain has been broken, but even so its existence in the past is a fact, so that in the arts no major area of Western thought or literature can be understood without some knowledge of the classics. This explains the existence of classics courses in the majority of universities, for some access to the classics is presupposed for any serious arts studies; hence, too, the great popularity of foundation courses and of options covering classical history and literature in translation. Most classics departments now offer a variety of combined studies degrees in combination either with modern languages, or with philosophy, or with English.

Language requirements vary between courses and universities. For literary studies prior knowledge of Latin or Greek is an advantage, but all universities make provision for beginners in one or both languages. You need a keenness to learn. All universities teach in varying degrees in translation, often exclusively in translation for history and philosophy, while in literature a combination of survey in translation with in-depth study in the original is typical. Many universities also offer courses in classical studies, in which the thought, literature, art, history and archaeology of the classical world play a dominant role. The best preparation for classics at university lies in Latin and, where possible, Greek; the various ancient history and classical civilisation A level, Higher Grade or equivalent courses are also useful. But all universities accept students from a wide variety of backgrounds, as long as they can show a genuine interest in the classical world. If there is no provision for language work at your school, get in touch early with the Joint Association of Classical Teachers for information on the many residential and non-residential courses for beginners in both languages.

Career Opportunities

In a recent survey of Classics graduates, 30% had entered further education and training and 60% had found full-time employment. Many graduates had entered teaching and a relatively high percentage became barristers and solicitors. The majority undertake business and commerce, with a third of all classicists entering accountancy, banking and insurance. Many enter marketing, sales, computing, personnel, the Civil Service and local government.

Related Degrees

Classical Studies, Classical Civilisation, Greek Studies, Classics with Study in Continental Europe, Latin Studies

Suggested Reading

The Oxford History of Greece and the Hellenistic World
- John Boardman et al, Oxford Paperbacks, 2001

The Oxford History of the Roman World
- John Boardman et al, Oxford Paperbacks, 2001

Early Greece
- Oswyn Murray, Fontana Press, 2004

The Oxford History of Classical Art
- John Boardman Ed, Oxford University Press, 2001

Renaissance and Renascences in Western Art
- Erwin Panofsky, Westview Press, 1991

Further Information

Institute of Classical Studies University of London
www.sas.ac.uk/icls/institute

Classical Association
www.classicalassociation.org

Joint Association of Classical Teachers
www.jact.org

Classical Association of Ireland
www.classicalassociation.com

Communications and Media Studies

Original article by Philip M Taylor, Institute of Communications Studies, University of Leeds

Introduction

Communications and media studies courses at British universities have expanded at a phenomenal rate in recent years. Frequently the object of unfair, not to mention ironic, derision in the media - largely on the grounds that they do not train graduates for the real world of the media, journalism or the communications industries in the broadest sense - these courses do in fact cover a variety of purposes. As a subject, communications is, by definition, multidisciplinary. Essentially, it involves the study of 'who says what to whom, when, with what purpose and with what effect'. Today's most effective communicators need to understand that although communication takes place in a technologically-driven environment, it requires creative applications that draw upon a number of traditional academic disciplines such as history, politics, sociology, law, psychology and even art, together with newer areas like cultural studies, graphic design and internet skills.

Degree Courses

Many university departments are interested in the media for their own sake, as part of an attempt to understand this significant aspect of our modern information society. These tend to concentrate on the theoretical aspects and should be of interest to students who want to be critics or analysts of the media, rather than practitioners. In the same way that students taking courses, say, in fine art, history or English literature, would not necessarily expect to make a career in those areas, these courses provide critical and analytical training of the mind and, as such, provide transferable skills that can be of use to many areas of society. Other departments concentrate largely on the practical or training aspects of the communications professions - from journalism to corporate or public relations. The most successful of these programmes do, in fact, have high rates of graduate employment in the media industries. Look for courses that enjoy accreditation with professional bodies - such as Skillset or the Broadcast Journalism Training Council - or which have close relations (including attachments) with the media industries. Bear in mind that communications is one of the fastest changing employment environments of our time and that therefore academic departments that are well resourced with the latest digital and multi-media equipment are most likely to provide you with industry-ready skills.

More importantly, remember that communications is about communicating *something*. It is not just about the medium. The message is vitally important, and communicators who understand the skills needed to communicate also need the intellectual ability to understand what it is they are trying to say. Because communicators have enormous influence in our modern society, they carry considerable responsibilities. Programmes therefore that combine both theory and practice - although the balance is often difficult to maintain - tend to be the most successful of all.

But they are also the ones that attract the most applicants, and therefore they tend to require high examination grades for admission. On the other hand, because of their competitive nature, if you get in you will find yourself surrounded by many of the brightest and best students of your generation. Whether you are merely interested in understanding the media as a force which shapes so much of our perception about the world we live in, or whether you feel driven to become a driving force within our information society, make sure you choose the course that is right for you. Students who already know what they want to do in life can choose from a variety of specific courses on offer. Or if you don't know yet which aspect of this lively and expanding area you want to join, go for the more generalised courses that will help you make up your mind further down the road.

Career Opportunities

One thing is certain. Communications and information are going to be to the 21st century what oil and coal were to the 20th. Understanding this significance, as well as mastering its skills and matching up to the responsibilities involved, is as important now as it has ever been in a world in which 'information overload' is already one of its greatest challenges.

Related Degrees

Publishing, Public Relations, Communication Studies, Information Studies, Creative/Interactive/Design Media, International Business Communications, Media Studies

Suggested Reading

Mass Communications in the Modern World
- Ken Ward, Palgrave Macmillan, 1994

The Media at War: communication and conflict in the 20th century
- Susan Carruthers, Palgrave Macmillan, 1999

Media Uncovered
- Catherine Harris, Trotman, 2007

Degree Course Guide: English, Media Studies and American Studies
- Trotman, 2007

Media Studies: Texts, Production and Context
- Paul Long and Tim Wall, Longman, 2009

Further Information

Media and Communication Studies Site, Aberystwyth University
www.aber.ac.uk/media

Communication Advertising and Marketing Education Foundation
www.camfoundation.com

Skillset
www.skillset.org

Broadcast Journalism Training Council
www.bjtc.org.uk

National Council for the Training of Journalists
www.nctj.com

National Union of Journalists (UK and Ireland)
www.nuj.org.uk

Irish Film and Television Network
www.iftn.ie

Computing and Information Technology

Original article by Chris Kimble and Jeremy Jacob, Department of Computer Science, University of York
Professor David Arnold, School of Information Systems, UEA, Norwich

Introduction

The study of computation and computers is a broad and rapidly changing discipline. The subject has grown from one that was only of concern to a few mathematicians and electronic engineers to one where almost everybody's life is affected by computers in some way.

In taking a degree in computing, you should gain an education in a broad range of theory, tools and applications. You will also find that it has now become humanly impossible to know everything about computing, so you are likely to have to make choices about the areas you go into in most depth. As well as deciding between computing courses by choosing a university on a wider basis (e.g. the location, the reputation, the social life, the cost and availability of accommodation), there are a number of other ways by which you might differentiate between computing degrees. These include:

(i) Professional Accreditation by the British Computer Society and the Institution of Engineering and Technology

(ii) Departmental Specialisations - usually demonstrated by the research interests of faculty

(iii) Balance between theory and practice; hardware and software; systems and applications

(iv) Lab provision - look at how much access undergraduates get

(v) Degrees with a year abroad (North America or Europe). This may affect the length and cost of the programme but also offers a wider educational experience

(vi) How much choice is there to take options in computing or options outside the faculty?

Traditionally, Computer Science has been the study of how to build machines that do computations efficiently. However, the term Information Technology (IT) is now used to describe the study of technologies used to store, communicate or manipulate information. Although related to computer science, the focus in IT is shifted away from technology used to process information and towards information and the uses that are made of it.

As a prospective student, you should make sure that you understand the different approaches to courses and course content before you apply for a course. If you do not appreciate the differences before you apply, you should certainly do so before you accept an offer.

Degree Courses

Growth and diversification in the Computer Science/IT area has led to the provision of a wide variety of courses and course names at universities. What is called 'Information Technology' at one university may be called 'Computer Science' at another. A course at one university called 'Software Engineering' may study more hardware in more detail than another university's 'Computer Science' course. Courses may be weighted towards the theory or more towards a vocational training in current techniques. How can you get behind the course title and find out what a degree is really about?

Is it a single subject, joint honours or an integrated degree?

Many Computer Science/IT degrees are single subject degrees, which tend to look at a particular subject area in greater depth than a joint honours or an integrated degree and often allow students to specialise in one particular area. For example, a single subject course may emphasise a particular sub-field such as artificial intelligence or computer graphics.

Joint honours degrees link Computer Science/IT with another subject. The usual partners are Mathematics, Electronics or Business Studies but other subjects can be linked to make some interesting combinations.

'Integrated' degree schemes attempt to overcome the problems that can be associated with joint degrees by teaching one or more topics as a single subject in a single department. 'Integrated' degrees may sound like a joint degree from their title but are more like single subject degrees. For example, Business Information Systems may be taught at some institutions as a joint degree, but be more integrated elsewhere.

Is it a sandwich course? Does it provide industrial experience?

Computer Science and IT are practical subjects; many universities will offer industrial experience as part of their course (a 'sandwich' course). In some sandwich courses the industrial experience will be a complete year (usually between the second and third years of study); in others a number of shorter periods are spent in industry. Engineering Council members, such as the British Computer Society or the Institution of Engineering and Technology set their own standards for training, and you are better off on a sandwich course whose training meets these standards. Most institutions will encourage relevant industrial experience even when they do not offer a formal sandwich course - ask the department when you apply.

Career Opportunities

A major issue is the significant decline in the numbers currently entering IT based courses: down by 50% since 2001. This trend has raised concern about a skills gap opening up, with the British Computer Society reporting a 25% shortfall of computer science graduates in 2009. The 'offshoring' of IT jobs to other countries has raised concerns that this will make job opportunities harder to come by. However, there is evidence that the IT sector is growing at a relatively fast rate. A report by Microsoft shows that the IT industry is growing five to eight times faster than other sectors and needs 150,000 new entrants each year. The mix of jobs is changing within IT: while jobs for lower-paid professionals such as help-desk and operations staff are migrating, the demand for higher-level jobs such as software engineering and project management is on the rise in the UK. This general 'upskilling' is reflected in the salaries for IT graduates, which are above average and continue to grow.

Related Degrees

Software Engineering, Information Systems, Business Information Technology, Network Computing, Business Computing, Internet Computing, Computer Security, Computer Games, Artificial Intelligence, Medical Informatics, Computer Modelling, Business Systems Modelling, Computer Aided Engineering, Computer Science Informatics, Software Development

Suggested Reading

Algorithms: the Spirit of Computing
- David Harel and Yishai Feldman, Addison Wesley, 2004
Computer Science: an Overview
- Glenn Brookshear, Pearson, 2008
The Internet Uncovered
- Hilary Nickell, Trotman, 2009
The Passionate Programmer: Creating a Remarkable Career in Software Development
- Chad Fowler, Pragmatic Bookshelf, 2009

Further Information

e-skills UK
www.e-skills.com
BCS, the Chartered Institute for IT
www.bcs.org
Irish Computer Society
www.ics.ie

Cybernetics

Original article by the University of Bradford

Introduction

Cybernetics, the science of information and its application, is concerned with systems and their control - whether they are technological, as in a robotic production line; involve humans, as in the control of body temperatures: or environmental. It is all about giving machines more 'intelligence'. The cutting edge of research is concerned with the connecting up of the computer to the human nervous system, thereby gaining direct access to the human brain, and in turn achieving thought control by computers.

Degree Courses

Undergraduate courses incorporate many aspects of traditional disciplines such as computer science, information technology and engineering. Courses in cybernetics can include the study of control, computing, electronics, measurement, mechatronics, robotics, artificial intelligence, virtual reality and new technologies associated with the internet. The applications are varied: from automated transport systems, aeronautics and space systems to health care and entertainment. You could study cybernetics alone or combine it with control engineering, emphasising the technological aspects of cybernetics and incorporating practical and project work. In combination with biomedical engineering, it is possible to study more human aspects of the systems and combine this with biological, ecological and human systems. Medical cybernetics could appeal to you if you have an interest in medicine and computing and can equip you to incorporate IT into healthcare.

Cybernetics and virtual worlds allow you to explore worlds of the future and to interpret simulated worlds as a reality. Further possibilities include genome cybernetics, computer science and cybernetics, and electronic engineering and cybernetics.

Career Opportunities

There are excellent opportunities available in various sectors and with companies either large and multinational or small and local. Graduates can work as production engineers or research and design engineers. Industrial placements are part of the four-year courses, which lead to either BSc or MEng qualifications. It is possible to obtain sponsorship for some of the undergraduate courses in cybernetics and to obtain a qualification professionally recognised by the Institution of Engineering and Technology, the Institute of Measurement and Control and the British Computer Society.

Related Degrees

Computer Control Engineering, Electronic Systems Control, Robotics and Automated Systems.

Suggested Reading

In the Mind of the Machine: Breakthrough in Artificial Intelligence
- Kevin Warwick, Arrow, 1998

Mind, Man and Machine: a Dialogue
- Paul T Sagal, Hackett Publishing, 1995

Natural-born Cyborgs: Minds, Technologies and the Future of Human Intelligence
- Andy Clark, OUP, 2008

How We Became Posthuman: Virtual Bodies in Cybernetics, Literature and Informatics
-Katherine Hayles, Chicago University Press, 1999

Further Information

BCS, the Chartered Institute for IT
www.bcs.org

Institute of Measurement and Control
www.instmc.org.uk

Medical Cybernetics
www.medical-cybernetics.de

Institution of Engineering and Technology
www.theiet.org

Irish Computer Society
www.ics.ie

Dance

Original article by Dr Richard Ralph, formerly of Westminster College, Oxford (now part of Oxford Brookes University)

Introduction

I like to ask students coming to audition: 'Is there anything else you could possibly be happy doing as a career?' If the answer is 'yes' I tell the student to do that, as without any doubt it would be easier than a training and subsequent career in dance. For dancing, like a religious vocation with which it has many parallels, chooses you rather than you choosing it. Young people suddenly discover that they need to move their bodies, to reach deep into their reserves of stamina, strength and courage - and to dance. It can come upon you at the advanced age of sixteen or seventeen or it might be something you wanted to do since infancy.

Degree Courses

The basis of most professional dance courses is the learning of dance technique (this is usually either ballet or contemporary dance technique: other forms include jazz). This takes at least three hours of every day always following the same pattern and gives you a basic movement alphabet - the building bricks with which a choreographer will be able to express his or her art through you, or with which you will be able to communicate with others through movement.

Technique is a bit like doing scales if you are a musician. It is a daily routine, which keeps the body fit, supple and responsive to the instructions your brain gives it. Of itself it is not necessarily artistic, but it makes art possible: for the choreographer will paint and compose with the dancers' bodies. It is important to emphasise the place of technique in a dance school because it consumes many of the dance student's waking hours. As the body is trained to master the full range of dance technique, it changes shape as the muscle is developed. The way that the movement is timed and phrased gracefully and beautifully in relation to music will also be learned and the inner ideas or 'feeling tones' and muscular habits connected with certain sequences become second nature. But learning to dance is a mental and physical activity requiring ferocious concentration and considerable endurance. It tests commitment severely and many fall by the wayside. In any professional dance course the main credit will be given on the basis of progress made in technique classes.

Physical aptitude is important; your body has to be strong, but people with less-than-ideal or 'difficult' bodies can work wonders, especially if they undertake an appropriately supervised course of corrective strengthening exercises. But there are certain weaknesses which carry the risk of injury and which rule out rigorous training. So a proportion of students are not accepted at audition for physical reasons. In ballet the stereotyped look is more necessary than in contemporary dance, which tends to be more individual with less emphasis on the corps de ballet.

The most important qualification and the secret of eventual success in dance is an appetite for movement. Even in an untrained body this can show itself in the height of the leap, the length or depth of an extension, the follow through of a movement or exercise, or in a general sense of joy or even ecstasy. However, facial and physical beauty are of themselves not enough. The body as a whole must need to speak out in movement.

What I have described is a study in itself: a full time job. But a course of theoretical studies as provided by most dance schools can speed your development as a dancer. Such subjects as music, anatomy and costume are relevant, dealing with the essential elements of the professional dancer's craft, but increasingly the dancer is being required to operate part-time as a community worker and teacher and so some preparation for teaching is necessary at dance school. A powerful sense of identity and self-confidence are necessary to contemporary dance in particular. The dancer is saying, 'Here I am; this is what I am doing; look at me.' And the 'I' is vital. There has to be somebody interesting to look at. All too often the hothouse intensity of the dance school produces a cold obsessiveness and a narrowing of horizons, which ends up by actually threatening artistic values. Keep your mind active and your interest in the world around you alive.

All the best dance schools have good libraries, record and video collections. It is vital that young dance students know something of the history of dance and about other art forms. Students need to go to museums, theatres, concerts and films, preferably with some guidance from the school. All of these art forms provide vital resources for any dancer.

Schools will give prominence to the creative and interpretative aspects of dance. Choreography is taught from an early stage. It is mainly a matter of individual ability, but there is a basic craft which will help dancers to understand the choreographers who will work with them in their professional careers. Even modest compositions can help dance students to develop as interpretative performers and to move creatively. It is an excellent preparation for professional life for students to work with other dancers on group pieces and to find ways of working through the inevitable artistic and personal tensions that arise.

Repertory - Once students have mastered the steps of a dance they learn how to perform it in front of other students and sometimes a public paying audience. It is important that students should always remember that they are studying a theatrical art form, which is designed to be performed, but too much performance early in the course is usually seen as inappropriate. The technical groundwork must be laid before it can be absorbed into interpretation. The dancer's training is very tough and requires much dedication. Should you not achieve your ambition of dancing professionally, there is now a range of interesting dance-related careers open to the well-trained dancer. Careful course selection when you are applying for your dance course can keep a range of career options open.

Career Opportunities

Professional careers call for those with outstanding ability and depend on a great deal of luck and determination to succeed. Some enter teaching - others enter the general graduate market. The skills of self-expression and self-confidence can be a considerable asset in many unrelated careers.

Related Degrees

Performing Arts(Dance), Physical Theatre and Dance, Art & Teaching of Ballet, Dance and Culture, Dance Studies

Suggested Reading

Performing Arts Uncovered
- Dee Pilgrim, Trotman, 2007

Conditioning for Dance: Training for Peak Performance in All Dance Forms
- Eric Franklin, Human Kinetics, 2003

Article 19
- Online contemporary dance magazine, accessible at *www.article19.co.uk*

Further Information

Dance UK
www.danceuk.org

Council for Dance Education and Training
www.cdet.org.uk

Dance Ireland
www.danceireland.ie

Dentistry

Original article written from material supplied by Dr S M Hooper, University of Bristol Dental School, and the British Dental Association

Introduction

There are 13 undergraduate dental schools in the UK and two in Ireland, each located in a major city. Dental courses last five years and lead to a bachelor's degree (BDS). The courses include a sound academic education combined with theoretical and practical training in all aspects of dental practice. Subjects studied include anatomy, physiology, biochemistry, pathology, behavioural sciences and dental materials science, as well as clinical skills in all dental disciplines. Some dental schools offer a 'pre-dental' year for suitable candidates lacking the relevant science subjects. Entry requirements to typical courses are likely to include AS/A Level or H Grade or equivalent Chemistry and Biology. A broad range of other science and arts subjects is encouraged. There are also some graduate-entry courses, usually taking four years to complete.

Degree Courses

Until relatively recently, the five-year course would start with two predominantly pre-clinical years, followed by three years of mainly clinical practice. Now, however, General Dental Council recommendations prefer early clinical exposure, together with integrated teaching of all subjects and a dimension of choice of special subjects by the student. The integrated nature of the programme means that basic science teaching relates to clinical practice and clinical teaching is underpinned by scientific understanding. This means that you should have contact with patients from the first few weeks of the first year and will be encouraged at an early stage to assume an appropriate level of responsibility for patient care.

A typical programme has three main components: the first consists of subjects common to medicine and dentistry, progressing from biomedical sciences through behavioural sciences, epidemiology, pathology and microbiology to human disease; the second includes oral and dental aspects of the biological sciences, leading to an understanding of the diagnosis, prevention and treatment of oral and dental diseases and disorders and the effects of systemic disease on the oral and dental tissues; the third consists of the clinical and technical aspects of dentistry, with the provision of comprehensive oral and dental healthcare for patients of all ages. These components are mainly integrated, although there is usually a larger proportion of basic sciences at first and a larger clinical component at the end.

In addition to learning the practical skills necessary to become a dentist, you would acquire communication, personal management and information technology skills, together with an appreciation and analysis of ethical and legal issues in dentistry.

At the end of year three, you may have the opportunity to take an 'intercalated' BSc degree, allowing you to pursue the subjects of your choice in greater depth.

You should note that, in addition to the normal academic entry requirements, most dental schools require you to take the UK Clinical Aptitude Test (UKCAT) as part of the admissions process. Visit the UKCAT website for full details.

Your personal statement is a significant factor in the overall assessment of your application. Schools will be looking particularly for evidence of appropriate commitment to, and realistic appreciation of, the academic, physical and emotional demands of a dental career. They would normally expect you to have undertaken some work experience in a caring environment and/or observation in a dental clinical setting. Communication skills and the ability to work successfully in a team are of great importance, while your interests, achievements and contribution to your community may be taken into account in addition to your academic ability.

It is rare for offers to be made without an interview, and you must be available for interview in order to be considered for admission. The interview is usually conducted by at least two senior members of the clinical and biomedical sciences staff, with the aim of assessing your personal qualities to find out whether you have the potential to become a successful member of the dental profession. In this context, strong interpersonal and communication skills are most important, particularly when you consider the relationships which dentists need to build with their patients.

Career Opportunities

After qualification there are a variety of areas in which you can choose to practise.

General dental practice - Most dentists choose to work as general dental practitioners (GDPs).

Hospital dentistry - This covers oral surgery, restorative dentistry, children's dentistry and orthodontics.

Community dental service - Provides dental care for patients with special needs.

Armed forces - Permanent commissions are available.

Dentists in industry - Some large companies (eg oil companies) offer a dental service to their employees

University teaching/research - Research may be combined with teaching at the dental school.

Related Degrees

Dental Technology, Oral Health Science, Dental Materials

Suggested Reading

Getting into Dental School
- Steve Piumatti, Trotman, 2009

Careers in Medicine, Dentistry and Mental Heath
- Judith Humphries, Loulou Brown Ed, Kogan Page, 2000

Oxford Handbook of Clinical Dentistry
- David and Laura Mitchell, OUP Oxford, 2009

Further Information

British Dental Association
www.bda.org

General Dental Council
www.gdc-uk.org

UKCAT
www.ukcat.ac.uk

Irish Dental Association
www.dentist.ie

Design and Technology

Original article by George Preston, Faculty of Applied Sciences, Bath Spa University

Introduction

If you are interested in studying an aspect of Design and Technology (D&T) in a higher education setting, do not restrict your research simply to courses that have D&T in their title. Many similar courses have titles as varied as electronic product design, fashion design technology, food technology and product design.

'Design' should be at the heart of all D&T courses, but what do we mean by 'design'? The term is unfortunately open to multiple interpretations. If we take as an example the design of an electric kettle, one interpretation of the design process can be considered to embrace everything to do with the development, production and marketing of the kettle. This will include technical aspects of the switch and heating element, the aesthetics and ergonomics of the body, the way the body will be manufactured, the way the product compares with other similar products, management of the development process, sourcing of materials/components and the environmental impact of the product.

If your interests are towards the technical aspects, you will be more interested in courses which focus on what is often referred to as engineering design. If, however, your interests lie in the aesthetic, functional and ergonomic aspects, you are more likely to be drawn to courses which emphasise industrial design. These are not the only aspects of design. Of increasing importance is the question of values in design that address the real impact, costs and consequences of a product. All products, for example, have an impact on the environment during every stage of their production, use and disposal. Considerable emphasis is now being placed on design which takes into account issues such as pollution and the use of finite energy resources. For example, if a component can be made from one material rather than two, there is a greater possibility that the component can be more easily recycled because expensive separation of the materials will be avoided.

There are few cases where one individual is responsible for the design, production and marketing of a product. Usually a number of people are involved in the development of a product and attention is given to the way people work together. *Concurrent or simultaneous engineering* sounds very technical and rather formidable but is primarily concerned with the way in which everyone with an interest can be involved in the design process at the same time. Traditionally, different aspects of the design process have tended to be dealt with in sequence. The concurrent approach makes the design process more effective and hence products can be brought to the market quicker with a greater degree of confidence that they will satisfy the needs of the user.

Degree Courses

In a typical course, first year students might take two very broadly based modules that give them experience of designing in a wide range of contexts such as food product development, resistant materials and textiles. Another important aspect of the modules is to ensure that students are familiar which a range of information technology tools that are increasingly important in all aspects of designing.

In the subsequent years, there is a range of modules that covers things such as design practice, working with resistant materials, materials and materials processing, design for manufacturing, control systems, designing with electronic multimedia, appropriate technology, product development in the food industry, marketing and satellite remote sensing.

Career Opportunities

Graduates enter specialist design studios, advertising agencies, teaching, newspapers, magazine and book publishing, product design in industry, printing, textile/fashion design, interior design and so on.

Related Degrees

Industrial Package Design and Technology, Textile Technology, Marine Sports Technology, Music Technology, Architectural Technology, Sustainable Technology, Paper Science, Environmental Technology, Industrial Product Design, Product Design, Theatre Design, Media Technology, Furniture Design/Production, Small Craft Design, Audio Technology, Sports Equipment Technology, Craft Design, Glass/Architectural Design, Model Design, Dental Technology, Prosthetics/Orthotics, Clothing Studies, Design for Digital Technologies

Suggested Reading

Design Uncovered
- Karen Holmes, Trotman, 2009

Getting into Art and Design Courses 2011 Entry
- James Burnett, Trotman, 2010

Manufacturing and Product Design
- Roger Jones, Trotman, 2009

Becoming a Product Designer: A Guide to Careers in Design
- Bruce Hannah, Wiley, 2004

Products 2: 50 Real-life Product Design Projects Uncovered
- Lynn Haller and Cheryl Dangel Cullen, Rockport, 2006

The Career Guide for Creative and Unconventional People
- Carol Eikleberry, Ten Speed Press, 2007

Further Information

Design Council
www.design-council.org.uk

Your Creative Future
www.yourcreativefuture.org

Chartered Society of Designers
www.csd.org.uk

Institute of Designers in Ireland
www.idi-design.ie

Dietetics and Nutrition

Original article adapted, with permission, from material supplied by the British Dietetic Association

Introduction

Dietetics is the application of the science of nutrition to the management and prevention of diet-related illnesses. This article is about professional courses which, when successfully completed, will provide you with eligibility for state registration as a Dietitian with the Health Professions Council. These courses last four years. If you already hold a degree in a life science subject you may be eligible for a two-year postgraduate course in dietetics. All courses include a period of practical training in hospital and community settings, approved by the Health Professions Council.

To start a degree course you will normally be expected to have obtained A Level, H Grade or equivalent passes in two or three subjects, preferably Chemistry and another Science subject or Mathematics.

Remember that colleges and universities will consider each application individually.

Degree Courses

A typical four-year course includes 24 academic modules and three mandatory periods of fieldwork placements in approved departments of NHS Trusts. You would be learning in a multidisciplinary environment with a long established tradition of training health professionals. Placements occur in years one and three. These years are therefore longer than the traditional academic year.

Year One modules:

Human Nutrition

Biochemistry

Laboratory Techniques for Biosciences

Physiological Basis of Health and Disease for Dietitians

Food Choice

Psychology of Eating

Food Studies

Welfare, Health and Inequalities

Introduction to Professional Practice

Year Two modules:

Human Nutrition

Clinical Medicine and Nutrition

Human Biochemistry

Evidence-Based Practice

Principles of Teaching and Learning

Social Dimensions of Health

Plus one option choice from a range of health-related subjects

Years Three and Four modules:

Health Promotion

Diet Therapy I

Community Dietetics and Nutrition

Diet Therapy II

Pharmacology for Healthcare Professionals

Management

Career Opportunities

State-registered Dietitians have a wide range of career options and can work as advisers, teachers and therapists in many different settings. Most work in clinical roles in the NHS, either in hospitals or primary care. Others find employment with local authorities, catering companies or the pharmaceutical and food industries. For graduates who opt to pursue postgraduate study, there is a variety of relevant Masters, MPhil and PhD programmes, in particular, the MSc in Advanced Dietetic Practice.

Related Degrees

Public Health Nutrition

Suggested Reading

Want a Career as a Dietitian?
- downloadable from the BDA website below

Manual of Dietetic Practice
 - Briony Thomas Ed, Blackwell, 2007

Pocket Guide to Nutrition and Dietetics
- Sarah E Byrom, Churchill Livingstone, 2002

Oxford Handbook of Nutrition and Dietetics
- Joan Webster-Gandy et al, OUP Oxford, 2006

Further Information

British Dietetic Association
www.bda.uk.com

Nutrition Society
www.nutritionsociety.org

Health Professions Council
www.hpc-uk.org

Irish Nutrition and Dietetic Institute
www.indi.ie

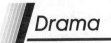

Drama

Original article by John Marshall, Bristol University

Introduction

Of all the arts, drama is perhaps the most public and popular. In the various forms of live theatre, film and television, more drama is seen now than ever before. Although this popularity may, in part, be attributed to the greater accessibility afforded by television, it cannot disguise the very real significance of performed drama to society. Why should this be so? What made London audiences flock to the public playhouses in Elizabethan England? Why do millions of people watch *Eastenders*? How did Shakespeare ensure that the audience not only watched and listened to his plays but also returned to see his next one? How do soap operas work in terms of character, story line, dialogue, subject matter, setting, camera angles, editing and so forth? The serious asking of these questions and the rigorous thinking, exploring and analysis required to answer them is, in very simple terms, what constitutes the study of drama.

To be able to comprehend fully the role of drama in society and to engage critically with text performance, it is necessary to gain knowledge and experience in a number of theoretical and practice areas which contribute to the informed study of drama. In the pursuit of textual analysis and practical criticism students may find themselves drawing on aspects of such diverse disciplines as art, architecture, history, religion, politics, physics, philosophy, psychology, sociology etc. This wide range of contributing knowledge is one of the exciting qualities of drama study at undergraduate level, which places it deservedly within the area of liberal arts education and distinguishes it from the more specialised and specific actor training with which it is sometimes confused.

Degree Courses

For the most part, drama degrees are not vocational; they are not designed to train students for particular professional posts in the theatre or television and should not be regarded as a fail-safe alternative to drama school. The candidate at interview who professes a yearning to act but wants a degree to 'fall back on' is unlikely to impress. It is rewardingly true that many drama graduates do proceed professionally but in most cases this follows an additional period of appropriate training.

The number of degree courses available in the subject has grown considerably since the first, more than 40 years ago; and although many may have 'drama' in the title, the courses may be very different in context and approach. It is, therefore, extremely important that candidates read course outlines very carefully in order to select the type of course which best suits their interest. For example, many departments acknowledge the significant contribution of television and film to the drama of the twentieth century and may incorporate not only the theoretical study necessary for the critical analysis of text and screening but also a complementary element of practical film or video making. Other courses may concentrate entirely on the process and products of the theatre. Similarly, the variety of courses reflects the variety of approaches available to the study of drama and, while most will combine a number of these, the emphasis on the historical, critical, sociological and generic approach may be different in each case.

Drama study, in common with its professional relations, theatre, television and film, is apparently glamorous but in reality extremely hard work, not only intellectually, but physically and emotionally as well. It is demanding in terms of time as well as effort, but it is also sociable and pleasurable, and to the outsider, enjoyment can sometimes be confused with easiness. Don't be confused; be prepared to work long hours at reading as well as rehearsing and to give a great deal of yourself, not merely for your own benefit, but for the collective advantage and development of others.

Career Opportunities

The employment record for Drama graduates is relatively good. Approximately 17% enter further courses of study and training. Of those entering direct employment on graduation, 50% enter the creative and entertainment fields, whilst others might take a PGCE to become a teacher, or train for journalism, editing, languages or administrative work. The skills of persuasion and self-confidence, gained through acting, can be of considerable value in a wide range of unrelated career fields.

Related Degrees

Drama in the Community, Speech and Drama Studies, Acting, Theatre Arts, Film and Drama, Visual Performance

Suggested Reading

Degree Course Guide: Music, Drama and Dance
- Trotman, 2007

Careers in the Theatre
- J Richardson, Kogan Page, 1998

The Career Guide for Creative and Unconventional People
- Carol Eikleberry, Ten Speed Press, 2007

An Anatomy of Drama
- Martin Esslin, Abacus, 1978

Modern Drama in Theory and Practice 1: Realism and Naturalism
- J. L. Styan, Cambridge University Press, 1983

The Empty Space
- Peter Brook, Penguin Classics, 2008

Further Information

National Drama
www.nationaldrama.org.uk

Equity
www.equity.org.uk

Theatre Net.com - the Performing Arts Centre
www.theatrenet.co.uk

Arts Council England
www.artscouncil.org.uk

Conference of Drama Schools
www.drama.ac.uk

National Council for Drama Training
www.ncdt.co.uk

National Association for Youth Drama in Ireland
http://nayd.ie

Irish Theatre Institute
www.irishtheatreinstitute.com

Ecology

Original article by Dr Louise Banton, Lancaster University

Introduction

Ecology is a complex area of biology concerned with how living organisms interact with each other and with the environment, including our own relations with other species and with the biosphere. It is an interdisciplinary subject drawing mainly from biology and environmental sciences but also from subjects like landscape history, economics, development studies and so on. It has its own rationale, methods and theory, particularly concerned with populations and communities. It is central to dealing with many problem areas such as pollution, climate change and resource conservation.

You may have the opportunity to specialise in different organisms (e.g. mammals, plants or insects) and in different environments (e.g. tropical or marine). You can study ecology to gain understanding of natural animal and plant communities and processes, and as the scientific basis for the sustainable management of the world's natural resources.

Degree Courses

At one UK university, the core first year units are based on workshops for numerical analysis, seminars and field trips, which play an important role in the programme. In the second year, you could take aquatic, marine, population and community ecology together with more ecology, evolutionary biology or environmental science units. Most third year units deal with applied aspects of ecology, such as fisheries, bioremediation and conservation. You would carry out a major independent research project during your third year.

At another university, 15 modules must be taken in the first year, including at least five in biology and five in environmental sciences. The remaining five modules can be chosen from biology, environmental sciences or other departments. There is a test at the end of each module. A similar pattern continues through the second and third years but the nature of the modules allows for increasing specialisation.

Some courses offer the chance of a year in another European state, in North America or in Australasia. There are also four-year industrial sandwich courses, in which you would spend the year between your second and final years working in a research laboratory or similar institution. While on your placement, you would be part of a research team and would be paid as such.

Career Opportunities

Ecology graduates usually have the experience and expertise to work in the related areas of ecology or conservation, possibly with organisations such as wildlife trusts, government or non-government conservation organisations, local government, environmental protection agencies and research agencies. There is a growing demand for ecological consultants, as environmental legislation and regulations increasingly require rigorous environmental audit and monitoring. There are also many opportunities in environmental education. While some graduates go straight into employment, others opt for further training at postgraduate level or seek short-term contracts to develop the breadth of work experience required for some areas of permanent employment.

Related Degrees

Animal Behaviour, Countryside Conservation, Conservation Biology, Environmental Science, Natural History, Wildlife Biology or *Zoology.*

Suggested Reading

'Rooting for a career in Ecology
- downloadable from the BES website below

First Ecology: Ecological Principles and Environmental Issues
- Alan Beeby and Anne-Maria Brennan, OUP, 2007

The Diversity of Life
- Edward O Wilson, Penguin, 2001

Ecology: Principles and Applications
- J L Chapman and M J Reiss, Cambridge, 1998

Conservation Biology
- Andrew S. Pullin, Cambridge University Press, 2002

Further Information

British Ecological Society
www.britishecologicalsociety.org

Institute of Ecology and Environmental Management
www.ieem.net

Ecology Foundation
www.theecologyfoundation.ie

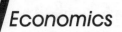# Economics

Original article adapted with permission from material supplied by Dr Hedley Rees of Bristol University

Introduction

Economics is the study of economic systems and the way people and businesses and other organisations react to economic events. It deals with, for example, the way labour markets determine wages and unemployment, why some countries take a bigger share of the world market than others, and the role of government in providing goods and services.

Many topics in economics are controversial. Should governments intervene to try to cut unemployment? Is there a risk of accelerating inflation if they do? How should the NHS be organised and financed?

Economics must be tested against the facts and applied to the real world. Econometrics is the statistical branch of economics which develops and applies the techniques for doing this and is an essential tool of modern economics.

Economists need to be good at working with figures. They should enjoy looking at a page of numbers and working out what they mean. Mathematical and information technology skills are essential.

Economists need to be able to explain their ideas simply, in plain English, to non-specialists. They should not be swayed easily by the views of others.

Economists need to be decisive, logical, quick-thinking and able to cope with pressure - they may, for example, be given only a few minutes to come up with a reasoned reaction to a set of statistics.

The work of professional economists varies considerably according to the sector in which they are employed, but there are certain tasks common to all jobs:

- All economists are experts in finding information from sources such as databases, libraries, newspapers and government departments. They manipulate data drawn from these sources, using mathematical, statistical and logical tools to find answers to questions such as: *What have the recent economic trends been? What are the driving forces behind these trends? What forecasts can be made for the future?*

- The problems economists deal with may be macro-economic - concerned with large economic units such as nation states; or micro-economic - concerned with the financial characteristics of firms, industries, individual households, and so on, and the way individual elements in an economy (such as consumers, or commodities) behave. A typical macro-economic task might be to forecast the GDP (gross domestic product) of the USA in the coming year, or to assemble the arguments for and against a change in interest rates, whilst the kind of question dealt with at micro-economic level could be concerned with predicting the demand for furniture in South East England over the next quarter, or analysing the costs and benefits of regulating or taxing some form of pollution.

Degree Courses

The current UCAS database lists 1425 UK degrees including economics. Careful research is therefore essential before you make a decision about where to apply. You could study economics alone or combine it with, say, a language, banking and finance, mathematics or any of a wide range of subjects.

A typical degree will have a modular structure and will allow an increasing number of option modules as the course progresses, such as four mandatory and two optional modules in year one, compared with two mandatory and four optional in year three.

There may be an option to spend a year abroad as part of your economics degree.

Bristol, for example, has reciprocal arrangements with partner universities in France, Germany, Spain and Italy.

Career Opportunities

Graduates pursue a great variety of careers, although most make choices directly related to their studies. Of recent economics graduates from Bristol, 65% went straight into employment, mainly in accountancy, banking, the City and the civil service. A further 21% went on to further study, especially in economics, law, finance and human resource management.

Related Degrees

Applied Economics, Business Economics, International Economics, Financial Economics, Economics with Econometrics, Political Economics, Political and International Economics, Agricultural Economics, European Economics, Philosophy. Politics and Economics, Politics/Economics/Language, Economics, Mathematics and Operational Research, Economics, Statistics, Computing and Operational Research, English, Economics and Management, Materials, Economics and Management, Technological Economics

Suggested Reading

The Wealth of Nations
- Adam Smith

The Origin of Economic Ideas
- Guy Routh, Palgrave Macmillan, 1989

The Principles of Political Economy
- John Stuart Mill

Ethics, Economics and Politics: Principles of Public Policy
- I M D Little, OUP, 2003

A History of Economics
- John Kenneth Galbraith, Penguin, 1991

Studying Economics
- Brian Atkinson and Susan Johns, Palgrave Macmillan, 2001

Blueprint for a Green Economy
- David Pearce, Anil Markandya and Ed Barbier, Earthscan, 1995

Further Information

Why study Economics?
http://whystudyeconomics.ac.uk

Royal Economic Society
www.res.org.uk

Royal Statistical Society
www.rss.org.uk

Biz/Ed
www.bized.co.uk

Institute of Economic Affairs
www.iea.org.uk

Economic and Social Research Unit, Ireland
www.esri.ie

Education (England, Wales, N.Ireland)

Original article by Professor Chris Husbands, University of Warwick

Introduction

This article is mainly concerned with programmes of teacher education in universities in England, Wales and Northern Ireland, since most education degrees fall into this category. Those aiming to work as teachers in the state system are required to have an appropriate degree and to have been awarded Qualified Teacher Status (QTS). There are two main ways of acquiring these qualifications: the postgraduate or the undergraduate route. (There are also employment-based and assessment-only routes but they are outside the scope of this article). For the postgraduate route, students can study for a degree in an appropriate subject, usually taking three or four years according to the discipline involved and they can follow this by taking a one-year Postgraduate Certificate in Education (PGCE) which provides them with experience in schools, a grounding in professional practice and policy frameworks and knowledge of the public education system. At the end of the PGCE programme, students are considered for the award of QTS.

The undergraduate route is to take a three- or four-year concurrent degree: either a BA/BSc(QTS) or a BEd. A concurrent degree means that students combine academic studies in their specialist subject(s) with professional studies and experience in schools throughout the period of the degree. In practice, the three-year degrees are often based on a longer academic year than the four-year degrees, so that the time involved in study is roughly the same. It is vital to check on the details of course length and course requirements before deciding on whether to apply for a three- or four-year concurrent degree.

In Scotland and the Republic of Ireland a somewhat different system of qualification exists, please see *Degree Course Descriptions*: *Education (Scotland)* and *Education (Ireland)*.

Degree Courses

All teacher training programmes are designed to equip you with the skills and knowledge you will need to teach successfully. Initial Teacher Training programmes focus on a number of themes, linked to the QTS standards. Whatever programme you choose, your initial teacher training (ITT) will involve:

- A knowledge and understanding of the relevant national curriculum programmes of study for your subject(s)

- Planning and preparing lessons and setting learning objectives

- Managing classes, promoting good behaviour and minimising disruption

- Using information and communication technology effectively

- Awareness of the professional values expected of teachers, in their attitudes and behaviour towards pupils and colleagues

Most trainee teachers (except for those on employment-based or assessment only routes) divide their time between a university or other higher education institution and a school, where they undertake supervised teaching practice.

All providers of teacher education work in close partnership with schools at all stages of the process: from curriculum design through to programme delivery and final assessment. Partner schools provide mentors from their staff to guide and develop students' work in schools.

All applicants for teacher education programmes must be interviewed to establish their academic, professional and personal suitability for teaching. As well as academic qualifications, applicants will be assessed at interview on their motivation and commitment to teaching as a career. Applicants are advised to gain some experience in an educational setting, possibly a local school, which will not only help them about making decisions about a possible career in teaching but will also provide valuable experience to discuss at interview.

Please note that a number of universities offer studies in education as a theoretical subject, which do not lead in themselves to qualified teacher status. For example, many institutions offer degrees in educational studies, business education, education and psychology, education and sociology.

Career Opportunities

The majority of those reading for BEd degrees and PGCE qualifications enter the teaching profession, where salaries and career prospects have become excellent, but quite a significant proportion use their degrees to enter the general graduate market. Careers in management, banking, insurance, commerce and retail sales management are all possibilities.

Related Degrees

Primary Education, Early Childhood Studies, Upper Primary, Lower/Primary, Nursery/Infants, Physical Education, Secondary Education, Outdoor Education, Community Education, Educational Studies, Science for Education, English Language Teaching, Education. Quality and Community Management

Suggested Reading

Directory of Teacher Training Courses 2009
- Trotman, 2008

Teaching Uncovered
- Karen Holmes, Trotman, 2010

The Newly Qualified Teacher's Handbook
- Elizabeth Holmes, Routledge, 2008

Further Information

General Teaching Council for England (but under threat of closure as we go to press)
www.gtce.org.uk

General Teaching Council for Wales
www.gtcw.org.uk

NASUWT
www.nasuwt.org.uk

Association of Teachers and Lecturers
www.atl.org.uk

National Union of Teachers
www.teachers.org.uk

Training and Development Agency for Schools
www.tda.gov.uk

General Teaching Council for Wales
www.gtcw.org.uk

Department of Education for Northern Ireland
www.deni.gov.uk

Education (Ireland)

Original article by Joyce Lane, educational consultant

Introduction

For almost all teaching posts in Ireland you need an eligible first degree and a recognised teaching qualification. This article gives some details of these qualifications and entry and training required. There is a lot of competition for teaching jobs so it is important to demonstrate interest and commitment. Relevant Work Experience such as time spent working voluntarily with children in schools or with youth people in clubs is recommended before application for teacher training.

Primary Teacher Training

Five Colleges of Education offer teacher training courses which last for three years and lead to a BEd degree. Up to 10% of places may be reserved for applicants from the Gaeltacht. Intake into the colleges is regulated by the Department of Education and Skills. It is also possible to qualify by completing an 18 month Graduate Diploma after graduating with another degree. Two centres offer a full-time postgraduate course in Primary Teaching: St Patrick's College, Drumcondra, Dublin and Mary Immaculate College, Limerick. After their first appointment all primary teachers serve a probationary period.

Entry and Training

Applicants must be at least 17 years old on 15 January in the year following their entry to a College of Education. A Leaving Certificate with 3 subjects at minimum grade C3 on Higher Level papers and 3 other subjects at minimum grade D3 on Ordinary or Higher papers. These must include at least grade C3 on a Higher Level paper in Irish (including the equivalent of grade C3 at the Leaving Certificate Oral Irish examination), grade C3 or an Ordinary Level or D3 on a Higher Level paper in English and grade D3 in mathematics at either Ordinary or Higher level.

All teacher training students in Colleges of Education must be proficient in spoken Irish and are required to attend a three-week course in the Gaeltacht at the end of their first year in training. It should be noted that this is a compulsory part of the course of training. In addition, students are subject to an oral Irish test at the end of their first year in training, a pass in which is necessary in order to continue to the second year of the course. Students who fail this oral Irish test may, at the discretion of the College, be allowed to repeat the test following attendance at the Gaeltacht course.

Secondary Teacher Training

The Postgraduate Diploma in Education / Graduate Diploma in Education / Higher Diploma in Education (Secondary) is a required qualification for all teaching posts in secondary, community and comprehensive schools.

The Postgraduate Diploma in Education is offered by the Education Departments of the four constituent universities of the National University of Ireland:

> University College Cork - National University of Ireland, Cork
> University College Dublin - National University of Ireland, Dublin
> National University of Ireland, Galway
> National University of Ireland, Maynooth

The Graduate Diploma in Education is offered by

> Dublin City University

The Higher Diploma in Education (Secondary) is offered by

> The University of Dublin/Trinity College

The Postgraduate Diploma in Education through Irish (Dioplóma Iarchéime san Oideachas) is available at

The National University of Ireland, Galway.

Admission Requirements

To be eligible to apply for the Post Graduate Diploma in Education / Graduate Diploma in Education / Higher Diploma in Education (Secondary), candidates must have obtained a suitable first degree. This is a degree or equivalent award from a State recognised university or similar third level college which is adequate to enable the holder to teach to the highest level (in the case of the majority of subjects, this is Leaving Certificate, higher level) in at least one subject on the post-primary school curriculum. The duration of such a degree programme must be at least three years of full-time study or equivalent. The Teaching Council must deem the applicant's degree eligible for the purposes of secondary school teaching.

Other Routes

If you are a primary or post-primary school teacher who qualified outside Ireland and you wish to teach in a recognised school in Ireland, you must apply for recognition of your qualifications prior to registration. However, you must be fully qualified in the country in which you did your training. Once your qualifications have been recognised, you may then apply for registration.

Primary teachers trained in another Member State of the European Union, whose qualifications have been assessed and accepted by the Department of Education and Science, but who do not possess an appropriate Irish language qualification, will be granted a five year period of provisional recognition to teach in national schools.

At Secondary level, there are aptitude tests/exams in areas where there is a shortfall between qualifications gained abroad and gained in Ireland. You are allowed 15 months after registration to take the appropriate test. The most common one necessary is the History and Structure of the Irish Education System, a knowledge of which is considered essential in the training of a teacher in Ireland.

Suggested Reading

Teaching Uncovered
- Brin Best and Sian Dover, Trotman, 2006

The Newly Qualified Teacher's Handbook
- Elizabeth Holmes, Routledge, 2008

Further Information

Department of Education and Skills
www.education.ie
Postgraduate Diploma in Education (NUI) Applications Centre
www.pac.ie/hdip.php
Teaching Council
www.teachingcouncil.ie
Irish National Teachers' Organisation
www.into.ie
Association of Secondary Teachers, Ireland
www.asti.ie
Qualifax: National Courses Database
www.qualifax.ie
Central Applications Office
www.cao.ie

Education (Scotland)

Original article adapted from material supplied by Teach in Scotland

Introduction

To work as a teacher in an education authority school in Scotland you must have a teaching qualification and be registered with the General Teaching Council for Scotland. This article gives details of the minimum qualifications you need to enter a teacher education course in Scotland and how to register when you qualify.

Primary Education

If you have the relevant Standard grades, Higher grades or other Higher level qualifications (e.g. HNC, HND), you could obtain a degree in any subject then do a one year postgraduate Professional Graduate Diploma in Education (PGDE) teacher training course.

To follow the PGDE route, you must have at least:

- A degree from a UK university (or an equivalent degree from outside the UK)
- Higher English at Grade C or above (or equivalent)
- Standard Grade Maths at Credit level (or equivalent)

The universities will also want to see evidence that you have studied at least two of the following subjects: Science, Social Studies, Expressive Arts, Religious and Moral Education, Technology and Modern Languages.

It's also essential that you get as much experience as possible of working with children of primary school age. For example, this could be as a classroom assistant or as a Brownie or Cub Group leader. If you are able to gain experience at after-school clubs or sports coaching or music tuition, this is also good to mention on your application form. You'll need to demonstrate a good understanding of the Primary Education system in Scotland.

An alternative route would be to undertake a four-year undergraduate Bachelor of Education (BEd) degree course in Primary Education. Entry requirements differ between universities depending on their admissions policy but are usually four Highers at BBBC or three Highers at ABB. You must have Higher English at level B and Credit level Standard Grade Maths (or equivalent). You should also try show that you have experience working with children, perhaps through voluntary work with youth groups, sports clubs and so on.

The Stirling Institute of Education offers an Initial Teacher Education (ITE) programme, which runs concurrently as part of a first degree programme. If successfully completed, this programme leads to a primary or a secondary teaching qualification recognised by the General Teaching Council for Scotland and by the Department for Children, Schools and Families (DCSF). The Stirling programme is the only one of its kind in Scotland.

Secondary Education

Your first step, in most cases, is to obtain a degree in the subject you wish to teach in Scotland, followed by the one-year PGDE. Some teaching subjects have specific requirements for entry to the PGDE course, so it is advisable to check with the university you want to apply to that the degree course you are thinking about undertaking will be suitable for teaching that subject.

If you don't want to go down the PGDE route, you can study towards:

- four-year Bachelor of Education (BEd) degree course in Physical Education, Music or Technological Education

or

- A combined degree (also known as a concurrent degree), which usually lasts around four years. The degree includes your main subject, study of education and some school experience

The entry requirements for BEd (Secondary) and combined degree courses are set by individual universities and vary by course and by university. To find out more, simply contact the university you are interested in applying to.

Career Opportunities

To teach in a school in Scotland you need to be registered with the General Teaching Council for Scotland (GTCS). You are guaranteed a teaching post with a Scottish local authority for a full school year, known as the Induction year, if you are a newly qualified teacher, who has graduated from a Scottish university and has been assessed as a home student for fees. You will be provisionally registered with the GTCS until you meet the Standard for Full Registration on successful completion of your Induction year.

Scotland wants to increase the number of teachers to 53,000 and has ambitious plans to reduce class sizes in Maths and English to 20 pupils in secondary schools, and 25 pupils in year one of Primary Education. It also has a target to increase the number of visiting specialist teachers in Music, Physical Education and Modern Foreign Languages. What's more, there are extra teaching opportunities in Physics, Technological Education and Home Economics.

You can choose five Scottish local authorities that you'd be willing to work in for in your Induction year. At the same time, local authorities work out the number of posts they have for probationer teachers. The selection process then chooses students at random and allocates them to teaching posts, starting with your first preference local authority. Unfortunately, your personal circumstances won't be taken into account during the process.

Suggested Reading

Directory of Teacher Training Courses 2009
- Trotman, 2008

Teaching Uncovered
- Karen Holmes, Trotman, 2010

Further Information

Teach in Scotland
www.teachinginscotland.com

General Teaching Council for Scotland
www.gtcs.org.uk

Learning and Teaching Scotland
www.ltscotland.org.uk

Electronic and Electrical Engineering

Original article by Dr R S Quayle, Manchester University School of Engineering

Introduction

Choosing a university can be difficult in areas such as electronic and electrical engineering, where there is a wide variety of courses available. It is important to consider the specialist interests of the department, as well as the structure of the courses and the topics covered to make sure that they meet your needs and interests.

Various universities and colleges have set up one-year foundation and conversion courses for young people who, for example, may have passes in subjects other than mathematics and physics.

Degree Courses

Electronic engineering is often referred to as 'light current' engineering, systems which use relatively low current and relatively low voltage and embracing technologies such as communications, broadcasting, computers, control, medical systems and many more. Electrical engineering, or 'heavy current', is concerned with relatively high current and high voltage, including electrical power generation, power distribution by the national grid, electrical machines and so on.

BEng and MEng Degree Courses - Most universities offer both the BEng and the more demanding MEng first degree courses. BEng honours courses may be of three years duration (or four in Scotland) plus an additional year of industrial experience. The MEng course is generally of four or five years duration, depending upon the time spent in industry. In many universities the BEng and MEng courses have common first years and transfer is allowed.

What sort of courses are there? - There are narrower electronic and electrical programmes and there are broad programmes that cover light and heavy current topics in a single degree - highly suitable if you do not know where your eventual interests will lie. Later you may realise that you will find yourself concentrating on a narrow aspect but need to have knowledge over a wider field. Take a radar system, for example. You may be involved in designing the high power electronics that produce a very short pulse of high frequency energy and so you may be an expert in radio frequency electronics. But a radar system has many other electrical and electronic component parts such as the aerial that will transmit and receive the radio frequency pulses, wave guides to connect the transmitter/receiver to the aerial and so on. The system you are working on will influence all of the others and all of the others will influence yours. **Programme content, what will courses contain?** - All electronic and electrical engineers must be able to analyse circuits, understand amplifiers, design analogue and digital systems, program computers and use computers as tools to aid other aspects of their work. Engineering is a practical subject, which requires work in laboratories to reinforce academic material, to provide expertise in the use of measuring and test equipment and to build confidence in your ability to design and construct working systems. This material is then enhanced with subjects such as power engineering, electrical machines, semiconductors and devices, software engineering and, for overseas programmes, tuition in a foreign language. Project work performed in groups or as individuals is undertaken in all years. In the final year, there is likely to be an individual design, development or research project, which forms a significant component of your final degree classification.

Career Opportunities

Graduates work at the forefront of modern technology and wealth creation. Most engineers are employed in research, development and design, often working with teams of scientists and other engineers. They also enter electronic communications, energy/power production, transport, (eg rail, shipping, aircraft fields), computing, automation, the NHS, the Ministry of Defence, marketing, sales of electrical equipment, teaching at college and university levels, or general commerce, banking and insurance.

Related Degrees

Electronic and Microelectronic Engineering, Telecommunications, Systems Engineering, Radio Frequency Engineering, Digital Systems Engineering, Broadcast Engineering, Communication Systems, Mobile Telecommunications, Instrumentation and Control Engineering, Electronic and Photonic Engineering, Electrical Power Engineering, Electronic Systems Control, Medical Electronic Engineering, Electronic Engineering with Music, Optoelectronic/Video Engineering, Electronics Manufacturing And Management, Mechanical Electronic Systems

Suggested Reading

Circuits, Devices and Systems: First Course in Electrical Engineering
- R J Smith and R C Dorf, Wiley, 1996

Degree Course Guide: Engineering
- Trotman, 2007

Electronics for Today and Tomorrow
- Tom Duncan, Philip Allan, 1997

How to get ahead in Engineering
- Trotman, 2006

Further Information

Engineering Council UK
www.engc.org.uk

Engology.com Engineering Careers
www.engology.com

Institution of Engineering and Technology
www.theiet.org

Electro-Technical Council of Ireland
www.etci.ie

Engineers Ireland
www.engineersireland.ie

Energy Engineering

Original article by Dr John Staggs, School of Process, Environmental and Materials Engineering, University of Leeds

Introduction

If you are concerned about our environment and fuel poverty and want to be part of realising a sustainable energy future, then energy engineering may be the course for you. Look for a degree accredited by the Energy Institute, which will train you to apply and design processes that reduce environmental damage. Courses may lead to a BEng or MEng qualification.

Degree Courses

Many universities now have all degree courses organised in a modular structure, with each year split into two semesters. In the energy engineering example below, 12 equally weighted modules are completed each year and each module consists of lectures, practical and associated course work.

Year one core engineering topics include fluid mechanics and heat transfer, and thermodynamics. Specialist topics include energy and the environment, renewable sources of energy, and combustion. There are options to study management and/or language subjects.

Year two core engineering topics include management and economics, design, measurement and control, and laboratory techniques. Specialist topics include waste processing, advanced renewables, managing aqueous effluents, and combustion-generated pollution.

In year three of the BEng degree, core engineering topics include industrial finance, safety management and hazard protection. Specialist topics include efficient use of energy, control of air pollution, advanced energy systems, wastewater engineering, law and the environment. You would also undertake a research project related to the field of energy and the environment.

In year three of the MEng Degree, core engineering topics industrial finance, safety management and hazard protection, computational aerodynamics, plant engineering and design. Specialist topics include advanced energy systems, efficient use of energy, and an industrially related research project with an associated business plan. You would continue this research project in more depth in year four.

In year four of the MEng Degree, you would extend your breadth of knowledge and undertake a considerable industrially related group project. You can choose from a range of intensively taught courses with industrial participation in their delivery. Other specialist modules offered include atmospheric process, control of air pollution, flames, explosions, and hazards.

Recent projects include engine emissions under real driving conditions, diesel particulate emissions and their effect on the urban atmosphere, and biomass combustion in a fluidised bed.

Career Opportunities

There are good career prospects in industries such as energy production, waste management, chemicals, sustainable design and development as well as with environmental agencies and consultancies. The fuel and energy supply and utilisation industry in the UK alone is worth over £40 billion and has wide ranging career opportunities. Examples of career paths of former students include assessment of environmental impact of energy production, improvement of efficiency of energy utilisation, energy equipment manufacturing, energy conservation and pollution consultancy. The broad-based nature of the degree also allows the student to pursue careers outside the energy sector.

Related Degrees

Energy Systems with Industrial Studies in Europe, Energy and Environmental Engineering, Fuel/Fire/Energy Engineering

Suggested Reading

The Bottomless Well: The Twilight of Fuel, the Virtue of Waste, and Why We Will Never Run Out of Energy
- Peter Huber, Mark P. Mills, Basic Books, 2006

A Brighter Tomorrow: Fulfilling the Promise of Nuclear Energy
- Pete V Domenici, Rowman and Littlefield, 2006

Tomorrow's Energy: Hydrogen, Fuel Cells and the Prospects for a Cleaner Planet
- Peter Hoffman, MIT Press, 2002

Sustainable Energy - Without the Hot Air
- David J.C. MacKay, UIT, 2008

Degree Course Guide: Engineering
- Trotman, 2007

Further Information

Energy Institute
www.energyinst.org

Energy Information Centre
www.eic.co.uk

Centre for Alternative Technology
www.cat.org.uk

Engineers Ireland
www.engineersireland.ie

Engineering

Original article by Dr A.M. Price BSc, PhD, C.Eng, MIMM., University of Warwick

Introduction

The range of available engineering degrees encompasses everything from Aeromechanics to Water Engineering; from very specialised degrees to those with a broader mandate. Virtually all programmes require A level/Higher/IB or equivalent mathematics or equivalent, many (but by no means all) require A level/Higher/IB or equivalent physics. Engineering degrees also recruit from a broad range of other qualifications.

The major disciplines are Mechanical, Civil, Electronic, Aeronautical, Production/Manufacturing Systems, Chemical and General. It is not possible to give detailed descriptions of each programme within this article but there are already individual articles on each of these major branches of engineering elsewhere in the Degree Course Descriptions.

- *Mechanical Engineering*
- *Civil Engineering*
- *Electronic And Electrical Engineering*
- *Aeronautical Engineering*
- *Manufacturing Engineering*
- *Chemical Engineering*

We can identify a number of generic features, such as design, science and engineering principles, analytical techniques, management and communication skills

Degree Courses

In general, accredited engineering degree programmes will award either a BEng or MEng qualification. The BEng degree is normally awarded after three years of full-time study (four in Scotland), whilst the MEng is awarded after four years (five in Scotland). The MEng degree is normally an enhanced or broader based degree than the BEng, and increasingly includes modules equivalent to postgraduate standard. Some programmes may also offer an exchange year abroad or sandwich programme, combining academic study with periods of employment. Under the criteria for accreditation, known as UK-SPEC, the Engineering Council has set the MEng degree as the normal route for those intending to apply for Chartered Engineer status. Many BEng degree programmes are accredited as suitable for meeting the academic requirements of Chartered Engineer status when combined with a one-year 'matching section', such as an approved MSc. Other degree programmes may set their objectives as meeting the academic requirements for Incorporated Engineer status and you should check the university prospectus to determine the level of accreditation granted to the degree.

With so many specialist degrees to choose from, it may seem odd that some universities also offer general engineering degrees. For some departments these represent a foundation year or 'Year 0'. For others, the different engineering disciplines exist within one unified department. These departments allow students to obtain specialist degrees, founded on common principles. This common material may extend for one or two years before specialisation is invited. Frequently there is also provision for studying a degree programme in general engineering for the full period.

In unified departments it is usually a mistake to equate the entry code with the degree at graduation, since the act of specialisation effectively moves students from one degree programme to another. Students use the common year to make their final choice of specialisation. This offers a clear advantage to the student who wants to read engineering, but cannot decide between the different branches. A good engineer has the knowledge and flexibility to work in the 'grey areas' found at each boundary between specialisations. Such an engineer has the capacity to apply basic engineering principles and concepts to a wide range of problems. General engineering degrees and unified departments seek to deliver these skills by careful development of the curriculum. Students learn how to model engineering problems across the spectrum. This gives the student the skills necessary to work effectively with other engineers on multi-disciplinary projects.

Career Opportunities

The types of work that engineering graduates enter are mainly directly related to their degree specialisms. However, a significant number go into a variety of other careers, including business. The Digest of Engineering Statistics from the Engineering Council reports that engineers as a whole are employed in a wide range of industries: 38% in manufacturing, 8.5% in construction and 54% spread through sectors such as finance and business, transport and communications, electricity and gas and water supply. Engineers are also increasingly needed for project management and leadership roles.

Related Degrees

Integrated Engineering, Engineering Foundation, Engineering with Business Management, Engineering with Overseas Study, Design Engineering, Forensic Engineering, Agricultural Engineering, Mathematical Engineering, Engineering/Economics/Management, Medical Engineering, Engineering with Product Design, Environmental Engineering, Railway Infrastructure Engineering

Suggested Reading

Higher Engineering Science
- W. Bolton, Newnes, 2004

Engineering Mathematics
- K A Stroud and Dexter J Booth, Palgrave Macmillan, 2007

Degree Course Guide: Engineering
- Trotman, 2007

Higher Engineering Mathematics
- J O Bird, Newnes, 2007

Further Information

Royal Academy of Engineering
www.raeng.org.uk

Enginuity - Engineering Careers Information Service
www.enginuity.org.uk

Institution of Engineering and Technology
www.theiet.org

Engineering Council UK
www.engc.org.uk

UK Standard for Professional Engineering Competence
www.engc.org.uk/professional-qualifications/standards/uk-spec

Engineers Ireland
www.engineersireland.ie

English

Original article by Professor Patrick Parrinder, University of Reading

Introduction

The initial attraction of an English course is likely to be the opportunity to immerse oneself in some of the most exciting works of poetry, fiction and drama in the language. Some of our motives for studying literature are quite properly introspective - a desire to know ourselves and to explore our cultural and psychic identity. But literary study is outward- as well as inward-looking. Literary criticism, as developed in the writings of such intellectual precursors as S T Coleridge, Matthew Arnold, T S Eliot and F R Leavis, combines formal analysis with the belief that literature offers a key to the nature of human experience.

The separation of literature from entertainment is central to the traditional justification of literary studies. Until recently, the need to demonstrate that literary students were not wasting their time on trivia led to a heavy emphasis on the intellectual and moral benefits of 'high culture'. Nowadays, it is acknowledged that all social life involves feelings and attitudes which are reflected in the culture's systems of symbolic expression. 'High' and 'Low' culture serve much the same functions in this respect. The notion of symbolic systems has permitted the extension of English studies beyond the canon of recognised major literary works to other texts including advertisements, popular romantic fiction and TV soap operas. Some teachers argue for a still broader redefinition of the subject. But the subtlety and complexity of the verbal creations of the greatest writers, from Chaucer to the Nobel Prize winning Caribbean poet Derek Walcott, remains the raison d'être of most English courses.

The reason why some kinds of writing are considered more literary than others is a question of language and form. Yet most varieties of current criticism give pride of place to the multiple meanings of literary texts, including below-the-surface meanings, the different meanings attached to them in different historical periods, and the meanings they may have for different readers. Since virtually every literary text contains moral, psychological, religious, political and philosophical layers of significance as well as evoking an aesthetic response, the number of valid critical approaches is very considerable. You are likely to be introduced to several approaches and you will have the opportunity to find out others for yourself.

Degree Courses

Which authors and texts will you be expected to study? Shakespeare is no longer invariably compulsory. You will meet a selection from the other canonical writers such as Chaucer, Donne, Milton, Pope, Swift, the Romantic poets, the Victorian novelists and the early twentieth-century Modernists. Such works as the *Canterbury Tales*, Spenser's *Faerie Queene*, Milton's *Paradise Lost*, Wordsworth's *Prelude* or the major novels of Dickens, George Eliot or Virginia Woolf may be studied in depth. The analysis of short unseen passages may be used to teach the skills of attentive reading and to develop versatility of response. In the final year, you are likely to be given the opportunity of writing a dissertation or series of extended essays on subjects of your own choice. Occasionally the study of some literature in another language is required.

The range of specialist options offered in many departments makes 'From Beowulf to Virginia Woolf' sound narrow. Anglo-Saxon, *Piers Plowman* and the Elizabethan sonnet sequences and verse romances continue to attract some of the best students, but the majority opt for the more modern subjects, which are likely to include American and post-colonial literatures, women's literature, 'minority' literatures, contemporary popular fiction, aspects of film and television studies, and literary theory. Broad intellectual movements such as feminism, structuralism and semiotics (ie theories of sign and symbol), hermeneutics (ie theories of interpretation), post-modernism and post-colonialisation have had a marked impact on the teaching of many degree courses. Current linguistic theories are probably less influential.

Many departments allow students to take part of their degree abroad. A possibility is a placement with a local firm. Creative writing and literary composition as such are very rarely part of the syllabus, though a number of departments run voluntary writing workshops. The creative atmosphere which a good English department can succeed in nurturing is a precious asset, but an English degree is only one course of study open to a future novelist or poet. English, like history and philosophy, is usually regarded as a humanities rather than a creative arts discipline, but even this generalisation is open to challenge, since the subject remains vigorous, argumentative and self-critical.

Career Opportunities

The skills you can gain through studying English are useful in a wide variety of career areas. Perhaps the major strength of all English graduates is communication skills, both in speech and in writing. However, you also learn to organise your workload, work to tight deadlines, convey meaning precisely, pick out the essential points from texts, interpret, assess and evaluate sources, lead and participate in discussions, work independently, think critically and develop opinions, propose ideas and theories, persuade others of your point of view, think and act creatively, and develop IT skills. Many English students write for student newspapers and magazines, get involved with student radio or film societies or volunteer in the community or local schools. Given that English is generally seen as a non-vocational course, the skills you develop outside your study could be critical in developing a rounded CV.

Last year, six months after graduation, 55% of graduates in English had entered paid employment. Many were in temporary jobs, mostly in clerical or catering jobs, to be used as a 'stepping stone' to gain experience for their longer-term aims. Of the graduates going into employment, around 50% went into professional or associate professional jobs. This included 8% entering marketing, sales and advertising, 8% entering managerial roles and 11% teaching and related roles.

Related Degrees

English Language, English Studies, English Literature, Literary Studies, English Language and Literature, Creative Writing, Script Writing

Suggested Reading

A Reader's Guide to Contemporary Literary Theory
- Raman Selden, Peter Widdowson and Peter Brooker, Longman, 2005

The Norton Anthology of English Literature (Vols 1 and 2)
- S. Greenblatt, Norton, 2006

Modern Literary Theory: A Comparative Introduction
- Ann Jefferson and David Robey Eds, Batsford, 1987

The English Studies Book
- Rob Pope, Routledge, 2002

How Poetry Works
- Phil Roberts, Penguin, 2000

The Common Pursuit
- F R Leavis, Faber Finds, 2008

Doing English: A Guide for Literature Students
- Robert Eaglestone, Taylor and Francis, 2007

Further Information

Society of Authors
www.societyofauthors.org

Irish Writers' Centre
www.writerscentre.ie

Environmental Health

Original article by Catherine Gairn, Faculty of Health and Environment, Leeds Metropolitan University

Introduction

Accredited environmental health courses all cover the same basic syllabus, although the emphasis varies from one university to another. Essentially, all involve accumulating operational skills and a fundamental knowledge of legal and organisational issues, understanding environmental and public health stressors and linking these with the principal realms of environmental health including food, housing, occupational health, environmental protection and public health.

As the course progresses, you will also acquire the qualities of confidence, independent critical judgement and leadership, and the ability to work as part of a team. These are all essential prerequisites for a career as an environmental health practitioner (EHP).

Degree Courses

When you apply for an accredited course, it is advisable to look for work-based learning opportunities as soon as possible. If you can find a placement before you begin the course, you will be able to complete a sandwich route and become qualified within four years (or in two years if you already have an appropriate science degree and have enrolled on an MSc course).

Work-based learning opportunities are available within a wide range of organisations including local councils, private sector companies, government departments and the NHS and its related agencies.

Universities offering accredited courses may be able to assist with finding work-based experiential learning places. Employers may notify universities of such vacancies. Newspapers too, are a good source of information.

If you cannot find a placement, you will still be able to enrol on the course and look for a placement whilst you are a student. If you still find it difficult to find a placement, you can complete your full-time accredited degree and then complete your work-based learning after graduation.

The main subject areas on accredited courses are: food safety, environmental protection, public health and housing. These subjects involve both theory and practical (laboratory) work and a variety of visits to such places as power stations, water sewage and water treatment plants and docks. You will also develop additional skills such as numeracy, literary, IT, research, communication and other transferable skills.

A 12-month placement of structured, practical training is required, usually integrated into the third year of the course, although it can be undertaken on completion of the three years of academic study. Work-based learning is an essential element towards professional qualification and this may be undertaken without time limits in any organisation that delivers an environmental health service. An opportunity to spend up to 12 weeks in another European country is available to students in their placement year, although a sound knowledge of the appropriate language is usually required. Throughout the placement year you'll also produce an experiential learning portfolio, which will be assessed as the precursor to the professional examinations, when you must satisfy the Chartered Institute of Environmental Health (CIEH) assessment prior to registration for professional practice as an EHP.

Career Opportunities

Local authorities, as the agencies concerned with the protection of public health (including food, housing, health and safety, environmental/pollution control) employ environmental health practitioners but there are plenty of other possibilities including: central government and its agencies, such as the Food Standards Agency, the Environment Agency and the Health and Safety Executive; the armed services; holiday companies (checking out foreign hotels etc); shipping and flight companies (ensuring passengers' on-board health and safety, for example); the National Health Service.

Beyond that, many EHPs work abroad. For example, the European Commission employs some, whilst others travel further afield to work in Australia, Canada, New Zealand and the US. A wide range of opportunities exists for EHPs in a world where pollution and danger to health have become vital international issues.

Related Degrees

Public Health, Trading Standards

Suggested Reading

Clay's Handbook of Environmental Health
- W H Basset Ed, Routledge, 2004

Environmental Health Practitioner - the professional magazine of the CIEH
- View the current issue at: *www.ehp-online.com*

Further Information

Environmental Health Careers
www.ehcareers.org

Institution of Occupational Safety and Health
www.iosh.co.uk

Charted Institute of Environmental Health
www.cieh.org

Health Service Executive, Ireland
www.careersinhealthcare.ie

Environmental Protection Agency, Ireland
www.epa.ie

Environmental Sciences

Original article by Malcolm Hudson, Senior Tutor, Centre for Environmental Sciences, University of Southampton, based on a previous contribution by Professor Ian F Spellerberg, Lincoln University, New Zealand (visiting Professor, University of Southampton)

Introduction

Environmental Sciences is a comparatively new approach to interdisciplinary science, based on various aspects of the traditional science subjects such as biology, geography, chemistry, geology and oceanography. Environmental sciences and environmental studies are concerned with both the natural and human environments but, whereas environmental sciences has a science component, environmental studies incorporates more aspects of social sciences and the arts. In reality, there is quite a bit of overlap between the two, depending on the interests of the university department and the choices available to the student.

Environmental sciences courses are interdisciplinary and multidisciplinary. In all the traditional science subjects there are topics of practical relevance to our understanding of the environment and the processes which take place in the environment. Such topics can be brought together in an integrated fashion and so provide the all-important interdisciplinary basis for informed and integrated management. For instance, academically valid studies of water pollution in rivers and estuaries require an interdisciplinary approach, incorporating relevant aspects of environmental biology, physical geography, environmental chemistry and marine ecology. Similarly, assessments of the environmental implications of alternative land use planning require a sound knowledge of carefully selected aspects of geography, geology, environmental biology and elements of subjects such as environmental engineering and environmental law.

Environmental sciences deal with current issues about the natural and the human environment, and as a result attract students with a wide range of interests, but clearly any such interdisciplinary studies and training are not a soft option or an easy way to get a degree. Although the component parts of environmental sciences are generally the same as those taken by students specialising in single subject degree courses, environmental sciences students have to think about the links between subjects and have to draw upon resources provided by more than one subject when tackling interdisciplinary assignments.

A major attraction is that you can either specialise in any one of the many areas or retain a more general approach. You might specialise, for example, in nature conservation, waste resource management, economic geology, coastal management, hydrology or irrigation, public health engineering, urban planning, ecological chemistry, land management, pollution control or sustainable development. Alternatively, many students choose environmental sciences because they simply want a good grounding in a broad variety of environmental topics. Many students come to the degree with a general interest in the area, and develop their own specialisms as their studies progress.

An interdisciplinary approach to the study of the environment has increasing practical relevance because of the growing concern for human activities upon the world we live in. There is an awareness now that 'everything links together;' for example, use of fossil fuels in the developed world can affect the climate thousands of miles away, or lead to the destruction of low-lying coasts or islands. Thus concern about many environmental issues (such as global warming, deforestation, desertification, disposal of toxic wastes and loss of biodiversity) has prompted the need for more research and better ways of managing our resources. The increasing awareness of environmental problems is resulting in a greater participation in environmental pressure groups and in the creation of more environmental legislation, which must be based on sound knowledge of environmental processes. At the same time, industry has begun to embrace the environmental agenda, with international corporations now routinely reporting on their environmental effects and setting targets for long-term improvement. Furthermore, environmental impact assessment of proposed major developments (eg motorways, marinas or chemical works) is now a comparatively new legislative requirement but has already stimulated the need for more people to be trained to manage interdisciplinary problems.

Degree Courses

Environmental sciences as a degree subject has a common core but, depending on where you study, there are different and unique components to the way that it is taught because the bias or structure will, in part, reflect the research interests of the teaching staff. This provides an added bonus of choice but it makes it essential that you find out all you can about the different courses. Checking out university web pages is a good place to start. All course admission tutors offer a friendly information service about teaching, research projects, field-courses, entry requirements and the careers of their graduates. Ask them for a reading list and in addition note the books mentioned below.

Career Opportunities

There is no single career path for an environmental sciences graduate, but recent years have seen a major expansion in the potential job market as employers have begun to recognise the value of interdisciplinary expertise. Pollution control (eg with the Environment Agency) or conservation management are two of the commonest areas for graduates to work in. There are increasing opportunities in consultancy, which may require some specialist knowledge (eg on contaminated land treatment or ecology) or interdisciplinary skills (in environmental impact assessment or planning).

While traditionally the water companies, along with the biotechnology and agrochemical industry have provided vacancies, other major industries now need environmental specialists for their sustainability programmes. International initiatives and the increasing challenges of managing our waste have produced many career opportunities in local government. There are even opportunities in unexpected areas, such as ecotourism. Some graduates enter teaching or take postgraduate courses, and some go on to an academic or research career after completing a PhD.

Related Degrees

Environmental Pollution/Protection, Environmental Conservation, Agriculture of the Environment, Environmental Biology, Environmental Chemistry, Environmental Technology, Environmental Physics, Environmental Archaeology, Marine Environmental Studies, Environmental Resources, Aquatic Science, Environmental Science with year abroad

Suggested Reading

The Human Impact on the Natural Environment
- Andrew Goudie, WileyBlackwell, 2005

Global Environmental Issues: a Climatological Approach
- David D Kemp, Taylor and Francis, 2007

An Introduction to Global Environmental Issues
- Kevin T Pickering and Lewis A Owen, Routledge, 1977

Further Information

Natural Environment Research Council
www.nerc.ac.uk
Environment Council
www.the-environment-council.org.uk
Institution of Environmental Sciences
www.ies-uk.org.uk
Environmental Sciences Association of Ireland
www.esaiweb.org

Equine Science

Original article by Dr Jeremy F Burn, University of Bristol

Introduction

Equine science is the study of horses from a scientific perspective. If you enjoy science and horses, then perhaps this could be the ideal subject for you. Since horses are animals, the areas of science that relate to them are broadly described as biological or biomedical sciences. These include such diverse subjects as anatomy (the study of the relationship between structural form and function), physiology (how body systems work), biomechanics (how the principles of mechanics such as Newton's laws can be applied to the animal body) and biochemistry (how chemical reactions are involved in everything from metabolism to muscle contraction). These are only a few examples of the way in which science helps us to understand horses and the way they work. If you are interested in horses and have read books on them, much of the information you will have learned has been passed down through generations of horsemen and women. Some of this information has a scientific basis, even though in most cases the originators of the information were not scientists. Some of the things you might have learned about horses do not have any scientific basis. An equine science degree course will allow you to differentiate between the two. You will learn the basic scientific principles that underlie, for example, behaviour, nutrition, reproduction, structural form, function, movement and husbandry of the horse. Hopefully, this will increase your appreciation and enjoyment of horses and may lead to a graduate career in horses either in industry or in research.

Degree Courses

The content of equine science courses varies widely between institutions so the first and important point to note is to shop around for the one that best suits your requirements. The reasons for the variation are firstly that, because equine science is a relatively new subject to be offered at degree level, there is not yet a consistent view of what an equine science course should contain. Secondly, the various institutions specialise in different areas of equine-related science and tend to focus their course around their internal expertise. Aspects of the courses that vary are typically (a) the amount of contact with live horses (which can vary from none at all to the opportunity to manage and ride horses) (b) the amount of business management in the course (which can range from none to several modules) (c) the areas of science covered (for example some courses might not cover genetics or biomechanics) (d) the significance and scope of the final year research project. Final year research projects will usually involve you working independently or in a small group on a piece of equine-related research. This is one of the most enjoyable parts of the degree course, as you are able to put the knowledge and skills you have learned during the course into practice. If you are particularly interested in an area of equine research, it might be worthwhile checking that your chosen institution is able to support a research project in that area.

Career Opportunities

A science degree is a general academic qualification that allows you to follow 'graduate entry' paths into finance, media, management, marketing, etc. In many cases there are specialist jobs in these areas relating to horses, for example within finance, you might work for a company that provides horse insurance, or in media, you might work for the natural history unit of a television company or an equine specialist magazine. Although the equine industry in the UK is large in both financial and employment terms, it relies predominantly on non-graduate employment and it is worth considering that a degree in equine science is not the best qualification for working with horses at a practical level. There are also specialist careers such as equine physiotherapy, chiropractic and osteopathy that have their own training programmes, and a degree in equine science is not usually the fastest route to qualification in these areas.

Related Degrees

Animal Science, Horse Management and Equitation, Equine Studies

Suggested Reading

Rose: the Athletic Horse: Principles and Practice of Equine Horse Medicine
- David R Hodgson and Reuben J Rose, Saunders, 2004

Equine Locomotion
- Willem Back and Hilary Clayton, Saunders, 2000

Equine Behaviour: a Guide for Veterinarians and Equine Scientists
- Paul McGreevy, Saunders, 2004

Equine Nutrition and Feeding
- David Frape, Wiley-Blackwell, 2010

The Domestic Horse: The Origins, Development and Management of Its Behaviour
- D. S. Mills and S. M. McDonnell, Cambridge University Press, 2005

Further Information

Equine Science Update
www.equinescienceupdate.co.uk

British Horse Society
www.bhs.org.uk

Irish Horse Society
www.irishhorsesociety.com

European Studies

Original article by Professor Juliet Lodge, Jean Monnet European Centre of Excellence, University of Leeds

Introduction

European studies exposes you to the many facets of life that have gone into producing the Europe of today and involves a broad examination of Europe's history, geography, culture, economics, philosophies, literature, politics and society. European Studies normally involves gaining fluency in at least one and usually two European languages besides your mother tongue. French, German and Spanish are the most popular but it is also possible to study Italian, Dutch, Russian etc. Language courses that form part of European studies degrees are increasingly practical in their orientation. Modern languages rather than linguistics or the literature of the 17th century are stressed, although you would also gain an appreciation of the literature of the country(ies) whose language(s) you were acquiring.

Comparative politics and political economy or economic history often form components of European studies degrees. The states most often studied include: Germany, France, Russia, the UK and possibly Italy, Spain and Sweden. You would normally learn about American and international politics as well. European studies degrees also normally involve a study of political philosophy from Plato, Machiavelli and Hobbes to Locke, Marx and Marcuse, for example. Major contemporary political trends - liberalism, socialism, communism, totalitarianism, fascism, feminism, etc - may also be studied from a variety of perspectives: literary, philosophical, historical, economic or political, for example.

Degree Courses

It is now possible to take degree courses in subjects like chemistry or maths, for instance, that have a European studies component in them. You can also combine European studies with languages, or with law, history, art history, environmental studies, business studies, management, sociology, economics or politics.

Normally, you would also spend a period of time in Europe either at a European university or working. Some courses sandwich two periods abroad into a four-year programme. During this time, you would be expected to write a dissertation of around 8,000 words (in English or one of your other European languages) on a topic relevant to your studies.

Departments in the field of social science now offer some of the most exciting courses in European studies. If you are keen on politics, lobbying, trade, international affairs and business, for example, you can now take courses which build in a 'stage' at the European Parliament. (A 'stage' is the European term commonly used to refer to a period of unpaid internship.) This means that, while continuing your studies in Brussels, you may also have working links with Members of the European Parliament. You get to see how Europe ticks. Periods working in Europe or as 'stages' or in partner European universities are highly illuminating, socially and personally rewarding. In addition, they are fun. As you become an active part of the trans-European student community, your circle of friends will grow, your intellectual horizons will alter and your experiences will challenge your preconceptions daily!

If you want such a course, make sure that you look beyond language departments. The social sciences, business and law, and increasingly English and science departments, provide rich hunting grounds. If your main interest is language you would do well to choose a course that has a high European studies component and one which does not restrict you to the study of European literature. Many departments now offer the chance to study commercial language alongside literature, culture and politics. Many allow you to study in another European university and gain an extra qualification or diploma.

In short, European studies courses offer you numerous options and they often benefit from excellent schemes such as *Erasmus*, *Tempus IV* and *Erasmus Mundus*, initiated by the European Union. *Erasmus* is the European programme for higher education, encouraging cooperation between institutions and boosting staff and student mobility for work and study. *Tempus IV* expands mobility and exchanges to 27 partner countries in Eastern Europe, the West Balkans, North Africa, the Middle East and Central Asia. *Erasmus Mundus* goes even further, extending scholarships and academic cooperation to the rest of the world.

In short, European studies is predominantly about understanding Europe today; how and why Europe is shaped as it is; what its role and place is in the world; where it is going; what problems it confronts; how it resolves them, whether they are economic, political, environmental, social, cultural, scientific, commercial or technical. Europe encroaches on all aspects of our lives and all aspects of education.

Career Opportunities

These courses develop interest and awareness of trends in overseas markets which are of value to employers with overseas interests. Graduates tend to favour jobs in the Fast Stream of the Civil Service, buying, selling, marketing, trading/retailing and banking organisations. Journalism, public relations, broadcasting, lobbying and EU consultancies in the private and public sectors are also popular. Increasing numbers of graduates enter law, accountancy, teaching and computing.

Related Degrees

European Law, Culture and Language, Contemporary Europe, European Studies with Languages, European Studies (History), Viking Studies, East European Studies, Welsh Studies, Celtic Studies, Irish Studies

Suggested Reading

The Penguin Companion to European Union
- Timothy Bainbridge and Anthony Teasdale, Penguin, 2004

The European Union: A very short Introduction
- John Pinder, Oxford, 2007

Understanding the European Union
- John McCormick, Palgrave Macmillan, 2008

Further Information

Europa (EU)
http://europa.eu

Erasmus, Tempus and Erasmus Mundus
http://ec.europa.eu/education/index_en.htm

Jean Monnet European Centre of Excellence
www.leeds.ac.uk/jmce

European Commission - the EU in the United Kingdom
http://ec.europa.eu/unitedkingdom

European Commission - the EU in Ireland
http://ec.europa.eu/ireland

Fashion Design

Original article written with help from Central St Martins College of Art and Design, now part of the University of the Arts, London

Introduction

A degree in fashion design should encourage you to explore your talents and individuality, helping you to develop the combination of innovation and design skills, technical ability and awareness of current trends and business objectives that you will need to succeed as a fashion professional in design, retail or production.

Many courses offer you a choice of subject routes to suit your career ambition, usually starting with a broad base in Year One and becoming increasingly specialised as you progress through Year Two.

In most cases, you would apply via UCAS after completing a foundation or access course. This would give you the opportunity both to explore a variety of creative options and to build a suitable portfolio. For fashion design, your portfolio should contain life, objective and fashion drawing. Admissions staff look for colour work, creative design ideas and development as well as evidence of how you have answered set briefs or initiated work for yourself. You would be encouraged to bring to interview sketchbooks, made-up garments and written work (essay and reports). In general, evidence of 3D work is more important than huge 'pieces' or folders full of patterns. A good tip is to set up your own fashion shoot - complete with accessories, hair and make-up - and present photographs rather than including too many completed garments.

Degree Courses

Fashion design studies are normally based on a mixture of studio and workshop practice, lectures, seminars, visits and personal study, with a typical ratio of approximately 80% practical work and 20% theoretical and historical study. You should have the opportunity to meet visiting designers and specialists, to take part in sponsored projects with major fashion companies and to gain experience in work-based placements. Many courses arrange overseas study trips for students, usually to international fashion centres such as New York, Paris or Milan.

Level 1 (first year) modules typically introduce the subject and are concerned with experimentation and the exploration of design language and process, while

Level 2 (second year) modules emphasise technical knowledge and creative development and include collaboration with designers and industry. During this level you may be asked to make your choice of subject route for Level 3, on some courses, while on others you may be asked to make this choice on entry.

For example, you may focus exclusively on fashion design or you may prefer to develop your business skills by combining fashion with marketing or retail management. If you are more technically inclined, you may choose to link fashion with product development.

During Level 3 study you will certainly be asked to undertake a self-directed project of your own choice that focuses your work in the direction of your intended career.

Career Opportunities

As a fashion design graduate, you should be able to work across a very wide spectrum. While you may not become the next Donna Karan, Stella McCartney, John Galliano or Tommy Hilfiger, you can still work successfully and influentially as a company designer, freelancer or consultant. Alternatively, you may pursue a fashion-related career as a journalist, stylist, photographer, illustrator, public relations consultant, pattern cutter, buyer or retailer. Career opportunities may depend to a certain extent on the pathway you choose.

Related Degrees

Depending on your interests, you may wish to consider courses in:

Textile Design, Interior Design, Industrial Product Design, Jewellery Design, Graphic Design. Alternatively, you might look at Photography, Journalism or Retail Management.

Suggested Reading

Getting into Art and Design courses 2011 entry
- James Burnett, Trotman, 2010

Fashion Design
- Sue Jenkyn Jones, Laurence King, 2005

200 Projects to Get You into Fashion Design
- Adrian Grandon, A & C Black, 2009

Fairchild Dictionary of Fashion
- Charlotte Mankey Calasibetta and Phyllis Tortora, Laurence King, 2003

Patternmaking for Fashion Design
- Helen Joseph Armstrong, Pearson Education, 2009

Women's Wear Daily
- access online at the WWD website address below

Le Book: international meeting point for fashion and photography
- access online at the website address below

Further Information

Can U cut it in fashion?
www.canucutit.co.uk

Laurence King Publishing
www.laurenceking.co.uk

Women's Wear Daily
www.wwd.com

Le Book
www.lebook.com

Fashion Net
www.fashion.net

Your Creative Future
www.yourcreativefuture.org

Irish Clothing and Textile Alliance
www.ibec.ie/icata

Institute of Designers in Ireland
http://idi-design.ie

Film Studies

Original article written with material supplied by the University of East Anglia

Introduction

Film Studies covers subjects ranging from the hundred-year history of cinema to the close analysis of film texts. Studying film requires you to investigate both visual and written materials, to master approaches from diverse disciplines and to apply ideas adopted from various intellectual perspectives. You might also have the opportunity to engage in practical film-making activities such as script-writing and video production.

Film Studies combines insights drawn from a range of disciplines - history, sociology, art history, comparative studies and aesthetics. The subject usually incorporates concepts from major theoretical perspectives such as semiotics, feminism, Marxism, psychoanalysis and post-colonial theory.

Degree Courses

Courses are usually modular in structure and often adopt broad topics such as:

- Aspects of film theory, examining the fascinating approaches that have been developed in order to think about, study and analyse films;
- Hollywood cinema, investigating the world's dominant system of film production;
- National cinemas - in particular, those of Britain, France, Germany and Spain - placing films within the broader contexts of the societies producing them.

Further modules might extend the scope to cover early cinema, experimental work, aspects of 'world cinema' and exploitation and cult films.

As you are unlikely to have any prior experience of film studies, Level 1 modules typically introduce the analytical terms and perspectives that would enable you to engage effectively with the programme. When you progress to Levels 2 and 3, you should be able to choose study options to tailor the course to your own developing interests. An 'extended essay' at Level 2 and dissertation at Level 3 would enable you to explore individually chosen topics of study under staff supervision.

Teaching normally comprises a mix of lectures, seminars, workshops, film presentations and tutorial support. You would be expected to develop your own programme of reading and film study and you would be assessed by essay, seminar presentation, study logs, dissertation and examination.

Career Opportunities

As a Film Studies graduate, you should be able to show a well-informed awareness of many of the cultural and social issues under debate in contemporary Britain as well as being able to demonstrate an in-depth knowledge of film. Your degree should give you advanced transferable skills in areas such as analysis and communication and could serve as a useful preparation for a wide variety of posts in media or other cultural industries. It could also lead on to postgraduate study. It is not, however, a vocational course providing technical skills.

Related Degrees

You might also consider *Media and Cultural Studies* or you could combine *Film Studies* with a related subject such as *English, Drama, American Studies, History, French, Spanish, Art* or *Sociology*.

Suggested Reading

Film Art: An Introduction
- David Bordwell and Kristin Thompson, McGraw-Hill, 2010

Film History: An Introduction
- Kristin Thompson and David Bordwell McGraw-Hill Higher Education, 2009

The Oxford Guide to Film Studies
- John Hill and Pamela Church Gibson Eds, OUP, 1998

The Cinema Book
- Pam Cook, BFI Publishing, 2008

Further Information

British Film Institute
www.bfi.org.uk

Film-Philosophy: International Salon-Journal
www.film-philosophy.com

Irish Film Institute
www.ifi.ie

Irish Film and Television Network
www.iftn.ie

Finance

Original article by David J. Collison, University of Dundee

Introduction

The terms 'finance' and 'accountancy' mean much the same thing to many people and are often used interchangeably. However, there are important distinctions between them, especially in the context of choosing a university course.

The term 'finance' relates to the ways in which organisations raise money to fund their operations and also to ways in which money is invested: the focus may be on individual organisations or on investments made in many organisations through financial markets (eg the stock exchange).

In contrast, 'accountancy' includes the preparation and communication of financial information about an organisation's operations (which could be in the private or public sector). Accounting information is needed to help manage an organisation and accountants are often part of the management team: accounting information is also needed by a variety of other users (eg employees, suppliers, bankers and other investors, tax authorities and other government agencies).

While there is a distinction between these two main areas of activity, there is also much overlap and people with an accounting background may work in finance and vice versa.

Degree Courses

The purpose of a finance degree is to provide an undergraduate education in an area in which the UK is, in many respects, a world leader. The financial intermediation sector is one of the largest industrial employers in the UK; the sector is also remarkable for its adaptability to changing economic conditions and hence for the flexibility required from its professional employees. The UK financial intermediation sector - banking, building societies, insurance and pension funding - employs just under one million people, and many more financial experts work in other industries. A finance degree will not only furnish an array of skills, techniques, knowledge of institutions and understanding of the often turbulent macroeconomics environment, but will also examine the theoretical and practical limitations of financial techniques.

The UK financial sector's development has been continued for decades and so there is no reason to think that the market for specialist finance graduates will not be sustained.

A distinctive feature of a typical finance course is the blending of financial economics-based and business finance-based courses to produce a course combination specifically tailored to the requirements of financial institutions. Potential employers among the financial institutions and the former UK Society of Investment Professionals (now the CFA Society of the UK), for example, were consulted about the content of the Bachelor of Finance degree at Dundee University.

The aim of a finance degree is to produce graduates with a deep understanding of the operations of financial institutions and a knowledge of the relevant techniques that will enable them to analyse operations at both microeconomic and macroeconomic level.

Career Opportunities

Graduates from these courses are well equipped to enter the financial sector. They enter accountancy, clearing and merchant banking, insurance, financial services, pension investment organisations, the Inland Revenue, building societies, stock and commodity markets. The scope is enormous in industry, commerce, central and local government.

Related Degrees

Banking and Finance, Business Finance, Financial Management, Insurance, International Finance and Trade, Investment, Finance and Risk, Accounting and Finance, Business and Finance (Marketing), European International Financial Management, Insurance/Banking, Economics.

Suggested Reading

Look at the financial sections of quality newspapers such as the 'Financial Times' and specialist journals such as 'Accountancy' or 'The Economist'.

Business, Administration and Finance
- Angela Youngman, Trotman, 2009

Progression to Economics, Finance & Accountancy 2011 entry
- UCAS/GTI, 2010

Economics for Business and Management: A Student Text
- Alan Griffiths and Stuart Wall, Prentice Hall, 2008

The Psychology of Money
- Adrian Furnham and Michael Argyle, Routledge, 1998

Quantitative Methods for Business and Economics
- Glyn Burton et al, Prentice Hall, 2001

Business Finance: Theory and Practice
- Eddie McLaney, Financial Times/ Prentice Hall, 2006

Further Information

CFA Society of the UK
https://secure.cfauk.org

Institute of Public Finance
www.ipf.com/finance

Biz/Ed
www.bized.co.uk

Chartered Insurance Institute
www.cii.co.uk

Institute of Bankers in Ireland
www.bankers.ie

Business and Finance Ireland
www.businessandfinance.ie

Food Sciences

Original article by Brent Murray, Procter Department of Food Science, University of Leeds.

Introduction

Courses bearing the title **"Food Catering"** or **"Food management"** are largely aimed at those seeking careers in the handling and distribution of food after production. They cover many aspects of food preparation, from large-scale preparation of meals to understanding nutritional and dietary issues and the running of a small business in the catering sector. Courses that carry the title **"Food Technology"** have a stronger focus on the production and processing of foods on a factory scale. They are likely to appeal to students with a greater leaning towards the engineering aspects of food production. **"Food Science"** degrees cover a broad range of basic science as it applies to food and the food industry. Students will improve their basic scientific skills in chemistry, biochemistry, physics, nutrition, microbiology and process engineering. All of these will be applied to the properties of foods and the processes of food production. **"Food Bioscience"** courses are similar to Food Science but have a more biological emphasis, looking towards the origins of the food as living material.

Degree Courses

Food Science/Bioscience students might learn about the chemical structure of vitamin A in a food chemistry module. Later, in a laboratory class on food analysis, they could expect to learn how to analyse foods to measure their content of this vitamin. In nutrition classes they would learn about the function of vitamin A in the human body and dietary requirements associated with vitamin A intake. In process engineering they could expect to learn about the effect of different techniques of the denaturation of this vitamin. In their final year they might undertake a project to improve vitamin A retention in a process. Finally they might be set the task, in a development project, to design in the control and preservation of this vitamin content. Vitamin A is of course just one example of the many nutrients and food components that the student will encounter during these courses.

Many university courses now have a strong emphasis on transferable skills. This is particularly true of vocational courses like food science. IT skills, presentation skills and writing skills are all likely to be prominent features of a food science degree.

Food Science/Bioscience is for many a vocational degree. The option to do a placement with a food manufacturer or retailer is an integral part of many food science courses. Often these placements take the form of a sandwich course: students spend a total of four years with a six-month placement in the second half of their third year. They cover all the modules studied by three-year food science undergraduates and also undertake a programme of management studies aimed at providing them with the skills to operate as project managers when they begin their career.

A number of universities also offer a European course. This enables students to study at another university within the EU for part of their studies. These courses include language training before the placement.

Career Opportunities

Students should investigate the degree of industrial contact that a prospective department has and should inquire about the careers of earlier graduates. Many food science departments work closely with the food industry and the regulatory bodies. Some have industrialists regularly lecturing on their courses throughout the degree programme. Good contacts with a university department raise the confidence of employers in recruiting graduates from them.

Related Degrees

Food Bioscience, Food Production and Quality, Food and Consumer Science, Food Science with Business, Food Biology, Food Technology Management, Food Manufacture and Management

Suggested Reading

Fox and Cameron's Food Science, Nutrition and Health
- Michael E.J. Lean, Hodder Arnold, 2006

Food: The Chemistry of its Components
- T P Coultate, Royal Society of Chemistry, 2008

Food Microbiology
- M R Adams and M O Moss, Royal Society of Chemistry, 2007

A Sociology of Food and Nutrition: The Social Appetite
- John Germov and Lauren Williams, OUP, 2008

Further Information

Institute of Food Science and Technology
www.ifst.org.uk

Food Navigator
www.foodnavigator.com

Teagasc Irish Agriculture and Food Development Authority
www.teagasc.ie

Food Safety Authority of Ireland
www.fsai.ie

Forensic Science

Original article by Dr Lee Chatfield, Department of Forensic and Investigative Science, University of Central Lancashire

Introduction

Forensic science has enjoyed an increase in popularity of late and has been the most rapidly expanding area of a key provision for science students. Forensic science is the application of scientific techniques and principles to matters pertaining to the law. It is primarily concerned with the scientific analysis of evidence from crime scenes and also provides an opportunity to place scientific principles and techniques within a vocational framework. The evidence criminal investigators collect varies depending on the case but it might consist of minute traces of paint or glass fragments, human hairs, footwear impressions, small samples of vegetation on footwear, fingerprints, different inks or handwriting, body fluids or chemicals or human remains. The analysis of these samples requires the application of scientific methods from different scientific disciplines.

Degree Courses

Forensic science encompasses four main areas of study as follows:

Forensic Investigation (Scenes of Crime) concerns itself with the collection and preservation of evidence from crime scenes. This evidence, usually of a physical nature, is subjected to a range of analytical techniques including fingerprinting, footwear impressions, ballistics, hair and fibre analysis, glass fragments and tool marks. This area of teaching also includes legal aspects of the collection and presentation of evidence in court.

Forensic Biology covers DNA profiling, the identification of individuals from bodily samples such as blood, semen or saliva and from other sources such as hairs or tissues. It also explores the application of other areas of biology, such as botany and entomology, to forensic investigations.

Forensic Chemistry entails the application of analytical techniques to fire investigation, detection and analysis of drugs, and trace evidence such as paint flakes or soil.

Forensic Anthropology concerns itself with the analysis of skeletal human remains and the recovery of buried or skeletal remains.

Forensic Pathology is also part of Forensic Science but applicants should note that a career as a forensic pathologist requires a medical degree and applicants interested in pursuing this as a career need to enter via a medical school rather than a forensic science degree.

At present there is a significant expansion in the number of forensic science degrees at universities. In general there are two types of forensic science degree and applicants are advised to delve into the course structures and contents of forensic science courses to distinguish between these. Firstly, many science departments are basing forensic science degrees around existing expertise in either chemistry or biology and these courses are focused primarily on these scientific aspects of the subject. The second type of forensic science degree tends to cover those aspects equally with scenes of crime and forensic investigation forming the core of that degree programme. Some courses will have specialist teaching from experts working in forensic science, most notably from one of the Forensic Science Service Laboratories, while the Police Service and the Home Office Pathology Department also provide students with the opportunity to spend time working with these services during their course. One good piece of advice is to check the module descriptions and course syllabus for the degrees to decide which would best suit your interests and aspirations.

Career Opportunities

Most students entering forensic science at university are aiming for a career as a scene of crime officer or employment in the Forensic Science Service. There is intense competition for places in these careers and therefore applicants are advised to consider alternative areas of employment should they be unsuccessful in these goals. Alternative areas of employment include the police service, where forensic science degrees are extremely appropriate for career opportunities, and in related areas such as customs and excise, the immigration service and the insurance and fraud industries. In addition, it is worth noting that forensic science degrees produce extremely well rounded science graduates with expertise in chemistry, biology and the physical sciences.

Related Degrees

Forensic Psychology, Forensic Analysis, Forensic Biology, Forensic Engineering, Forensic Technology, Forensic Investigation with Law, Chemistry with Forensic Analysis, Chemistry with Forensic Chemistry, Forensic, Fibre and Colour Science, Forensic Studies, Forensic Psychobiology, Forensic Science and Toxicology

Suggested Reading

Forensic Science: An Introduction to Scientific and Investigative Techniques
- Stuart H James and Jon J Nordby Eds, CRC Press, 2009

Principles and Practice of Criminalistics: the profession of forensic science
- Keith Inman and Norah Rudin, CRC Press, 2000

Criminalistics: An Introduction to Forensic Science
- Richard Saferstein, Pearson Education, 2010

Crime Scene to Court: the essentials of Forensic Science
- Ed Peter White, Royal Society of Chemistry, 2010

Fundamentals of Forensic DNA Typing
- John M Butler, Academic Press, 2009

Further Information

Forensic Science Service
www.forensic.gov.uk

Forensic Science Society
www.forensic-science-society.org.uk

Forensic Science Laboratory
www.forensicscience.ie

Forestry

Original article by Ken Reynolds, specialist writer on careers and higher education

Introduction

Forest ecosystems are important components of the life-support system of the planet. Trees and forests not only provide us with many of our most important raw materials such as timber and paper, but also supply much of the oxygen we breathe, contribute to our most precious landscapes, act as habitats for much of the world's wildlife and provide welcome resources for recreation, particularly in and around urban areas. Increasingly, we are also recognising their vital contribution to the regulation of the world's climate. Many people take these benefits for granted but it is the job of the forester to manage these precious natural resources in such a way that they provide the maximum benefits to society.

Today's forestry is therefore concerned with environmental protection, conservation of habitat for wildlife and meeting recreational needs as well as the traditional use of forests for the production of domestic and industrial raw materials. The benefits provided by forests include the conservation of biodiversity, the protection of soils and water and the production of wood and other marketable goods. Forests play an important part in the landscape of many countries and are used for formal and informal recreation, with beneficial effects on the emotional and physical health of visitors. Modern foresters need a wide range of skills such as plant identification, knowledge of how trees grow and develop, conservation issues, computer literacy, planning and management skills and an ability to work with many different groups of people.

Degree Courses

The main subjects for starting the study of forestry include the science of renewable resources, geology and sustainable land management, moving on to soil science, community ecology, plant physiology and diversity and economics. From these roots, students can branch into silviculture, forest measurement, forest planning, wood science, harvesting and wood use, forest ecology, social forestry and research skills, together with the opportunity to take a year out with the Forestry Commission or another forestry organisation. There may also be the possibility of spending a year on an overseas project.

The final year usually involves the preparation of a forest management plan that allows the skills and knowledge acquired during the earlier years to be put into practice. An individual research project is also completed.

Successful completion of the course should give you exemption from the Institute of Chartered Foresters Part I examinations.

Career Opportunities

Traditionally, there has been a strong demand for well-motivated and educated individuals in all aspects of forestry. The predicted doubling of wood production in Britain over the next 15 years can only make career prospects brighter. Presently, about half of forestry graduates become foresters within the state and private sectors in Britain; the remainder progress to urban, environmental or social forestry, timber processing, forest management overseas or research.

Forestry professionals are employed in most parts of the world, perhaps protecting delicate ecosystems in the tropical rainforests, managing large productive areas of plantations, creating attractive urban forests from industrial wasteland, caring for individual trees in towns and cities or managing natural tree cover in National Parks and nature reserves.

Related Degrees

You might also consider: *Agriculture, Arboriculture, Biology, Ecology, Landscape Architecture* or *Surveying*.

Suggested Reading

Woodland Management: a Practical Guide
- Christopher Starr, Crowood Press, 2005

The Woodland Way: A Permaculture Approach to Sustainable Woodland Management
- Ben Law, Permanent Publications, 2001

Forestry: the Journal of the Institute of Chartered Foresters. Five issues per year

Further Information

Royal Forestry Society
www.rfs.org.uk

Forestry Commission
www.forestry.gov.uk

Institute of Chartered Foresters
www.charteredforesters.org

Royal Scottish Forestry Society
www.rsfs.org

Society of Irish Foresters
www.societyofirishforesters.ie

French

Original article by Professor Alison Saunders, University of Aberdeen

Introduction

French can be studied as a single honours subject in its own right; as half a joint honours degree with another language, or with a non-language subject like history, philosophy or politics; as the major component of a major-minor combination like French with film studies or as the minor component, like law or chemistry or business studies with French.

In cases where French is an adjunct to the main subject, usually only the language is studied, but in other cases, while the language component is obviously very important, it is only a part of the degree programme. Equally important are the 'content' courses, which form the other part of a French degree. Traditionally language degrees used to be described in terms of 'lang. and lit', but nowadays 'content courses' mean something much more wide ranging than just the study of French literature, although this is usually still an important feature. French culture, politics, institutions, film, linguistics - to name only some areas - may also figure in the range of topics available for study. In some universities francophone African or Caribbean literature and culture may also be studied. The division between language and content is, of course, an artificial one, since the two complement each other. Linguistic ability is necessary in order to read and understand works in French, but equally the more widely we read, the more we enrich our linguistic awareness and increase our own communication skills. Cultural awareness and understanding is vital to anyone contemplating a career in translation or interpreting, or any career which involves working closely with French-speaking people. Whilst most Honours degrees in French will require an A level (or equivalent) pass in the subject, a number of universities now also offer Honours courses in French to beginners or to people who have not studied the subject beyond GCSE (or equivalent).

Degree Courses

Language is usually taught in smallish groups, and an important feature of most French departments is the presence of young French native speakers who take responsibility for oral work. Accuracy in the use of language is very important at university level, but so also is the ability to select the appropriate register of language according to circumstances (the language used in casual conversation with friends is different from the more formal language used, for example, to impress a potential employer at interview). So, as well as traditional translation and composition work, students learn to write letters, summaries or reports, to use the telephone, to make speeches and presentations, all of which have their own conventions. Students also exploit a range of other aids to language learning: magazines and periodicals; video and television; computer packages.

Content courses are taught differently. Like language courses they may or may not be taught in French: practice varies from university to university; from level to level; from course to course. Some parts of the content courses will often be taught in big lectures. These are backed up by work in smaller groups in tutorials and seminars, with the focus on student presentations and in-depth informal discussion on pre-arranged topics; the material covered in lectures provides a starting point.

While language study is normally a compulsory core course throughout the degree programme, this is less often the case with the content courses. Sometimes a common core is compulsory in the earlier stages, but normally thereafter a range of optional courses is available, from among which students select those which most interest them. Very often a dissertation forms an important part of the course, and for this students usually have considerable freedom in their choice of topic.

Most honours degrees in a language require a period of residence in France itself, or French-speaking Belgium or Switzerland or even francophone Africa or Caribbean. The time may vary from as little as one month to nine months, but it is best to spend as much time as possible in a French speaking country, whether as part of the course or during the vacation. Students frequently seek employment in France during the summer vacation to supplement their official period of residence. The most common ways of doing the official period of residence are either to spend a year as a language assistant in a French school; to spend a year or less studying in a French university; or going on a work placement.

Career Opportunities

Modern languages currently enjoy one of the highest employment rates of all degree programmes.   According to the latest statistics only 5% of modern languages graduates were unemployed six months after graduating.   The majority went straight into employment - often abroad - rather than undertaking further training.   Many went into business, and particularly popular areas of employment included finance, advertising, media, marketing, management, commerce and public relations.   Fewer than 10% went into teaching.

Suggested Reading

The best way to prepare for a course is to spend as much time as possible in a French-speaking country, to read French novels, poetry, plays, newspapers, journals, and to listen to the radio, watch television, films, plays and so on.

For a more general approach towards Modern Languages, see *Degree Course Descriptions: Modern Languages* by Professor Dennis Ager, Aston University.

Francothèque: A Resource for French Studies
- Gareth Thomas Ed, Hodder Education, 1997

Compo 2000: French Language Essay Writing
- Rod Hares and Genevieve Elliott, Hodder Education, 1997

101 French Idioms
- Jean-Marie Cassagne and Luc Nisset, McGraw-Hill Contemporary, 2009

Further Information

CILT - the national centre for languages
www.cilt.org.uk

Alliance Française de Londres
www.alliancefrancaise.org.uk

Fédération des Associations Françaises en Grande-Bretagne
www.fafgb.org

Franco-British Council
www.francobritishcouncil.org.uk

Alliance Française - the French Institute Dublin
www.alliance-francaise.ie

Genetics and Molecular Genetics

Original article by Dr John Kay, School of Biological Sciences, University of Sussex

Introduction

Molecular genetics is the study and manipulation at the molecular level of the DNA sequences that encode the genetic potential of all living things and allow the transmission of inherited characteristics from one generation to the next.

The genetic information for a simple bacterium resides in a thousand or so different genes, averaging about a thousand base pairs each, laid out along a single giant DNA molecule - a huge encoded message written using just four letters. The instructions to form a human are more complex still, requiring several thousand different genes, spread along 23 pairs of chromosomes (and interspersed with ten times the amount of what appears to be meaningless non-coding DNA). Complete DNA sequences are now known for many types of viruses and bacteria and several small nucleated organisms - yeasts, insects and a nematode worm. The Human Genome Project - to identify all the 20,000-25,000 genes in human DNA and determine the sequences of the 3 billion chemical base pairs - was completed in 2003, with most of the sequencing performed in universities and research centres from the United Kingdom, United States and Canada. The mapping of human genes, an important step in the development of medicines and other aspects of healthcare, remains one of the largest single investigational projects in modern science.

This mass of information is of real practical value. Just one wrong letter in this huge mass of information present in the germ cells from which we develop can cause crippling disease, and tiny alterations in the DNA occurring in just one of our billions of cells can lead to a cancer that destroys the whole individual. Every week there are reports of new discoveries of the defects responsible for one or another of the thousand-plus inherited human genetic disorders known or those that underlie one of the multitude of cancers that may afflict us. We then at least know what has to be done to correct the problem, though gene therapy is still in its infancy. Discovery of features in the genome that vary from one individual to another has led to genetic fingerprinting, with applications ranging from fighting crime to investigating breeding patterns in frogs and blue tits. In every field of biology the ability to sequence genes and characterise the nature and function of their protein products after expression in laboratory bacteria or tissue culture cells has had enormous impact.

The molecular genetic techniques that have enabled this astonishing expansion of our knowledge (to the extent that huge computers accessed via the internet are required to store and analyse the mass of information obtained) are surprisingly simple in principle, encompassed in degrees in biochemistry or related biological sciences. However, most biochemistry students will have little opportunity to learn to use them at the practical level. Molecular genetics as a degree creates numerous employment opportunities for a new group of specialists in a whole range of large-scale projects, ranging from basic medical and agricultural research to the biotechnology industry, developing discoveries into novel treatments and products.

As well as the required academic grades, enthusiasm for the biological and chemical sciences, an active and inquiring mind, self-discipline and commitment to your studies are far more important than any specific formal qualifications.

Degree Courses

Most university genetics courses are of three or four years duration. In the *earlier years*, you would probably study core modules in Genetics, Biochemistry, Ecology, Evolution, Molecular Engineering, Molecular evolution and Ecological Genetics.

The *final year* is likely to include a Project and Coursework. The Project would be original work carried out under the supervision of a member of the university department.

In all years, expect to be offered other modules, some of them optional and even modules from other departments. which may be related or unrelated ones.

Career Opportunities

Work in the expanding field of genetic engineering is growing rapidly and many opportunities exist in the NHS and in medical research. General graduate opportunities in finance, manufacturing and commerce are also available.

Related Degrees

Medical Genetics, Human Genetics, Genome Science, Molecular Biology

Suggested Reading

The Selfish Gene
- Richard Dawkins, Oxford University Press, 2006

The Double Helix
- James D Watson, Penguin, 2008

Concepts of Genetics
- William Klug, Michael Cummings et al, Pearson Education, 2008

The Language of the Genes
- Steve Jones, Flamingo, 2000

Further Information

British Society for Human Genetics
www.bshg.org.uk

Irish Society of Human Geneticists
http://irishsocietyofhumangenetics.blogspot.com

Geographic Information Systems (Cartography)

Original article by Giles Darke, Oxford Brookes University

Introduction

The traditional, patient, painstaking world of the cartographer or map maker - where a single map sheet could take many weeks or months to prepare - has been totally transformed by the development of Geographic Information Systems (GIS).

GIS are computer systems that handle maps and geographical information in digital form. They link maps, remotely-sensed images, statistics and other information about the world around us. Once combined in computer format, a GIS can be used to analyse the human and natural world. For example, a GIS may combine a detailed map with statistics on health, allowing us to discover patterns of the incidence of disease.

Remote sensing and digital terrain modelling are subjects related to GIS and you would normally study both as part of your course. Remote sensing is the science of observation of the Earth's surface using images obtained from sensors on board aircraft and satellites. Examples of remote sensing range from weather satellite images to low altitude air photos used in ecological mapping or urban planning.

Using remote sensing technology, you would learn to map and monitor both local and remote areas and to further your understanding of our natural environment and human impact upon it.

Remote sensing has been used to map deforestation, to measure the extent of the ozone hole, to monitor the tracks of hurricanes and even to map movements of icebergs to assist shipping.

Digital terrain modelling uses computer systems and graphics to represent the Earth's surface, often using 3D display.

To use a GIS effectively, you need to understand something of the nature of geography and of the patterns of the natural and human worlds, and there is a large element of applied geography in this discipline. As part of a combined honours degree, GIS can be combined with any one of a wide range of subjects. It combines especially well, for example, with Physical Geography, Geography, Computing and Business.

You should note that many universities offer GIS only at postgraduate level and you may wish to consider this option while researching undergraduate degrees.

Degree Courses

The aim of a typical GIS course would be to produce graduates who are skilled in using GIS and understand how to apply and interpret the results of a GIS query. Such an approach focuses on applying GIS, rather than being based on computer science or programming, although you would be introduced to the computing environment.

Year 1 would give you an introduction to GIS, looking at how maps reflect the human and natural landscapes, and would familiarise you with basic skills of data measurement and analysis. In Years 2 and 3, core modules would further advance your knowledge of analysis using GIS. They would also look at the applications of GIS and the practical issues surrounding setting up and using GIS. A GIS project would give you the opportunity to apply your skills to a major study. In addition, optional modules would explore how to present GIS data and design good GIS maps, 3-D visualisation in GIS, and would give an introduction to remote sensing.

Career Opportunities

Opportunities for graduates with skills in GIS are continuing to grow around the world. Areas of local and national government (planning, education and health departments, for instance) are a good source of vacancies, together with the utilities, environmental monitoring, insurance, cartography and digital map management, not to mention other areas where the geographical nature of information is important.

The **British Cartographic Society** publishes a useful booklet entitled *Careers in Cartography*. You can download a copy of the sixth edition (2008) from the BCS website given below. You can also order from the same address: *Cartography - an introduction*.

Related Degrees

Surveying and Mapping Science, Hydrography, Geomatics, Surveying, Topographical Science

Suggested Reading

Mapping: Ways of Representing the World
- Daniel Dorling and David Fairbairn, Prentice Hall, 1997

Introduction to GIS
- Ian Heywood et al, Prentice Hall, 2006

Principles of GIS
- Peter Burrough et al, OUP Oxford, 1998

Further Information

British Cartographic Society
www.cartography.org.uk

International Cartographic Association
http://cartography.tuwien.ac.at/ica

Ireland GIS Resources
http://gislounge.com/atlas/blireland.shtml

Ireland Organisation for Geographic Information
www.irlogi.ie

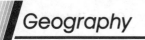

Geography

Original article by Dr Alex Gibson, Exeter University

Introduction

Geography constitutes one of the more popular undergraduate degrees and can be studied at most UK and Irish universities, although the precise nature of the degree does vary significantly. Entry requirements tend to be quite high, and competition for some degree programmes can be fierce.

For many students, and indeed employers, geography's particular attraction lies with its breadth. Most degree programmes will cover a wide range of topics, from hydrology and coastal geomorphology through to tourism and economic geography, and successful students will have had to demonstrate high levels of numeracy and literacy. Geography is not a vocational subject - indeed, a substantial minority of students find it necessary to undertake a further year's postgraduate training to prepare them for particular vocations (such as teaching or planning) - but it is widely acknowledged by employers to impart the broad range of transferable skills that is required of today's graduates.

Degree Courses

Degree programmes in geography vary enormously from one institution to the next, and applicants should take care to ensure that their particular strengths and interests match both the content and structure of the programmes on which they wish to enrol. Most degree programmes are built upon compulsory first year courses, which seek to provide a broad introduction to the full range of geographical enquiry. Thereafter, students are usually permitted to select from a range of options those which they find most stimulating or relevant. Sometimes this specialisation is postponed until the final year, and sometimes choice may only be available between predetermined 'study routes', but the courses available in the second and third years will usually reflect the particular research interests of academics in the department. Geography covers such a diversity of topics that few departments can cover the entire subject at an advanced level. Many, in fact, have chosen to focus in particular on relatively few 'themed areas' for the purpose of research and this, given the relationship between research and teaching, tends to have an impact on the nature of second- and, in particular, final-year courses. At Exeter, for instance, we have particular research strengths in hydrology, Quaternary geomorphology, historical geography, contemporary social geography and tourism studies. Whilst a wide range of second and third year option courses is offered, a significant number are influenced by these particular research foci. Careful attention to the detailed course descriptions provided by departmental prospectuses is essential for applicants with established interests in particular aspects of geography.

This attention to detail is also required to distinguish between the wide variety of degree structures that are available, both within and between institutions. One university may offer more than one degree course in geography. BA and BSc courses could both be available and will often be subject to different entry requirements and regulations.

Courses can be assessed by a variety of mechanisms; most incorporate tutorial support for students from arrival through to the final examinations, and most include compulsory fieldwork. Differences between institutions in these areas can be marked. The emphasis placed on tutorials, practicals and fieldwork varies significantly from place to place. Similarly, many departments require students to undertake personal research by means of a dissertation. This often contributes very significantly to a student's final assessment profile, but different departments take different views on how dissertations should be supported and assessed.

It should be clear that there is no 'standard' curriculum that underpins the study of geography at university. In terms of both content and structure, there is enormous variation between institutions and the only way to ensure that you end up with a course which suits you is through careful preliminary research. It is only through a careful study of departmental prospectuses, websites and other publications that the sometimes subtle but always important differences between departments will become apparent. It is also always worth attending the open days put on by departments in which you are seriously interested.

Career Opportunities

Typically, 60% of graduates enter permanent employment in the Civil Service, Armed Services, local authorities, industry and commerce. Approximately 100 graduates each year enter chartered accountancy; others join banks, insurance and finance companies, retail chains, transport management, administration, sales and marketing. Others qualify as town planners or surveyors. Social welfare, meteorology, water distribution, environmental research, and the National Environmental Research Council provide other opportunities.

Related Degrees

Physical Geography, Human Geography, Marine Geography, Environmental Geography, Development Geography, Topographical Science, Social Geography, Geographical Science, Population Studies

Suggested Reading

The Student's Companion to Geography
- A Rogers, H Viles and A Goudie, WileyBlackwell, 2002

The Dictionary of Human Geography
- S Whatmore, D Gregory, R Johnston, G Pratt and M Watts, WileyBlackwell, 2009

An Introduction to Human Geography: Issues for the 21st Century
- Peter Daniels, Michael Bradshaw, Denis Shaw and James Sidaway, Prentice Hall, 2008

Physical Geography and Global Environmental Change
- O Slaymaker and T Spencer, Longman, 1998

An Introduction to Physical Geography and the Environment
- Joseph Holden, Prentice Hall, 2010

The Earth Transformed
- Andrew Goudie and Heather Viles, Blackwell, 1997

Further Information

Royal Geographical Society
www.rgs.org

Geographical Society of Ireland
www.ucd.ie/gsi/index.html

Geology and Earth Sciences

*Original article by Dr R Gayer, Department of Earth Sciences, Cardiff University
(with contributions from Oxford Brookes University)*

Introduction

Geology and the Earth Sciences are courses that study the planet Earth; its composition, structure, internal and surface processes and history. It is difficult to generalise about these courses since each course will have many unique features. Careful study of prospectuses, departmental brochures and websites is therefore essential.

Degree Courses

Many courses offer a holistic view of the Earth, basing some of the modules on "Earth Systems" and major global processes and issues. Some courses are research-led, so that major new initiatives or research findings can be introduced rapidly into the course by active researchers to stimulate enthusiasm. The first year subjects aim to introduce you to the main aspects of a study of the Earth and in particular bring students who have not previously studied the subject at A Level or H grade into alignment with those who have. Where more than one degree scheme is offered in the Earth Sciences it is usual for the first year of these schemes to be common.

Modules might include:

Planet Earth (the structure and composition of the planet and of its origins, evolution and principal internal processes), *Introduction to Rocks, Geological History of the British Isles, The Fossil Record, Geological Structure and Maps, Sediments and Sedimentary Rocks.* In addition a range of optional modules is usually offered. These might include *Geological Chemistry, Geophysics, Computing for Geologists, Geology of Natural Resources, Oceanography* or *Global Change.*

In later years, modules are usually designed to reinforce those which you took in the first year, allowing you to gain an in-depth understanding of the different aspects of the subject. This is the "power house" year. Modules are introduced which separate the various degree schemes, so that progressively you will diverge from students taking one of the other schemes. For example, several modules could be included in the field of:

Environmental Geoscience, Exploration Geology and *Geology.*

In the last year a typical scheme could include:

Geochemistry and Petrogenesis, Sedimentology, Tectonics and Structural Analysis, Palaeobiology and *Macroevolution.*

There is a greater emphasis on project work, with certain individual modules consisting entirely of projects. As an example, modules in Exploration Geology include: Industrial Placement Project where you could carry out a carefully supervised study in the work place of an industrial sponsor.

Throughout any Earth Sciences Degree scheme there is a major emphasis on field training, which is important not only for the study of Geology but is required by many potential employers. Most Earth Sciences degree schemes include at least a week's residential field course in year one, two weeks in year two and period of at least four weeks independent field project work in the vacation between years two and three.

Many universities offer a 4-year Master of Geology (MGeol) or Earth Sciences (MESci) first degree for students who aim to enter a career in research geology, whether in industry or as an academic. These courses usually follow the first two years of the BSc degree before diverging into specialist areas that normally incorporate a major research project in the fourth year.

Some departments encourage students to spend one or two semesters in a partner European University. You can study a European language before taking part in the exchange.

Career Opportunities

Many degree schemes are accredited by the Geological Society or other professional bodies, so that your degree will lead to a further qualification after a period of professional work (e.g. Chartered Geologist). A significant number of graduates go on to higher degrees, which are needed in some areas; others undertake postgraduate teacher training. Opportunities exist for geologists in the public services, including the British Geological Survey, local government and water companies. The oil industry is a major employer. Graduates may work for oil companies or for contractors who undertake well-logging, seismic interpretation and other tasks. The mining industry employs geologists as exploration and mine geologists, while expanding areas of employment for Geology graduates exist in the civil engineering, construction and water industries.

Related Degrees

Geoscience, Exploration Geology, Geophysics, Applied Geology, Environmental Geology, Earth and Planetary Science, Geological Oceanography, Engineering Geology, Geochemistry, Exploration Geophysics, Earth System Science, Palaeobiology

Suggested Reading

Understanding Earth
- Frank Press et al, W H. Freeman, 2006

Earth Systems: Processes and Issues
- edited by W G Ernst, Cambridge University Press, 2000

Geology, New Dictionary of
- Philip Kearey, Penguin, 2005

The Way the Earth Works
- Peter J. Wyllie, Wiley and Sons, 2002

Further Information

British Geological Survey
www.bgs.ac.uk

Geological Society
www.geolsoc.org.uk

Institute of Geologists of Ireland
www.igi.ie

History

Original article by Dr Maurice Keen, Balliol College, Oxford University

Introduction

History opens at the moment when the person studying the past can establish contact with statements that come direct from an articulate individual who lived in a past period and who can tell us of his or her internal reactions to the contemporary external environment. History is not just about man's experience as a species, but also about the experience of individuals with inner feelings and opinions and ambitions which are still communicable, even across major barriers of time.

Your first duty as a historian, therefore, will be to learn to listen critically since you will hear a great many people talking, and people in the past were just as divided as they are now by differences of status, situation and attitude. They were often the victims of their own prejudices, and they were prone to handling the truth carelessly. This is as true of historians themselves as it is of the people who made history, which is why in the study of history there is no substitute for the original sources. Naturally it is important to read what historians have said about their own fields, but history books are not infallible. They are valuable as interpreters, to put you in touch with the past to form your own judgement about it. The final test of a history book is whether what the author says rings true when his or her words are set alongside those of the people about whom he or she is writing.

Languages will be important to you as an historian. This is obviously true in the superficial sense: to specialise in French or Spanish history, for example, you must be able to catch the special nuances of people's words. But an historian must also learn to speak the 'language of the past'. The different environments of past ages and the differences in the range of possibilities in social, economic and technological terms caused people to value different priorities and to talk and think about their situation in ways that are different from those natural to us. The historian must be able to grasp these differences imaginatively in order to understand what the people that he or she studies are saying.

This is what makes history an educational subject in the best sense of the term. Many problems in any age arise from people's inability to appreciate and to make allowance for differences of opinion and attitude that stem from differences in upbringing, in physical and economic environment, in cultural background and in individual reactions. The study of history cannot solve the problems that arise thus, but it should teach us to approach them in an intelligent way. The study of long past history can be highly relevant and educational: seeking to understand the ways of those remote in time is a useful introduction to understanding modern people who are divided from us, by barriers of distance and culture. The process is a two-way one: what anthropologists can tell us about primitive societies of our own time may illuminate, for example, the thought-world of the early Anglo-Saxons.

Listening and looking imaginatively with a critical ear and eye are the keys to understanding **how** things happened in the past. Just how different that is from understanding **why** things happened remains debatable. You have to form your own judgement about it. Does history have an inner logic of its own? To what extent do such impersonal factors as physical environment, technological development and economic relations allow individual endeavour and action to have a decisive impact? In the past 100 years, a powerful school of historians, influenced by Marx, has believed and taught that we can perceive a coherence in history, based in the dynamic working out of impersonal factors, and that in the understanding of this lies the key to the improvement of the human condition. Other historians, as I myself, do not believe that history shows as efficient a measure of coherence as this, and claim simply that its study is a humanising exercise. These are only two lines of approach, around which a lot of debate has focused: there is an infinity of alternative approaches. History is a very broad and important subject and it is bound to raise controversy.

History is a subject that requires a lot of patient work, and there are a number of ancillary skills which are very helpful. In terms of A levels (or Scottish Higher, or the IB), you will be wise to offer history and, if at all possible, a modern language (or Latin). Mathematics or economics can be very useful: historians nowadays are much more statistically minded than they once used to be. Geography is another subject that can directly cross-fertilise with history. Classical studies or classical civilisation can be helpful, especially if the degree course covers ancient history.

Degree Courses
Degree courses vary enormously in their subject matter and approach, so it is essential to study prospectuses with great attention to detail to ensure you select a course which will suit your own needs and interests.

Career Opportunities
Historians develop valuable skills in the balanced assessment of historical evidence, which are of great value to them in their ultimate careers. Of some 10,000 History graduates each year, around 10% enter further academic studies, 5% teacher training and 6% other training including law. Major employment areas include commerce, accountancy, banking, insurance, industry, local government, the Civil Service and lecturing/teaching.

Related Degrees
Modern History, Contemporary History, Victorian Studies and Church History, History with Study in North America, Ancient History, European History with year abroad, Economic and Social History, American History, Scottish History, Jewish History, Economic History, Political History, Social History, Cultural History, Welsh History, Intellectual History, Ancient and Medieval History, History, Philosophy and Politics, Historical Studies, Irish History, History and Philosophy of Science, Mediaeval History

Suggested Reading
The Hedgehog and the Fox: Essay on Tolstoy's View of History
- I. Berlin, Phoenix, 2009

Constructing the Past: Essays in Historical Methodology
- Jacques le Goff Ed, Cambridge University Press, 1985

The New Penguin History of the World
- J M Roberts, Penguin, 2007

Further Information
Institute of Historical Research
www.history.ac.uk

Historical Association
www.history.org.uk

Archives Ireland
www.archives.ie/prof_body.html

History of Art

Original article by Professor W H T Vaughan, Birkbeck College, London

Introduction

Because it emphasises art as an historical product, art history is to be distinguished from art appreciation - which has as its object the closer knowledge of individual works for the edification of the individual and is concerned with evaluation. History of art is not concerned with making value judgements about works of art - although it has to take into account the value judgements that have been made and are still being made by others. History of art is also to be distinguished firmly from the practice of studio art. While many courses do combine the two, they are not dependent on each other, and the premier sites for history of art teach the subject on its own. While historians of art are not expected to practise an art form themselves, they do have to pay special and minute attention to the processes whereby works of art are made. They also have to develop their visual awareness of how effects are achieved. This is the side of the subject that has traditionally been known as 'connoisseurship'. Although such a name might imply it was a skill that was only of use for collectors and in the salesroom, it does mean the close critical reading of pictures in a manner similar to that of the close reading of texts in literary studies.

What, then, do art historians do? They must first become aware of how works of art are made and the different ways in which images and other artefacts have been used over the centuries. This involves close looking and note taking. There should be a constant habit of going to museums and art galleries as well as visiting sites. Above all, you must keep your eyes open as relevant objects might be seen at any place.

It has already been remarked that close reading and knowledge of objects is important. But equally important is a knowledge of the ways in which pictorial language has developed and changed. While we always feel we 'know' what is in a picture because we can see it, we have frequently lost the knowledge that enables us to interpret it. In a society where there are rapid cultural changes, this knowledge can quickly become lost. We are no longer in a society that would immediately recognise a woman holding a child as a 'Madonna and Child' - and we have long passed the time when people could read the subject matter in Greek sculptures. But changes can be more subtle than this. Pictures of daily life of the past - Dutch seventeenth century pictures of interiors, for example - might look as though they were simple pictures of people at home. But in fact, they depict elaborate moralities. They would have been evident as such to people of the time, but no longer to us. When we think of the visual imagery that we also interpret from our own culture (think, for example, of advertising and how incomprehensible much of it would be to people outside our society) one can see how much of the job of the historian of art is to reconstruct the visual culture of a society as well as the physical reconstruction of objects.

Traditionally in this country the history of art has largely covered Western art. This comes from the time when it was supposed that great art was primarily a Western achievement. We have a very different perspective on this now, and there is an increasing tendency to include the art of other cultures - particularly those of the East. But it is still the case that most specialist courses of this kind are taught within institutions that specialise in the language and culture of the West.

Degree Courses

Traditionally, the history of art has involved the study of 'high art', with painting, sculpture and architecture taking pride of place. Over the last two decades, however, there has been a great expansion of new areas of study. Perhaps the most notable of these is design history. This can now be studied as a separate subject, but it is also being incorporated far more into history of art courses. An area which has only been explored patchily is that of popular and folk art. Here there has been a tendency to expand into areas which involve mass production (such as prints and photographs), but not into painting. Photography and film history are now studied far more than they were and often within an art historical context.

History of art is now seen familiarly as an aspect of cultural history and is therefore studied more and more as a symptom of a whole social structure rather than as a practice on its own. This can have the disadvantage of taking students away from the object and undermining their capability to make fine judgements and analyses of artefacts. On the other hand, it makes clear the extent to which aesthetic valuations are related to the wider values of a society and thereby presents a more exciting and challenging context within which to study. Issues of gender and race are amongst the important ones that have been coming into courses increasingly in recent years.

History of art is only offered in a minority of schools so candidates are rarely expected to have a detailed knowledge of the subject when they apply to university. They are of course expected to show an interest in history and art, and these tend to be the areas explored when candidates are called for interview.

While not being essential, it is an advantage to have done some historical studies at school before, and also to have knowledge of at least one other language. Not much of the art studied will be from English-speaking countries (traditionally French and Italian art have been studied most, and these languages are particularly useful, as is German).

At its best, history of art is a challenging intellectual subject that involves a wide range of social and cultural issues. It encourages the development of visual acuity and the ability to handle complex and challenging arguments. It also provides the satisfaction of being brought into close contact with some of the greatest of human achievements.

Career Opportunities

As with other arts subjects, employment opportunities in areas directly related to the study are limited. It does nevertheless open the way to careers in teaching (at all levels), working in art galleries and museums, working in the trade with dealers and auctioneers, in publishing and in various forms of arts administration as well as leading to careers in general management, administration, commerce, finance, public relations, advertising, and so on.

Related Degrees

Art, History and Culture, History of Decorative Arts, History of Art and Design

Suggested Reading

Art and Illusion: A Study in the Psychology of Pictorial Representation
- E H Gombrich, Phaidon Press, 2002
The Story of Art Pocket Edition
- E H Gombrich, Phaidon Press, 2006
Careers in Art History
- Association of Art Historians, 2006, content and purchase details from their website below

Further Information

Association of Art Historians
www.aah.org.uk
National Gallery
www.nationalgallery.org.uk
Arts Council England
www.artscouncil.org.uk
Irish Antique Dealers' Association
www.iada.ie
Arts Council, Ireland
www.artscouncil.ie

Horticulture

Original article by Dr Eunice Simmons, Wye College, University of London, now Imperial College Wye, with additional material from the Institute of Horticulture

Introduction

Horticulture is the science of plant production, not only for food but also for recreational purposes. In addition to the commercial production of fruit, vegetables and flowers, horticulturists are engaged in the establishment of parks and gardens and in the conservation of the countryside. Horticulture impinges on the lives of everyone. Beyond the science, it's a huge industry encompassing both the commercial production of vegetables, fruit, flowers and plants, and the establishment and maintenance of vast areas of parks, sports grounds, open spaces, amenity and roadside plantings, private estates and botanical gardens. It also supports and services one of the nation's main leisure pursuits - gardening.

Loosely, there two main branches of horticulture, but there is no precise division.

Environmental (or Amenity) **Horticulture** embraces the establishment and management not only of our parks and open spaces but also the vast areas of recreational turf from county cricket grounds to the local bowling club. And, of course, some sectors of it are highly commercialised such as landscape design and construction, interior plant displays, etc.

Commercial Horticulture on the other hand, embraces the actual production of vegetables and fruit both outdoors and under the protection of glass and plastic, flowers (for cutting), bedding and pot plants and nursery stock.

All the aspects of horticulture have many basic features in common.

Degree Courses

Several universities or colleges offer degree courses involving horticulture and it would be wise to consult prospectuses before making your choice. Several of the universities offer straightforward horticulture as a three-year course, with an alternative of a four-year course involving a year of work experience. Another possibility is a four-year course 'Horticulture with Studies in Europe'.

Here is an example of a degree course in Horticulture. The *foundation* courses form a vital introduction to the international nature of the industry. They include principles of plant propagation, an introduction to ecology, design and analysis of experiments and surveys, principles of marketing management, horticultural biology, microbiology and genetics. Lectures are complemented by practical work and visits.

In the **second and/or third year**, courses in amenity horticulture and crop production form the core of the teaching: plant growth in relation to the environment, crop pests and diseases, soils, horticultural crop production, landscape and ornamental plants, and hardy ornamental nursery stock production. Practical work and visits to horticultural enterprises and gardens form an integral part of the teaching, and an overseas tour is arranged in the Easter vacation, often to the Netherlands or to the Loire Valley in France. The option is available to all students to do a 'sandwich' year between the second and final year in College. Such students have to produce a report on the work undertaken during their year away from College and this is taken into account in assessing their overall performance.

Students decide whether they want to specialise during their *final year* in amenity horticulture or horticultural crop production. Nevertheless, the opportunity exists for students with broad horticultural interests to study both. All students have to produce a comprehensive report, which could be a literature review or a research project involving experimental work. Current work at this university involves countries in all the continents.

Career Opportunities

Opportunities are forecast to increase in commercial horticulture. Ever-growing technological demands are creating a need for high-level skills in information and production technologies as well as the ability to understand and operate complex production systems. There is also a demand for graduates with business management and marketing abilities. The amenity side is slightly less positive, with local authorities in particular cutting back staffing levels. Specialised skills associated with historic gardens, restoration and environmental conservation are, however, in increasing demand.

Related Degrees

Crop Management, International Horticulture, Floriculture, Environmental Horticulture Management, Commercial Horticulture Management, Turf Science

Suggested Reading

Principles of Horticulture
- C R Adams et al, Butterworth-Heinemann, 2008

A Handbook for Horticultural Students
- Peter Dawson, Dawson 2006

Further Information

Grow Careers
www.growcareers.info

Environmental and Land-based Careers
www.afuturein.com

Royal Botanic Gardens Kew
www.kew.org

Royal Botanic Garden Edinburgh
www.rbge.org.uk

Institute of Horticulture
www.horticulture.org.uk

Royal Horticultural Society of Ireland
www.rhsi.ie

Hospitality Management

Original article by Clive Robertson, Head of the School of Hotel and Restaurant Management, Oxford Brookes University

Introduction

The provision of hospitality to the traveller has always been important and can be traced back at least as far as ancient Rome. Today, the hospitality industry is enormous and diverse, providing accommodation and food and drink for millions of people each day - from a local pub to complex leisure resorts, from bed and breakfast to luxury five star hotels, from large international conferences to weekend breaks, from catering for students to catering for company chief executives, from patients in hospital to up-market restaurants. It is a truly international industry, whether in terms of the customers it serves or the opportunities for travel and career development internationally which it offers.

Successful hospitality businesses are concerned with meeting the needs of consumers. Managers must harness and develop the skills of their staff and use all the resources at their disposal (buildings, equipment, technology and finance) to provide the hospitality expected by customers.

Degree Courses

More than 70 universities and colleges offer degrees, foundation degrees and higher national diplomas in hospitality management across the UK. Most of the degrees are four-year sandwich programmes, including a year spent in industry. Some degree programmes are linked to specific areas of the hospitality industry, such as event management and licensed retail, but the majority provide a broad vocationally oriented business education leading to a wide range of career opportunities. A common core of most degree programmes is operational experience and the development of operational management skills. Thus, students have 'hands-on' experience of information technology systems and software used in industry, and they work in training kitchens and restaurants within the university or college and spend a year working outside in hotels and restaurants, with opportunities to work overseas. Many students also work part-time in the hospitality industry to extend their range of experience and develop a wide perspective of the industry.

Feeding into the operational core, and drawing from it in terms of examples of current practice and contemporary issues, programmes include studies in financial management, human resource management, marketing, information systems, legal aspects and strategic management. To capitalise on career opportunities internationally, students should ideally have fluency in a second language, and many degree programmes are designed to enable students to study a second language.

To be successful on a programme which includes a wide range of subject areas requires enthusiasm and motivation, important attributes of a hospitality manager. At the same time, working in training kitchens and restaurants and work experience in the hospitality industry requires other important attributes, a desire to work effectively with other people and a passion to provide hospitality of the highest quality. The hospitality industry is a people industry, you will be working with people and for people. You also need to be prepared to be working at times when others are enjoying the hospitality you provide: weekends, evenings and holiday time!

Career Opportunities

Vacancies in the hospitality industry outnumber the supply of graduates each year and hospitality management graduates are in great demand. You might decide to work for an international hotel company, or in contract catering, where you could be involved in anything from restaurants for city executives to supplying an oil rig, or feeding university students. You could work in a chain of high street restaurants, or in a country house hotel. In all cases, your education and development doesn't end with your degree. You will normally be offered a company graduate training scheme and should expect to continue your professional development as your career progresses. This could include studying for an MBA or another masters degree from those now available in hospitality management. You could also register with a university to undertake research, full-time or part-time, towards a PhD. A complex, diverse and growing industry needs research evidence to underpin its future development and approaches to providing hospitality.

Related Degrees

Food Industry Management, International Hospitality Management, Catering Management

Suggested Reading

Hospitality Management and Organisational Behaviour
- Laurie Mullins, Longman, 2001

Successful Event Management
- Anton Shone and Bryn Parry, Thomson Learning, 2004

Working in Hospitality and Catering
- VT Lifeskills, 2008

An introduction to the UK Hospitality Industry: A Comparative Approach
- Bob Brotherton, Butterworth-Heinemann, 2003

Food and Beverage Management
- Bernard Davis et al, Butterworth-Heinemann, 2008

Introduction to the Hospitality Industry
- Clayton Barrows and Tom Powers, John Wiley, new edition due February 2011

Further Information

Institute of Hospitality
www.instituteofhospitality.org

Springboard UK Ltd
http://springboarduk.net

Irish Hospitality Institute
www.ihi.ie

Human Resource Management

Original article by Sharon Herkes, Aston Business School

Introduction

Understanding the human side of organisations is central to their performance and effectiveness. As organisations change, grow, divide, develop and operate internationally, professional knowledge of the part played by their people is essential at both operational and Board levels.

Human Resource Management considers how people, processes and structures inter-relate. It focuses on the crucial part played by individuals and groups in organisation processes, such as decision making, planning and managing new technology. On a degree course in this area, you would develop an appreciation of the central importance for all organisations of effective human resource strategies, set within the legal, institutional, national and international contexts within which organisations operate. You would also gain a sound understanding of employee development, relations, resourcing and reward and of how these specialisms are integrated into wider corporate strategies.

You should seek out a course that will give you exemption from the Core Management exams of the Chartered Institute of Personnel and Development (CIPD).

Degree Courses

Your first year might be shared with students intending to follow other specialisms in business and management. You would study a range of subjects to ensure that you have a broad foundation of management awareness, considering the economic, financial, human and legal issues managers deal with, together with the tools and techniques they use. You would be introduced to the key areas of business as well as carrying out project work to help draw together the subjects you have studied.

First year modules could therefore include such topics as: Foundations of Management; Introduction to Economics; Business Computing; Business Decision Analysis; Organisational Behaviour; Contract Law; Economic Environment of Business; International Perspectives in Organisations; Principles of Operations Management; Quantitative Techniques.

In your second year, you would concentrate on developing critical, vocational and analytical skills, focusing more on the management of people and the strategies of human resource management. At the same time, you would develop sound theoretical bases for considering the ways in which people behave and can contribute to organisations.

In your final year, you would typically explore how organisations relate to their wider context, from both a socio-psychological and socio-economic perspective. You might examine, in particular, how changes in the external environment (social, financial, competitive and legislative) relate to the processes of management.

You may opt to benefit from a four-year sandwich programme, incorporating a full year in a paid professional placement in a relevant role, gaining valuable practical experience. This usually comes at the end of the second year of your studies.

Teaching and learning methods would include lectures, seminars, workshops, group work, computer-assisted learning, case studies, video and other multimedia presentations. Self-directed study and independent learning materials are also used in some modules. Assessment would be by a combination of written assignments, group presentations, poster sessions and time-constrained examinations.

Career Opportunities

Entry to careers in human resource management is highly competitive, a message which reinforces the importance both of the sandwich year and of gaining CIPD recognition. If you can demonstrate that you have a thorough understanding of organisations and of issues related to change and development, that you possess advanced literacy, numeracy and IT skills, and that you can work in teams and groups, you should be particularly well suited to today's rapidly evolving employment market.

Related Degrees

Personnel Management, Emergency and Disaster Management

Suggested Reading

Human Resource Management: Theory and Practice
- John Bratton and Jeffrey Gold, Palgrave Macmillan, 2007

Human Resource Management at Work: People Management and Development
- Mick Marchington and Adrian Wilkinson, CIPD, 2008

Human Resource Management
- Derek Torrington et al, Financial Times/Prentice Hall, 2007

Further Information

Chartered Institute of Personnel and Development
www.cipd.co.uk

International Journal of Human Resource Management
www.tandf.co.uk/journals/routledge/09585192.html

Irish Management Institute
www.imi.ie

CIPD Ireland
www.cipd.co.uk/branch/ireland/default.htm

Information and Library Studies

Original article by Dr Anthony Booth, Loughborough University and Dr Chris Baggs, Aberystwyth University

Introduction

What do courses in information and library studies offer students today? First, they provide a sound professional education that enables students to take up posts in the wide range of information careers now available. Information professionals are eagerly sought by all kinds of organisations, including libraries and information services, in both the public and private sectors, as well as all those organisations developing the management of their information resources, in such wide-ranging fields as marketing, charity and welfare education or commerce. The market for information professionals is expanding rapidly, as the significance of information increases in our society, and the young information worker can anticipate a challenging and varied career.

Degree Courses

The emphasis in most courses today is on the exciting developments in information management, made possible by the increasing sophistication of technology. This means that computer literacy is essential for students: IT skills are developed in students from the very beginning of courses.

Knowing how to organise information is one of the key skills to be developed (and expected by employers), but equally important is knowing how to manage that information in the context of a library or information service. The kinds of management skills developed in students are therefore very similar to those you would find on a business studies course, as all libraries today are in the business of information provision. Many libraries or information services are also engaged in selling their services: university libraries, for example, are being encouraged to market their business information services to local industries. Courses include a considerable element on the basic management skills needed to achieve this: resource management, managing people and marketing.

Inevitably, information professionals will spend a great deal of their time in communicating to users, to other information services through the extensive national and international information networks, and also to information providers such as publishers or database producers. It is therefore essential to learn how to communicate effectively, whether verbally or in writing. Report writing and abstracting, and presenting skills, feature considerably, as do languages.

So far, we have concentrated on the development of the various necessary skills. There are as well huge areas of knowledge that you will gain. The history of knowledge and of information transfer is intrinsically fascinating and you will be introduced to the contribution made to our culture by authors, publishers, libraries and other learned institutions. In addition to the 'core' areas of study, such as organising information, and managing libraries and information services, there is also a range of optional elements for specialist study, which caters for students' particular subject and career interests.

Students are encouraged to take up work placements during the long vacations; to take a sandwich year out, either in the UK or in institutions overseas; and to undertake project work in libraries and information services as part of their course assessment.

Career Opportunities

CILIP (see below) accredits undergraduate and postgraduate library and information courses in England, Wales and Scotland. Successful completion of an accredited course will help you secure professional posts in the UK and elsewhere in the world. It will also enable you to register for progression to Chartered status with CILIP.

As an information professional/librarian, you would be at the heart of the information revolution. There are many other people equally eager to succeed in information management, so you will need to stay abreast of new developments and consider some strategic career moves if you are seriously ambitious.

Related Degrees

Museum and Galleries Studies, Communication and Information Studies, Media Technology, Information Management, Business Information Management

Suggested Reading

An Introduction to Library and Information Work
- Ann Totterdell, Facet Publishing, 2005

The Enduring Library: Technology, Tradition and the Quest for Balance
- Michael Gorman, ALA Editions, 2003

Your Essential Guide to Career Success
- Sheila Pantry and Peter Griffiths, Facet Publishing, 2003

Further Information

Chartered Institute of Library and Information Professionals (CILIP)
www.cilip.org.uk

Library Association of Ireland
www.libraryassociation.ie

International Relations

Original article by Professor Trevor C. Salmon, Department of Politics and International Relations University of Aberdeen

Introduction

International relations is concerned with issues involving life and death for individuals and nations. Traditionally, the focus has been on the great issues of war and peace. Indeed, for much of the twentieth century, certainly from the end of World War 1(1918) to the end of the Cold War (1989-1991) war and peace were the issue of international relations. Increasingly, however, there has been a recognition that issues such as world poverty, hunger and the environment also require co-operative or collective action by states or groups of individuals acting across state boundaries.

The main preparation for the study of international relations is not particular courses at school but a genuine interest in the world and what makes it tick. Similarly, it would be wrong to study international relations just because you desire to work for the UN, EU or the Foreign Office. In today's world a wide range of careers require an awareness of the European or international dimension. It is also true that many believe that, given the nature and complexity of today's world, international relations is best studied in conjunction with a range of other subjects.

Typical international relations courses focus upon the relations between states, nations, political systems, organised groups or multinational corporations and even individuals as they try to deal with the issues confronting humanity. Most of the discipline focuses on international politics (and in most cases departments or units are entitled International Politics or Relations regardless of focus). International politics is concerned with the nature, distribution and use of power to resolve disagreements. Those disagreements can cover a range of issues: territorial or ethnic disputes, tariff or quota disputes, or perceived threats to peace and security; but most importantly they require power in one form or another to resolve them. That may involve fighting a war, threatening to use force, the use of economic sanctions or embargoes, or just persuasion - i.e. diplomacy. The resolution of such disputes may only involve the parties involved, but it may also involve international institutions, international courts and law, or mediation. Indeed, states may often seek to obviate disputes by coming together in voluntary organisations to discuss pressing matters. Most of these organisations exist to defend the interests of the members and to help them resolve the tensions between an insistence on sovereignty and independence and having to survive in an inter-dependent, shrinking world environment. Some of the organisations are heavily institutionalised, others may be largely ad hoc, even informal.

Degree Courses

Different courses increasingly tend to focus on different aspects of the subject, or even to diverge on the whole approach they take to the teaching and study of international relations.

Some courses, reflecting the influence of political philosophy, diplomatic history and law in the development of the discipline, put an emphasis on seeking to analyse developments, institutions, policies and concepts such as war in an empirical or descriptive manner. This is not to be equated with 'current affairs' since the prime motivation is to look beyond, say, the day-to-day events in Israel or Iraq to extrapolate what these events tell us about the role of the UN, NATO or EU; the nature of alliances;

the utility of military power or economic sanctions, and the issue of when it is legitimate to intervene or not etc. Other courses take this extrapolation much further and treat international relations as a social science. Some courses fall somewhere in-between these two ends of the spectrum. Students should, therefore, take care to determine what the actual content and focus of each degree programme is.

However, there is no one truth. Explore, enquire, experiment and enjoy - that is the motto of international relations.

Career Opportunities

Very few careers are available in related political and international organisations. Approximately 50% of international relations graduates enter the general graduate employment market and 25% go on to professional careers as teachers or lawyers, after further specialist training.

Related Degrees

International Studies, International Politics, Peace Studies

Suggested Reading

Globalisation and Fragmentation: International Relations in the 20th Century
- Ian Clark, OUP, 1997

Contexts of International Politics
- Gary Goertz, Cambridge University Press, 1995

The Globalisation of World Politics
- John Baylis and Steve Smith, OUP, 2008

Introduction to International Relations: Theories and Approaches
- Robert Jackson and Georg Sorensen, OUP Oxford, 2010

Further Information

Foreign and Commonwealth Office
www.fco.gov.uk

European Union
http://europa.eu

United Nations
www.un.org

Department of Foreign Affairs, Government of Ireland
http://foreignaffairs.gov.ie/home/index.aspx

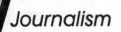

Journalism

Original article by Ken Reynolds, specialist writer on careers and higher education

Introduction

Learning about journalism is like working as a journalist: both offer an experience that is varied, fast-moving and challenging. A vocationally oriented degree course should give you the chance to learn about and practise the core journalism skills of writing, reporting and researching, underpinning these practical elements with factors such as the development of news organisations, news values, sources, language, regulation, ethics and the uses and influences of news. Look for a department with a long history of journalism teaching, close links with the media industries - including guest lectures by leading national media figures - and staff with experience of working as professional journalists.

It is important that you research courses carefully and consider why you want to take a degree in journalism. Some courses, for example, focus exclusively on journalism and are accredited by bodies such as the National Council for the Training of Journalists and the Broadcast Journalism Training Council. Other courses may be less vocationally specific, combining the study of journalism with another subject, such as English, a foreign language, economics, psychology or sociology.

You may be invited, as part of the admission process to some of the more popular courses, to submit a 500-word typed essay and up to three examples of your written work, published or unpublished. If you are successful at this stage, you could be invited to visit the university for practical tests and an interview.

Degree Courses

During the first two years of a vocational course, you would learn the basic skills of reporting and writing for all the main news media. This would involve news gathering, reporting, editing and production for newspapers, online sites, radio and television. In your third year, you should have the opportunity to specialise and pursue routes that reflect your interests or career aspirations. Third year options usually include newspapers, radio, television or online journalism or a dissertation. You must also learn about media law, regulation and ethics and public administration. News both reflects and contributes to society and culture, and you would study these relationships from historical, political, economic and organisational perspectives.

If you are pursuing a vocational option, seek out a course offering work placements in the media industries.

Much of your learning should take place in specially equipped newsrooms and digital radio and TV studios, where you would undertake realistic projects, reporting events and issues for your own newspaper, online sites and radio and television bulletins.

Many of the combined honours courses have a stronger academic emphasis, especially on your other subject in the first year, leaving you significantly less time to develop your skills in practical journalism.

Career Opportunities

Journalists are trained to research complex issues, pick out the main threads quickly and explain them in a straightforward way. Studying journalism as a combined honours subject could be suitable if you want to acquire valuable communication skills in preparation for careers in areas such as information dissemination, book production or magazine journalism. This is a less suitable route, however, if you intend to start a journalism career in the traditional way through news reporting. Should this be your intention, you might prefer to consider a single-subject journalism programme, although the combined honours route could lead to various forms of specialist journalism or to a place on a postgraduate course. There is an argument that learning to write as a good journalist is helped by reading both widely and critically. This is one of the reasons that, say, journalism and English literature provide a popular combination of subjects.

It should be said that most journalism graduates seek careers in the professional media and many succeed in gaining employment with national and regional newspapers and magazines, radio and TV stations.

Related Degrees

Multimedia Journalism, Broadcast Journalism, Writing for Media Arts, International Journalism

Suggested Reading

A Career Handbook for TV, Radio, Film, Video & Interactive Media
- Shiona Llewellyn and Sue Walker, A & C Black, 2004

In Print: the Guardian Guide to a Career in Journalism
- Chris Alden Ed, Guardian Books, 2004

The Media in Britain: current debates and developments
- Jane Stokes and Anna Reading Eds, Palgrave, 2003

The Penguin book of Journalism: Secrets of the Press
- Stephen Glover Ed, Penguin Books, 2000

My Trade: A Short History of British Journalism
- Andrew Marr, Pan Books, 2005

Further Information

Skillset
www.skillset.org

Broadcast Journalism Training Council
www.bjtc.org.uk

National Council for the Training of Journalists
www.nctj.com

National Union of Journalists (UK and Ireland)
www.nuj.org.uk

Landscape Architecture

Original article by Alistair Taylor BSc DipLD ALI, Head of Landscape Architecture, Leeds Metropolitan University

Introduction

Landscape Architecture is a design-based discipline concerned with promoting, designing and conserving the external environment. It seeks to achieve a balance between human needs and a respect for the earth's natural systems.

Historically, landscape architecture was concerned with the design of parks and gardens born out of the traditions of the great families and houses of Europe. The garden of Louis XIV at Versailles and the 18th century landscape style parks in Britain are examples of this art. The park designers of these eras altered the configuration of the land form, created lakes and used plants and structures to define space and delight the eye of the beholder. Today, landscape designers are still designing parks but the people who use them have different demands and values from the privileged aristocratic patrons of Versailles and the English parkland. The notion of landscape now covers all scales of outdoor space, from courtyard to countryside and from rural locations to city centres. The emphasis now includes landscape assessment, landscape planning and the environmental and land arts.

David Lowenthal sums up the demands a landscape architect has to meet, *'to do this well they (landscape architects) must command an awesome sweep of subjects: art, architecture, engineering, sociology, politics - perhaps alchemy and magic as well'*. He might have added *ecology*. In an increasingly environmentally conscious world, the relationship between development and environment presents man with a great challenge. The landscape architect works at the interface between development and the environment.

Degree Courses

Most landscape architects begin by completing an undergraduate or postgraduate course accredited by the Landscape Institute. Successful completion of the course leads to Associate Membership of the Landscape Institute, the first step on the path towards becoming a chartered landscape architect.

The next step is to undertake a period of mentored experience as part of the Pathway to Chartership (P2C). The Pathway is about developing the knowledge, understanding and professionalism required to practise as a chartered landscape architect in the UK. Individuals can progress at their own pace and previous learning and experience is also taken into account - but most people will need two years on the Pathway in professional practice before they are ready to go forward to the final stage of the Pathway, the oral examination.

Successful completion of the Pathway means you are eligible to become a full Member of the Landscape Institute and may use the initials MLI after your name. An MLI is allowed to use the title Chartered Landscape Architect, a designation which is protected by law.

Becoming an MLI is a milestone rather than the end of a landscape professional's learning and development. As with other chartered professions, being a chartered landscape architect involves making a commitment to keeping one's skills up to date. All landscape architects are required to complete at least 20 hours continuing professional development each year.

The curriculum design and content of landscape architecture courses will vary from school to school and will usually reflect the discipline of the parent school (i.e. Schools of Art, Architecture and Design, Town and Country Planning or one of the Environmental disciplines).

Landscape Architecture is typically taught as an art and design based discipline within the context of producing socially and environmentally responsive landscapes. Most Landscape Architecture courses are studio based and use landscape design projects as the principal learning focus.

The degree begins by developing a student's critical awareness and understanding of landscape and introducing landscape design processes and skills. Students acquire an appreciation of the principles and theories underlying the historical development of landscape architecture and of the natural processes affecting the landscape. A basic understanding of the potentials and constraints of landscape materials and technologies is also introduced.

In the second year, students will further develop creativity and technical abilities through a range of landscape design projects which focus on site planning and engineering, site design and design with hard (construction) and soft (plants) materials. This work is undertaken in the context of exploring the contribution of landscape to urban and rural locations. Students also develop their understanding of the relationship between cultural and natural processes. Techniques of landscape and environmental assessment are introduced.

The final year emphasises self direction and the application of design skills to real situations.

Career Opportunities

Around 50% of landscape architects work in private practices - others are employed by the public sector, for local authorities or government agencies such as Natural England, Scottish Natural Heritage and Countryside Council for Wales. There are also numerous opportunities to work overseas.

The increased emphasis at local and national level on the importance of the environment, green spaces, sympathetic and aesthetically pleasing development means that landscape architecture is a rapidly expanding profession and the demand for qualified chartered professionals has been outstripping supply for some time.

Related Degrees

Landscape Design and Conservation, Garden Design, Landscape Planning, Exterior Spatial Design, Marine Resource Management

Suggested Reading

Design with Nature
- Ian L. McHarg, Wiley, 1995

Cities and Natural Process: a Basis for Sustainability
- Michael Hough, Routledge, 2004

The Landscape of Man: Shaping the Environment from Prehistory to the Present Day
- G and S Jellicoe, Thames and Hudson, 1998

Designing the New Landscape
- Geoffrey Jellicoe and Sutherland Lyall, Thames and Hudson, 1997

Further Information

I want to be a landscape architect
www.iwanttobealandscapearchitect.com

Landscape Institute
www.landscapeinstitute.org

European Foundation for Landscape Architecture
http://europe.iflaonline.org

Irish Landscape Institute
www.irishlandscapeinstitute.com

Law

Original article by Professor Geoffrey Wilson, Warwick University

Introduction

The common reason for reading law is that students are thinking of becoming solicitors or barristers. For those who eventually decide to practise as lawyers, a law degree has the advantage of providing them with the opportunity of getting exemption from the First Part of the professional examinations as well as giving them a better idea of what might be involved in practice, and laying a foundation of legal knowledge that should stand them in good stead as lawyers in future years. One does not have to take a law degree to be a lawyer, but three or four years on a law degree does provide the chance of a more thoughtful and grounded introduction to the way the law works than can readily be acquired by practising it; taking the first part of the professional examinations after leaving university means more time and money. An alternative for those who do not wish to spend three years reading law is to look for a mixed degree, providing that it is the right law to secure an exemption from the first part of the professional examination. Each law department will know if this is the case.

Degree Courses

Most law schools would agree that the study of law has advantages for students who do not intend to practise. They would point to the intellectual training involved in the close reading of texts, statutes and the judgements in decided cases, in the isolation of the relevant from the irrelevant and the identification and disposal of the main issues in complex problems and situations, and in the practice of rational argument according to the ground rules of English legal reasoning. They would emphasise too the special characteristics of legal reasoning that it is not simply abstract and academic, not simply logical, but reasoning with a view to reaching a decision; that even though it is conducted in an academic environment, it is dealing with real-world problems, real legislation, real cases, real facts, real judgements. It is reasoning of a practical kind. In this respect, law as a degree subject can provide a convenient halfway house between school and the real world.

To the arguments that law is a suitable subject of study for future lawyers and when done well provides a good general training in rational analysis, discussion and decision, most law schools would probably add the importance of law and the legal profession in the community. Here it stands with other subjects which study important aspects of society, such as economics or politics, looking at society from one important perspective, that of the part law plays in it. Along with law go the legal profession and the machinery of justice, criminal and civil. Individuals, companies and groups cannot avoid the impact of law and lawyers, which extends into family life, labour relations, the organisation of companies, commercial and business relationships, taxation, social security, the environment, consumer questions, the business of buying, selling and renting houses, and all the millions of contacts between them and public authorities of one kind or another. In other words the study of law is as important as the law itself.

The growing interest in foreign legal systems has been accompanied by the creation of formal links between UK law schools and law departments in foreign universities and the introduction of special degree courses which include a year abroad. For students with modern language skills, a law course with a year abroad is one of the best legal courses at present, subject to proper preparation beforehand and good provisions for supervision by the host university when abroad.

Law schools vary in their strengths and weaknesses. Different schools emphasise different aspects of legal study and, as with other subjects, one needs to follow up a general interest in the prospect of studying law with a closer look at what each has to offer. It is important for those who want variety to see what options are available.

Courses in international and comparative human rights, the environment, media, medicine, women and the law and even sport can add a bit of excitement to the hard core.

Competition for places to read law is exceptionally strong and university admissions tutors expect high grades at A level/Advanced Higher, Higher or equivalent. No particular subjects are specified. You will have to take the National Admissions Test for Law (LNAT) to secure a place on a Law degree at eight of the most prestigious UK universities (plus NUI Maynooth if you apply as a mature student).

Equally important to what is offered is the spirit of the place and here one is pretty well bound to be dependent on rumour and reputation, but even a day's visit may help and this goes for the question of studying law itself. Although there is a lot of law around for those still at school, it is largely invisible, but although it is invisible it is not inaccessible. All courts are open to the public. Many solicitors' firms welcome inquiries and some even offer opportunities for part-time work. Visits of this kind can help to give some idea at least of the atmosphere in which the professional lawyer works.

Career Opportunities

In addition to the legal professions, law degrees open doors to a wide range of careers in the Civil Service, police, social services, community legal services, accountancy, industrial and commercial management, teaching/lecturing, local government, politics etc.

Related Degrees

European Law, Business Law, Taxation and Revenue Law, Criminal Justice, Legal Studies, American Legal Systems, Conveyancing and Executive Law, Law with French or German or Italian Law, Law with Legal Practice Management, Politics, Economics and Law, Law with Criminology

Suggested Reading

Law and Modern Society
- P S Atiyah, Oxford, 1995

Learning the Law
- Glanville Williams and A T H Smith, Sweet and Maxwell, 2010

The Law Machine
- Marcel Berlins and Clare Dyer, Penguin, 2000

Getting into Law
- Carl Lygo, Trotman, 2010

Further Information

Legal Education
www.legaleducation.org.uk

National Admissions Test for Law (LNAT)
www.lnat.ac.uk

Law Society of Scotland
www.lawscot.org.uk

Faculty of Advocates
www.advocates.org.uk

Law Society of Ireland
www.lawsociety.ie

Bar Council, Ireland
www.barcouncil.ie

Leisure and Sport Studies/Management

Original article by Gill Lines, University of Brighton

Introduction

During the last decade there has been an increase in leisure and sports related university courses. These come from a variety of academic disciplines such as Recreation Studies or Maritime Leisure Management. The type of course selected is likely to be determined by the student's interests, expertise and career aspirations.

Degree Courses

Here are examples of two different degree courses. A leisure and sport studies degree is firmly based on leisure studies with a social scientific approach, and an emphasis on physically active forms of recreation; a leisure and sport management degree has a stronger emphasis on the acquisition of relevant administration and management skills.

The modular structure provides a common core area of study for all students across both courses: Social Perspectives on Physical Culture; Leisure in Society; Leisure and Sport Organisations: Providers and Policies; Sport and Recreation in the Community; The State and Policy Provision; School Community Partnerships; Applied Studies: Leisure and Sport; Sport, Leisure and Work and Critical Perspectives on Leisure and Sport Policies.

All students at our illustrative establishment have the opportunity to study a foreign language at the University's Language Centre. This distinctive feature is perceived by students to increase their potential career opportunities, especially in overseas leisure markets. For those students particularly interested in physically active sports and dance participation, there is the opportunity to select practical performance modules across a range of areas. There is a long-standing exchange programme. Students on both courses can be considered for exchange study visits to Europe, USA and Canada.

The Leisure and Sport Studies course relates theory to practice and balances the in-depth academic study of selected aspects of leisure and sport with appropriate vocational emphases.

A strong feature of a Leisure and Sport Management course is the Off-Campus Study Period, which enables students to develop workplace experience and skills whilst applying theoretical skills and knowledge to a practical situation. This 12-week placement includes public, private and voluntary sector hosts in areas ranging from sports development to marketing. These may be taken either close to the University or in the student's home area. Each year some students have the opportunity to take their placement abroad.

University based modules include two hours contact time per week. This involves a range of teaching and learning methods; tutor led lectures, seminars and group discussion, workshops, role-plays, group work, visiting speakers, case studies, debates and student presentations.

The 4 hours per week of independent non-contact work includes: guided reading, small-scale research projects, investigative tasks, presentation and assessment preparation time.

A range of assessment methods operate within the modular scheme: multiple choice/short answer examinations, seen/unseen examinations, essay, case study, report assignments, presentations and practical/ coaching performance related tasks. Assessments can also be individual, pair and/or group based. As this varies according to each module students might select modules according to their assessment strengths.

Career Opportunities

Graduates from both courses are equipped for a variety of careers in the public, private and voluntary leisure sectors. Posts might include recreation manager, leisure services co-ordinator, sports development officer events promotion officer and sports coach. Students also have the opportunity to take postgraduate studies, eg in teaching.

Related Degrees

Leisure and Tourism, Leisure Management, Golf Management, Events Management, Leisure Studies

Suggested Reading

Researching Leisure, Sport and Tourism: The Essential Guide
- Jonathan A Long, Sage Publications, 2007

Research Methods for Sports Studies
- Chris Gratton and Ian Jones, Routledge, 2003

A Guide to Jobs and Qualifications in Sport and Recreation
- John Potter, John Potter Publications, 2000

Sport and Fitness Uncovered
- Beryl Dixon, Trotman, 2007

Internships, Jobs and Careers in the Sports Industry
- Glenn M. Wong, Jones and Bartlett, 2008

Working in Sport
- James Masters, How To Books, 2007

Career Opportunities in the Sports Industry
- Shelly Field, Checkmark Books, 2010

Further Information

SkillsActive
www.skillsactive.com

Institute for Sport, Parks and Leisure
www.ispal.org.uk

Irish Sports Council
www.irishsportscouncil.ie

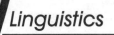

Linguistics

Original article by Professor Richard Hudson, University College London

Introduction

Linguistics is the scientific study of language. People are often surprised to hear that there's anything in language to study, and are even more surprised to hear that it can be studied 'scientifically' but there is actually a wide range of researchable topics and of active research. The topics range from physics (How does a 'd' sound move through the air?), through physiology (How do we make a 'd' sound?), to psychology (How do we plan a 'd' sound?) and then through grammar (How do we use 'd' sounds to show tense, as in 'walked'?), and lexicology (Which verbs use 'd' to form past tenses?), to history (How long have we been using 'd' to form past tenses?) and philosophy (What do we mean by 'past tense'?), not to mention sociology (How do we use past tenses to show politeness?) and, of course, other languages (How do other languages mark, and use, past tenses?)

Degree Courses

It is impossible to generalise too widely about linguistics courses. However, one course in Linguistics goes as follows:

Early Years:

- **Pronunciation** (Phonetics and Phonology) - Speech sounds - how to classify and transcribe them, how we make them, how they affect each other when combined in words.

- **Sentence-structure** (Syntax) - Word-patterns in sentences - how to diagram them, how to write a grammar to explain them.

- **Meaning** (Semantics and Pragmatics) - The nature of meaning - how to use the notation of logic, how we extract information from what we hear and read.

- **Principles of linguistics** - The aims, methods and discoveries of linguistics.

Later in the course:

A choice of courses on other parts of linguistics:

- **Sociolinguistics**: socially significant variation, politeness, prejudices.

- **Language Acquisition**: child language and how it grows: nature or nurture?

- **Applied Linguistics**: how to teach (and learn) a foreign language.

- **Computational Linguistics**: how to program a computer to analyse sentences.

- **Language Structures**: the structure of some language (e.g. Esperanto) as viewed by a linguist.

In the Final Year:

As above, plus a project, e.g. the accent or dialect of your home town; a study of a child's language; differences between a few male and female speakers; a survey of ideas on the meaning of tense.

In other departments you may find other optional subjects. Even the following list is incomplete:

- **Language Processing**: how we plan, produce and understand speech and writing.

- **Morphology**: patterns of roots and affixes within words.

- **Discourse Analysis**: how we organise speech beyond the sentence.

- **Historical Linguistics**: how languages change, and the history of particular languages.

- **Typology**: how do the world's 5,000-odd languages vary?

- **Language and Gender**: differences between men and women.

- **Language and Ideology**: how language transmits ideologies.

Career Opportunities

Linguistics graduates are well equipped to teach languages but also have skills of communication, analysis, logic and debate, which can be valuable in many careers. Some train as lawyers, librarians, social workers - others enter commerce, the Civil Service, management services, computing, finance, public relations, marketing, etc.

Related Degrees

Linguistic Science, Psycholinguistics

Suggested Reading

Invitation to Linguistics
- R. Hudson, Wiley-Blackwell, 1993 - What's it like to be a linguistics student?

The Language Instinct: How the Mind Creates Language
- Steven Pinker, Harper Perennial, 2007 - A superbly written guide to some big issues

The Stuff of Thought: Language as a Window into Human Nature
- Steven Pinker, Penguin, 2008

Teach Yourself Linguistics
- Jean Aitchison, Teach Yourself Books, 2004 - A clear and helpful introduction

The Cambridge Encyclopaedia of Language
- David Crystal, CUP, 2010 - A marvellous collection

Further Information

Linguistics Association of Great Britain
www.lagb.org.uk

International Association of Applied Linguistics
www.aila.info

Irish Association for Applied Linguistics
www.iraal.ie

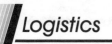

Logistics

Original article by Ken Reynolds, specialist writer on careers and higher education

Introduction

Getting the right product to the right place in the correct quantity at the appropriate time, in the best condition and at an acceptable cost, is the challenge of logistics. It is the strategic management of the total supply chain, which goes from raw material via the resulting product and its availability to the consumer and ultimately to its recycling. When new products are in the development stage, logistics professionals are often involved in helping to ensure that the product will have an efficient supply chain. The wide range of functions, each with its own challenges and associated skills are interdependent and logistics experts work together to manage, coordinate and continuously improve the total supply chain. Supply chains are often complex and their smooth operation depends on high-level managerial skills, coupled with effective communication systems utilising information technology. The latest developments in e-commerce demand extremely effective supply chains and, in addition today, professionals working in the logistics field are required to combine business development with a sustainable approach to the environment.

Degree Courses

There are different types of courses in logistics: some cover all aspects whilst others may concentrate on core topics and incorporate aspects of a European language programme. There are also courses which enable you to specialise in a specific area such as transport management, maritime or even e-logistics. There are both three- and four-year courses, with the longer ones incorporating a paid professional placement or study abroad. In addition it is possible to do a one-year course in Logistics as a top-up to a relevant Higher National Diploma. Some of these courses are fully accredited by the Chartered Institute of Logistics and Transport, so that in completing the course you will qualify for Corporate Membership. Following relevant practical experience, you will be eligible to become a full member of the profession. In a logistics course, you study human resource management, financial management, systems analysis and information technology. You will also develop a wide range of managerial skills to enable you to meet the challenges facing manufacturing organisations as well as learning about transport planning and economics and studying different forms of freight transport operations, including rail, air and sea.

The first year at one university offering a range of Logistics degrees, gives you a broad grounding in core business subjects. Logistics is a cross-functional subject and draws from marketing, operations, finance, accounting and corporate strategy. You develop knowledge of a range of business issues and academic skills that provide the foundation for more specialist study.

In the second-year core modules, your study focuses on the principles and practices of logistics and supply chain management and of distribution and warehouse management. Supply chain managers need a comprehensive grounding in the foundations of the discipline so that they can make informed decisions about future strategic developments.

All the Logistics programmes at this university provide the opportunity either to spend your third year abroad (at an institution where the teaching is in English) studying your specialist subject in an international context, or to enhance the value of your programme by taking a work placement year before returning to your final-year studies.

In the final year, you focus on global freight movement and international collaboration, on how e-business influences supply chain integration and on the modelling of supply chains. A choice of optional modules also allows you to specialise further in logistics or broaden your studies with related subjects.

Career Opportunities

There is currently a shortage of appropriately qualified logistics graduates in the UK. Graduates can follow careers in logistics and supply chain management with a variety of companies, including specialist providers of logistics and distribution services, airlines, major industries and retail management. They often join management training schemes and quickly take on managerial roles. They work in Local and Central Government as well as in the Health Service and the Armed Forces.

Related Degrees

Transport Management, Transport and Logistics Management, E-logistics, Business (Logistics), Purchasing and Logistics, Maritime Business with Logistics, European Logistics Management, Logistics and Supply Chain Management, Logistics with French/German.

Suggested Reading

International Journal of Logistics Research and Applications
- Journal of the Chartered Institute of Logistics and Transport. See website for subscription rates

Graduate Career Guide to Logistics and Transport Management
- downloadable from the Chartered Institute of Logistics and Transport website below

The Dictionary of Transport and Logistics
- David Lowe, Kogan Page, 2002

Further Information

Chartered Institute of Logistics and Transport (UK)
www.ciltuk.org.uk

Careers in Logistics
www.careersinlogistics.co.uk

National Institute for Transport & Logistics, Ireland
www.nitl.ie

Supply Chain Management Institute, Ireland
www.ipics.ie

Management/Business Studies

Original article by Professor Dom Wilson, Professor of Strategic Management and Director of the Management Research Institute, School of Management, University of Salford

Introduction

Every university and Higher Education Institute in the UK offers at least one **Business** or **Management** degree course and most offer several. The advantage of this to students is that there is a huge variety of courses on offer in what is now a very competitive market. The downside is that you face a lot of work (including visits and asking searching questions) to get behind the marketing rhetoric to make a sensible choice of what is right for you. Some courses are particularly academic and self-directed, usually at the more research-oriented universities, which expect students to ask critical and challenging questions. Other courses are aimed at those who require a more practical, skills-oriented and disciplined programme, with often less option choice, where you are told more precisely what to do and how to do it. This relative emphasis on academic and practical priorities is not always as marked as it used to be, but it is still a significant factor to consider.

Degree Courses

An important benefit of studying management or business at university is that you can combine the subject with almost anything you can think of in joint or mixed degrees (e.g. with languages, sciences, humanities, technology) - so you do not have to give up subjects that fascinate you just to pursue a degree with better job prospects.

Some courses offer sandwich arrangements, where students spend time (watch out for exactly how long and what you would be doing) in an organisational placement to develop practical experience of management. Surveys suggest that prospective employers do value this experience element but it can be gained in other ways too, such as vacation work (preferably something more than the usual bar work, fast food sales, call centres, and shop work), project work based on real cases, and what you do in a gap year.

Many courses now provide opportunities to spend some time (from a few weeks to a full year) studying management in overseas partner universities. This does not always mean studying in a foreign language - as some foreign universities teach management in English - but you should expect to be treated in the same way as an indigenous student. Studying overseas is also valued by many employers, not least because it takes maturity, self management and confidence to get the most from such opportunities while it also develops sensitivity to cultural differences, boosts language skills, and generally broadens your horizons. My own experience is that students returning from a year overseas or in a sandwich placement seem to have significantly better insight into management issues and greater self-confidence, which means they often perform better in assessments also.

Business and Management are complex mixes of many other subjects. Some see Economics (both macro and micro) as perhaps the most important component, reflected also in such topics as competition in markets, business efficiency, and the effect of the general economic climate on business. Mathematics and statistics are important too, for example in helping to forecast market changes, understanding the vast amounts of data available to managers, and in choosing between alternative investment decisions and strategies. Psychology, sociology and management of people are central to the study of management because of the necessary focus on organisational behaviour, leadership and group work. Finance and accounting cover the ways in which organisations, markets, sectors and economies are regulated and monitored, as well as how alternative investment opportunities are evaluated. Obviously, legal issues are important to management too, especially with respect to the increasing influence of EU and international law. Many would argue that management is fundamentally about understanding exchanges of products and services (marketing), which will involve individuals as well as other organisations and is as relevant internally as externally within the many market places of an organisation's myriad activities. International issues also now form an important aspect of most business and management degree programmes, not only with the usual language options but also in a more general sensitivity to issues of cultural diversity and the globalisation of markets and economies. Finally, while all courses assume a basic IT competence, some place particular emphasis on this, with options in IT systems designed specifically to assist management decision making and organisational efficiency. Nevertheless, given the huge variety of courses available in the UK (and beyond), and the vast scale of the management field (which cannot be crammed into a single degree programme), there are still excellent courses around which do not require particular strength in economics, mathematics, languages, or IT.

Career Opportunities

Graduates from these degree courses are in considerable demand. They enter public administration, the Civil Service, transport, communications, industry, commerce, accountancy, banking and insurance, the armed forces, not-for-profit organisations. In fact management is highly relevant to any career stream you can think of. So unemployment rates are very low for those who make the most of the opportunities provided by a business or management degree. But with so many business/management graduates emerging from UK universities, it is increasingly what you do with these opportunities, and not just possession of the degree, that distinguishes the successful student.

Related Degrees

Management Science, Business Analysis, E-Business Commerce, Business Administration, Business and Finance, Business Studies, Business and Management, European Business Management, International Business Management

Suggested Reading

The business, commerce and management pages of any serious newspaper
The Winning Streak Mark II: How the World's Most Successful Companies Stay on Top Through Today's Turbulent Times
- Walter Goldsmith and David Clutterbuck, Texere Publishing, 1998
The Goal: A Process of Ongoing Improvement
- Eli Goldratt and Jeff Cox, Gower Publishing, 2004
Inside Organizations: 21 Ideas for Managers
- Charles B. Handy, Penguin, 1999
The Machine that Changed the World
- James Womack, Daniel Jones and Daniel Roos, Simon & Schuster, 2007
Getting into Business, Economics and Management Courses
- James Burnett, Trotman, 2009 (new edition due February 2011)

Further Information

Institute of Business Consulting
www.ibconsulting.org.uk
International Institute of Management
www.iim.org
Chartered Institute of Marketing
www.cim.co.uk
Public Appointments Service, Ireland
www.publicjobs.ie
Chartered Institute of Personnel and Development in Ireland
www.cipd.co.uk/branches/Ireland
Irish Management Institute
www.imi.ie

Manufacturing Engineering

Original article by Dr Ian Pillinger, School of Manufacturing and Mechanical Engineering, University of Birmingham

Introduction

To study Manufacturing Engineering at University, you will normally be expected to obtain high grades at A level/Higher/IB or equivalent in Mathematics and two other subjects. If you have achieved good grades, but have not studied Mathematics, you may still be able study Manufacturing Engineering by undertaking a preliminary Foundation Year. This year will be designed to bring you up to the required level in this subject and so you would need to have good GCSE, SCE Standard or equivalent passes in Mathematics and Physics (or Double Science).

Degree Courses

Accredited university degree programmes in Manufacturing Engineering are now generally of four years duration, at the end of which you obtain a Master of Engineering (MEng) degree. During the first two years, you study the fundamental subjects of Engineering Science, Manufacturing Processes and Technology, Manufacturing Systems (the organisation of manufacturing installations), Industrial Automation, Operations Management (controlling the flow of products and materials) and Metrology (measurement techniques and methods). Underpinning all these subjects will be the study of Mathematics. You may take various other subjects that Manufacturing Engineers need to know about such as Ergonomics, Economics and Accounting. Some of the time you will be attending lectures, but you will also be carrying out laboratory work and computer exercises, and undertaking personal study such as working through quizzes set by the lecturer or researching a topic in the library. There will also be the opportunity to develop professional skills like report writing, making presentations, working in teams and time management, through various mini-projects and assignments.

After your first two years, you may choose to take a year out to work in industry in order to gain some of the experience you need to become a Chartered Engineer.

During the final two years of your degree programme the core subjects you studied during your first two years are continued at a more advanced level, and in addition you will be able to choose from a range of specialised topics such as Experimental Design, Statistical Process Control, and Computer Aided Production Management. An important element of the final part of your degree studies will be the undertaking of a major project. The subject of this may well be related to the research your lecturers are doing, and you could find yourself working alongside a research team. Alternatively, it may be a problem you have brought back from a placement in industry.

There are many variations to this basic outline. For example, many universities allow you to study a foreign language or business-related topics in addition to the Manufacturing Engineering subjects. In some places, the mid-course year out is compulsory; in others it is optional. (Most universities would, however, be happy for you to work for a year in industry before starting your degree programme, and you would be encouraged to find industrial placements during the summer vacation.) Part-time study is also possible, generally by interspersing blocks of time (a term or a year) at university with similar periods in industry.

Career Opportunities

Graduates are well qualified for work in industrial production/management, in analysing the performance and efficiency of companies, in solving operational problems and establishing good working practices. These skills can also be used in banking, accountancy, insurance, commerce, local/central government, marketing, purchasing and in a wide range of businesses or management consultancies.

Related Degrees

Industrial Engineering, Product Design Engineering, Manufacturing Engineering and Management, Food Manufacture and ManagementMechanical Engineering

Suggested Reading

The Engineer's Conscience
- Professor M W Thring, Thring Publishing, 1992

Mechatronics Principles and Applications
- Dr Godfrey Onwubolu, Butterworth-Heinemann, 2005

Progression to Engineering and Mathematics 2011 entry
- UCAS, 2010

Manufacturing Engineering and Technology
- Serope Kalpakjian and Steven Schmid, Prentice Hall, 2009

Further Information

Institution of Mechanical Engineers
www.imeche.org

Engineering Employer's Federation - EEF: the Manufacturers' Organisation
www.eef.org.uk

Engineering Council UK
www.engc.org.uk

Institute of Industrial Engineers, Ireland
www.iie.ie

Engineers Ireland
www.engineersireland.ie

Marine Biology

Original article by Dr David N. Thomas, School of Ocean Sciences, Bangor University

Introduction

Marine biology encompasses many biological disciplines covering the range of organisms found from viruses through to blue whales: microbiologists study bacteria and fungi; botanists look at plants of the ocean that range from unicellular algae to giant kelps 60m long. Zoologists look at everything from microscopic organisms to crustaceans, molluscs, fish and marine mammals. Some choose to concentrate on a group of organisms, although others look at systems as a whole studying the ecology and the interaction between groups of organisms and the factors that influence long- and short-term changes.

Marine biologists increasingly rely on sophisticated technology to carry out their investigations. Modern molecular and biochemical techniques are common in most established marine laboratories. Chemical analysers and light and electron microscopes are all tools commonly used. Marine biologists are often required to span several biological disciplines, and even several scientific disciplines. The biologist has to understand the chemistry and physics of the system marine organisms find themselves in. In turn, the biology affects the chemical properties of the seas.

It is not just an academic curiosity that drives this search but a realisation that the biology of the oceans may be the source we have to turn to in order to feed the world's increasing population; to find novel chemicals for the pharmaceutical industry; and as a buffer to combat the global warming induced by increasing levels of carbon dioxide.

Marine biologists have a key role in deciding how to manage fish stocks around the world. This involves long-term monitoring work and liaising with both politicians and fishermen. The oceans are no longer a place that we can indiscriminately use as a dumping ground. Marine biologists monitor the effects of previous dumping of waste.

Degree Courses

Most marine biology degrees in the UK are based on a modular system. During the course of a three- or four-year study, a degree will provide experience in many of the major biological disciplines, including genetics, ecology, zoology, botany, microbiology and biochemistry. Often in the first year there are more general modules to cover the basics in these disciplines, which can be built upon in second and third year modules. In addition to the different biological aspects, there will be modules designed to give the necessary background in marine chemistry and oceanography, where details will be given of the forces dictating the tides, waves, optical properties of water and circulation patterns. Modules are designed to describe how the physics, chemistry and biology interact to determine what is found in the various seas and coastlines.

Most marine laboratories are near or at the coast, and so many courses have a large fieldwork component involving working on rocky shores, beaches, salt marshes, mudflats and estuaries. If the facilities include a research vessel, this is used to collect water samples and marine organisms to analyse during field trips and laboratory practical classes.

Increasingly, there is the need to acquire skills in information technology, together with the skills required to enable scientists to interact as part of a team. So, as well as learning the basics of marine science, varied transferable skills will be learnt and honed during the degree. This is one of the clear advantages of studying such a multifaceted subject as marine biology.

Courses are generally based on a lecture series plus practical classes and fieldwork. In most cases assessment is by continuous assessment of practical and course exercises as well as end-of-course examinations. Frequently, final year students are expected to carry out an independent piece of research under supervision. This is a highlight of the degree course, giving the opportunity to express ideas, derive hypotheses and test them in experiments. Normally this work has to be written up as a small thesis, and an oral presentation of the project is also part of the assessment.

Marine biology is a degree in which there are plenty of opportunities to get your hands dirty. In many cases it also means getting wet, and at times cold. But that does not seem to matter so much when you are able to get to grips with understanding the overwhelming diversity and sheer fascination of the plants and animals that live on our shores, in coral reefs, in salt marshes and mangroves and of course in the vast expanses of ocean that stretch from the poles to the tropics.

Career Opportunities

A few graduates enter research or continue with further academic study, but the majority find employment in finance, administration and operational management, marketing/buying, medical and technical sales, computer programming, environmental health, laboratory work, technical journalism etc. Very few careers opportunities are available which directly involve this biological specialism - but the monitoring of the marine environment will call for more graduates eventually.

Related Degrees

Marine and Freshwater Biology, Marine Biotechnology, Coastal Marine Biology, Aquatic Biology, Aquaculture, Marine Zoology

Suggested Reading

Mapping the Deep - The Extraordinary story of Ocean Science
- Robert Kunzig, Sort Of Books, 2000

Cod- A Biography of the Fish that Changed the World
- Mark Kurlansky, Vintage, 1999

An Introduction to Marine Ecology
- R S K Barnes and R N Hughes, WileyBlackwell, 1999

Marine Biology: Function, Biodiversity, Ecology
- Jeffrey S. Levinton, OUP USA, 2008

Further Information

MarineBio
www.marinebio.com

Society of Biology
www.societyofbiology.org

Marine Biological Association of the UK
www.mba.ac.uk

Institute of Biology of Ireland
www.ibioli.net

Marine Technology

Original article by Emeritus Professor J. B. Caldwell, Newcastle University

Introduction

This study area is about the sea, and mainly about designing and building things that go to sea. Ships, of course, but other things too; from boats and barges to the large structures and systems which will be needed as mankind looks increasingly to the sea for a multitude of purposes. The oceans have been described as our last resource, and the exploring and harvesting and preserving of this resource will pose some fascinating challenges to the marine technologists of the future.

Their work is a reflection of, and a response to, our need to use the sea. Throughout history the principal uses have been firstly to move people and goods and weapons around the globe, and secondly to harvest some of the many varieties of food which exist in the sea. The centrepiece of these activities is the ship in its multifarious forms, sizes and functions. Through many centuries the art of creating ships evolved by trial and error and experience, but with the Industrial Revolution came the need to design and build ships in new materials with new forms of propulsion, without the benefit of prior experience. And so there emerged the profession of naval architecture, signalled formally by the founding of the Institution of Naval Architects some 150 years ago. Since then the main task of the naval architect has been the designing and building of all kinds of ships and crafts for both civil and military uses, from ferries to frigates, tankers and trawlers, icebreakers and hydrofoils, containerships to cruisers. What is particularly fascinating is that, despite the antiquity of shipping, new concepts continue to appear. Wave-piercing catamarans and SWATH ships (small waterplane area twin hull) are recent examples.

Nor should we overlook the part played by naval architects in the growing business of leisure activities at sea, whether on luxury cruise ships, or just messing about in boats. The design of both types of vessel depends on the same basic principles of naval architecture.

The marine engineer - and this is where the definitions can get a little confusing -can have two fairly distinct roles. One is as an operator of the machinery and systems on board ship; the other, which is the real counterpart of the naval architect, is as the designer and builder of this equipment. Again, variety is a feature of this work: ships can be propelled by steam turbines, gas turbines, slow- or medium-speed diesel engines and electric motors, and many combinations of these are possible. The basic source of energy to push a ship along has changed through the centuries from wind, muscle-power, coal, oil and other special chemical fuels to nuclear fission. It is one of the fascinations typical of marine technology that the days of wind propulsion, or of coal used in new forms, may come again if technological developments and relative fuel costs make them feasible and economic. More futuristic ideas currently being researched include 'magnetohydrodynamic' propulsion, and even harnessing the energy in waves to push ships along!

Degree Courses

Marine engineers and naval architects work closely together, and the professional education and training they receive reflects their common interest in engineering for the sea. Mathematics and science - especially physics - provide the basis for degree-level education, not as ends in themselves, but for their usefulness when applied to solving the problems confronting the marine technologist. A foundation year of engineering science, mathematics, computing and some introductory work in marine technology is followed by an increasing emphasis through the second and third years on 'professional' studies. In the final year there may be a wide choice of specialised marine topics, and the student can begin to look forward to various career possibilities in choosing subjects for advanced study.

Career Opportunities

Employment opportunities are many and varied. This widening tapestry of marine activity now includes offshore, or ocean, engineering. This embraces a whole complex of engineering activities ranging from seabed technology (placing foundations for ocean structures, or pipes or cables) through underwater engineering (problems of submersible design, communication, visibility, life-support, safety etc.), up to engineering on the surface (mothering craft, production platforms, artificial islands, protective structures, wave-energy devices etc.).

Related Degrees

Marine Engineering, Naval Architecture, Marine Technology/Fisheries, Nautical Science, Marine Operations

Suggested Reading

Careers in Naval Architecture
- at the Royal Institution of Naval Architects website below

Introduction to Naval Architecture: Formerly Muckle's Naval Architecture for Marine Engineers
- E. C. Tupper, Butterworth-Heinemann, 2004

Sea your Future - a guide to Marine Careers
- downloadable from the Institute of Marine Engineering, Science and Technology website below

Introduction to Marine Engineering
- D A Taylor, Butterworth-Heinemann, 1996

Oceans of Opportunity
- careers information at the Society for Underwater Technology website below

Further Information

British Marine Federation
www.britishmarine.co.uk

Institute of Marine Engineering, Science and Technology
www.imarest.org

Society for Underwater Technology
www.sut.org.uk

Royal Institution of Naval Architects
www.rina.org.uk

Irish Maritime Development Office
www.imdo.ie

Maritime Studies

Original article by Dr Alston Kennerley, Plymouth University

Introduction

The development of undergraduate courses in Maritime Studies (at some universities called Marine Studies or Nautical Studies) has taken place in response to the increasing use of the seas for transportation, resource extraction (fish, energy, minerals), recreation and military purposes, and the growing awareness of the importance of their waters to the well being of the planet Earth. Typically, course structures allow for the interdisciplinary study of marine subjects, spanning the sciences, technology and business. Though such courses bear titles not usually found in school curricula, admission tutors accept quite a wide selection of A level/Higher/IB or equivalent subjects. Some of the Maritime Studies subject components have in recent years been developed as separate undergraduate degrees, which are highlighted below, but the ability to combine subjects suited to employment in many maritime industries is preserved through modular structures. Maritime undergraduate courses are designed taking account of the advice received from a wide variety of employers active in the maritime world. The courses are concerned with mankind's activity on and under the surface of the sea, and of necessity, with the interface between land and sea, the coastline and ports. Most degrees are traditional three-year "through" courses, though sandwich arrangements are usually possible. One or two have been developed as two-year courses to cater for advanced entry qualifications, or as foundation degrees.

Degree Courses

Most established undergraduate courses in maritime studies have been built around the transportation use, having the ship as a focus. The range of marine subjects involved is surprisingly wide. The design, building and propulsion of ships and other marine structures such as offshore oil and gas rigs, is now grouped under *Marine Technology* or *Ship Science*, or *Ship Design*, though some courses still carry the titles *Naval Architecture* or *Marine Engineering*. In the engineering world they may be viewed as sub-specialisms of mechanical and electrical engineering, despite involving unique areas such as ship stability. Guiding a ship safely around the world involves the study of *Marine Navigation*. This broad scientific subject is equally important in recreational sailing. The core study involves positioning, using navigational charts, astro- and electronic navigation, together with navigation management and marine communications. It also involves aspects of oceanography (particularly tides and currents) and marine meteorology. A slightly different emphasis will be found in *Merchant Shipping Operations and Marine Operations*. The surveying and mapping of the oceans involves the specialist study of *Hydrography*. This is also a science-based subject, which ranges from the study of the shape of the earth and the principles of map projections to the practical business of marine surveying and marine chart production. *Oceanography*, the study of the chemical composition and physical movement of the waters of the world, including sedimentology, is important, for example, in the understanding of the impact of marine pollution. Some courses use the title *Ocean Science*, because they also cover aspects of fisheries and the legal regime, such as coastal zone management. Closely related is *Underwater Studies*. Courses in *Marine Biology*, also including elements of Oceanography, are concerned with the biological study of all forms of marine life. Because the progression from A level/Higher/IB or equivalent courses is so obvious, this tends to be a popular option. But the study of the commercial sea fisheries and fish farming or aquaculture, *Fisheries Science* or *Fisheries* or *Fisheries Science & Aquaculture*, although including Fish Biology, may also include Fishing Technology (the study of fishing equipment and boats), and Fisheries Business (the commercial and regulatory dimension of the fishing industry).

All the degree courses mentioned so far tend to draw on backgrounds in the sciences or mathematics, but applicants with other backgrounds are also catered for through courses in Maritime Business, Marine Law and Maritime Recreation. The finance, ownership and commercial operation of ships are topics at the heart of *Maritime Business*, with *Marine Law* as an essential component. Courses also include elements of economics, management and personnel, and variants deal with port operations. Marine Law is a specialism having ancient roots and significant international dimensions. Britain has a significant maritime past, and there is at least one degree in *Maritime History*.

The long established courses in Marine Navigation and Maritime Business have provided many students with a valuable foundation for careers in maritime recreation. But recent years have seen the design of degree courses tailored more closely to the needs of this important industry. Degrees in Maritime Recreation combine relevant maritime aspects of business, management, tourism, and sport. Even individual sports are beginning to be treated as degree course subjects. Examples include *Applied Marine Sports Science* and *Surf Science and Technology*, which both require a background in the sciences, and involve the study of selected elements from marine science and technology as well as the study of the sports and their equipment. For a non-science based approach try *Maritime Leisure Management*.

Many of the degrees mentioned in this article can be found at Plymouth, Southampton Solent and Liverpool John Moores (Lairdside Maritime Centre) Universities.

Career Opportunities

Apart from the provision for seagoing careers, there are upwards of three thousand vacancies annually ashore in industries and businesses which in some way are connected with the maritime world. There are always opportunities in the commercial world of shipping, mainly in London, in ship operation, ship broking, chartering, marine lawyer practices and marine insurance. Ports also offer a range of jobs in management, conservancy, hydrographic survey and marine traffic management. Government and international agencies also have departments concerned with the maritime world and need suitable staff. Marine equipment suppliers need technical and sales staff versed in maritime affairs. Water companies employ marine scientists. Indeed, think of a field for employment and there will be a maritime dimension to it. Another option is postgraduate study. There are taught masters degrees in most of the subjects noted here. Examples include *Applied Marine Science* and *International Shipping*

Related Degrees

Ocean Science, Oceanography, Hydrography, Marine Navigation, Ocean Studies

Suggested Reading

To explore the content of maritime studies a little further, start with one of the few books providing something of an overview. *The Times Atlas of the Oceans*, edited by Alastair D Couper (Van Nostrand Reinhold, 1987), despite its date, is particularly useful and should be found in larger reference libraries. It has short articles on almost all of the subject areas noted here and provides suggestions for further reading. *The Oxford Companion to Ships and the Sea*, edited by Peter Kemp and I. Dear, (OUP, 2006) also contains concise articles on most subjects.

Further Information

British Marine Federation
www.britishmarine.co.uk
Irish Maritime Development Office
www.imdo.ie

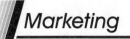

Marketing

Original article by George Long, Lancaster University

Introduction

Marketing is concerned with one of the most fundamental human activities - exchange. In primitive societies, as soon as individuals produce more than they require, or make something better than anyone else, it pays them to exchange goods and services in order to have a richer variety of things to consume. As societies become more developed, and individuals more specialised, the requirements for sophisticated and complex exchange increase and markets emerge. So marketing management is not just advertising or public relations or selling. It is the management of the whole set of decisions which help to create successful exchanges between a firm and its customers. As examples, marketing involves decisions about market analysis, product development, market structuring, pricing, distribution channels, product features and promotion. You can take a single major degree in marketing or a degree in advertising and marketing. Degrees are offered in marketing with studies in a foreign language (e.g. French, German, Spanish, Italian). Whereas most degrees are three- or four-year courses, those in which marketing is combined with a foreign language often include an additional year spent abroad. You will find other courses in which marketing is combined with subjects such as economics, advertising, law, computer sciences and many others. Some courses involve a placement in industry or in North America.

Degree Courses

A typical degree course will teach skills as well as knowledge. General transferable skills would include problem solving, computing, data analysis, report writing, market research techniques, interviewing and case study analysis. Among the learning experiences would be computer-linked market research exercises, business games, live market research and consultancy exercises for industry and other organisations. A major object of these experiences is to bridge the gap between university and the world of work by working in small groups, developing teamwork and presentational skills.

Departments are likely to have close contacts with industry and commerce, partly due to their consultancy work and research. In choosing a university, it is worthwhile investigating the research interests of its staff and matching them with your own interests.

Career Opportunities

A degree in marketing does not limit you to marketing management as a career. Many graduates work in managerial positions in advertising agencies, market research companies, the National Health Service, theatre management, and organisations such as British Gas and NPower. Nevertheless, a high proportion of graduates will acquire posts in large companies ranging from supermarket organisations and other retail firms to computer manufacturers and manufacturing companies.

Related Degrees

Marketing Management, Food Marketing, Leisure Marketing, Retail Marketing, International Marketing, Advertising and Marketing, Public Relations, American Studies and Business Economics with Marketing, Agricultural and Food Marketing

Suggested Reading

Marketing Uncovered
- Andi Robertson, Trotman, 2009

The Marketing Plan Workbook
- John Westwood, Kogan Page, 2005

The Hidden Persuaders
- Vance Packard, Ig Publishing, 2007

New Marketing Practice: Rules for Success in a Changing World
- David Mercer, Penguin, 1997

Marketing Today
- Gordon Oliver, Prentice Hall, 1995

Further Information

Institute of Sales and Marketing Management
www.ismm.co.uk

Communication, Advertising and Marketing Education Federation Ltd
www.camfoundation.com

Chartered Institute of Marketing
www.cim.co.uk

Enterprise Ireland
www.enterprise-ireland.com

Marketing Institute of Ireland
www.mii.ie

Materials Science, Materials Engineering and Metallurgy

Original article by Vernon John, formerly of City University

Introduction

Today the spectrum of engineering materials is very wide, comprising a large range of metals and alloys, a continually increasing number of polymer materials, ceramics (including many new industrial ceramics) and glasses, stone, concrete, bituminous materials and very many composite materials.

The pace of development in both materials and processing techniques is rapid and exciting. Some examples of developments in recent years include new materials for the electronics industry with impurity levels measured in parts per billion; single crystal turbine blades capable of operating at temperatures very close to their melting temperatures for high performance aero gas turbines; ceramics which may be formed into complex shapes using processes similar to those for polymer materials; polymers for high temperature service; and carbon fibre and other high performance composites.

Degree Courses

The subject matter of degree courses in Materials Science, Materials Engineering or Metallurgy develops from a knowledge of physics, chemistry and mathematics. Some of the degree courses are orientated more towards science while others lean more towards engineering. In the first year of many degree courses there are further studies in aspects of physics, chemistry and mathematics, together with specialist materials science studies and, in many cases, an introduction to engineering studies. Practical work forms an essential part of all the courses. In the later years the courses cover a wide range of topics: the structure of materials and the relationships between structure and properties, the production and fabrication of materials, and the behaviour of materials and components in a wide variety of service conditions. Other important topics are failure mechanisms and failure prevention, corrosion, chemical and microbial attack, joining technology, test and evaluation methods, selection criteria and quality assurance. Economics and management studies feature in courses with a major bias towards engineering. Many universities have links with institutions throughout Europe and in North America and there are possibilities to have a study period abroad. On many courses, there are opportunities to have industrial training periods either in the UK or abroad.

Before selecting a course you need to decide whether to practise as an engineer or to remain fairly firmly within the world of science. Most of the degree courses available are accredited by the Institute of Materials, Minerals and Mining for the Engineering Council. These are the 4-year MEng and the 3- or 4-year BEng but some BSc courses are not accredited and will not lead directly to the professional qualifications of CEng or MEng.

Career Opportunities

The possession of a degree in Materials and/or Metallurgy can lead to employment in industry, the public services or the armed forces. There is a wide range of career possibilities including research, development, manufacturing, management, marketing or teaching in spheres as diverse as microelectronics, aerospace, off-shore engineering and general manufacturing industry. Many graduates register with the Engineering Council for the professional qualifications of either Chartered Engineer

(CEng) or Incorporated Engineer (IEng), after which they follow a period of monitored Initial Professional Development (IPD). This comprises training, learning from experience and taking responsibility in appropriate roles. When the IPD phase is completed, usually about four years after graduation, the final assessment for the young engineer is a Professional Review. This normally includes presentation of a written report and an interview with suitably qualified and experienced professional engineers and is the final hurdle before being registered as either a Chartered or Incorporated Engineer.

Related Degrees

Ceramics, Polymer Science and Technology, Ceramics Science and Engineering, Recycling Technology, Materials, Economics and Management

Suggested Reading

Materials Science and Engineering: An Introduction
- William D. Callister, Wiley, 2007

The New Science of Strong Materials or Why You Don't Fall Through the Floor
- JE Gordon, Princeton Science Library, 2008

Degree Course Guide: Engineering
- Trotman, 2007

Progression to Engineering and Mathematics 2011 Entry
- UCAS, 2010

Further Information

Engineering Council UK
www.engc.org.uk

Cogent Careers for the petroleum, chemicals, nuclear, oil and gas and polymer industries
www.cogent-careers.com

Institute of Materials, Minerals and Mining
www.iom3.org

Engineers Ireland
www.engineersireland.ie

Mathematics

Original article by J C Ault, University of Leicester
With contributions by Louis Billington, University of Hull and by Sheffield Hallam University

Introduction

All university mathematics courses are based on a core of pure mathematics consisting of topics from mathematical analysis and abstract algebra. Broadly speaking, analysis is that part of the subject which deals with limiting processes and includes concepts such as differentiation, integration and continuity of functions, while algebra deals with finite processes such as addition and multiplication and the solution of polynomial and simultaneous linear equations. It is in this core that you will learn the rigour of formal proofs and the logical thinking needed for the rest of the course. You will also have the opportunity to study other topics from pure mathematics and from some or all of the other main areas of the subject: applied mathematics, numerical analysis, mathematical statistics and computation.

Degree Courses

Usually the first year is fairly prescribed and most departments will take the opportunity to provide courses to help with the transition to university. In the second, third and, where applicable, fourth years an increasing choice of modules is provided, allowing you to concentrate on the areas of the subject which interest you most (or perhaps to avoid those that appeal to you least). The range of modules on offer will vary from department to department and from time to time and will depend on the interests and strengths of the staff, but you can expect a wide range of topics from at least three of the main areas.

The teaching of mathematics is normally by a combination of lectures, tutorials, problem classes and workshops. The whole class attends lectures, while tutorials and problem classes are organised for smaller groups and there is more interaction between tutor and students. Most workshops in mathematics tend to be in a computer laboratory, where you would be learning to use a specialised mathematical package or a spreadsheet, but there are also situations where you could be working with a small group of fellow students to investigate a problem. You will be expected to work on your own as well and to hand in solutions to exercises for assessment on a weekly basis. Assessment is generally by written examination but most mathematics courses also include a certain amount of coursework (typically 10% or 20%) and some may be assessed entirely on written reports of project work.

A typical university course offers a choice of studying mathematics for three years for the BSc degree, or for four years to obtain the MMath (Master of Mathematics) degree and these can often include a year abroad, in Europe, Australia or the USA. It can also be combined with many other subjects, among which astronomy, computer science, physics, education and economics are the more obvious ones, but this is by no means an exhaustive list.

By varying the choice of modules, it is also possible to concentrate on pure or applied mathematics including statistics, computer modelling or a number of other fields. There are also four-year degrees that have been developed in collaboration with mathematics staff in Germany, France and Spain. These involve students spending a year abroad. In each of these mathematics/language degrees, the mathematics load is reduced in the first two years so that you can take language modules that will enable you to enjoy living abroad in your third year when you are taught mathematics in the foreign language.

At another university, there are three choices of course to follow (*BSc Mathematics, BSc Mathematics and Technology* and *BSc Mathematics with Biomedical Sciences*). Whichever of these you enrol on, you do not need to make your final choice until the end of the first year. In all courses you are strongly advised to do a one-year industrial placement, which can be a great help in gaining employment after graduation. Although you must initially register on one of the courses, you retain the right to transfer within the mathematics programme at that stage.

Career Opportunities

The completion of a degree course opens the door to a wide range of careers. As well as those open to holders of any non-specialised degree, there are opportunities in areas requiring numerical skills and a capacity for organised and logical thought.

Related Degrees

Mathematical Sciences, Pure Mathematics, Applied Mathematics, Business/Finance Mathematics, Computational Mathematics, Industrial Mathematics, Mathematics with Study Abroad, Actuarial Science/Studies, Statistics, Economics/Mathematics and Statistics, Foundation Mathematics, Mathematical Engineering, Mathematics and Theoretical Physics, Mathematics/Statistics and Computing, Operational Research

Suggested Reading

Archimedes' Revenge: The Joys and Perils of Mathematics
- Paul Hoffman, Ballantine Books, 1997

Mathematics: A Very Short Introduction
- Timothy Gowers, Oxford, 2002

What Is Mathematics?: An Elementary Approach to Ideas and Methods
- R. Courant and H. Robbins, OUP, 1996

From Here to Infinity
- Ian Stewart, Oxford, 1996

Further Information

Enriching Mathematics
http://nrich.maths.org

London Mathematical Society
www.lms.ac.uk

Royal Statistical Society
www.rss.org.uk

Operational Research Society
www.orsoc.org.uk

Actuarial Profession
www.actuaries.org.uk

Institute of Mathematics and its Applications
www.ima.org.uk

Irish Statistical Association
www.maths.may.ie/lsa

Irish Mathematical Society
www.maths.tcd.ie/pub/ims

Mechanical Engineering

Original article by Dr Ian Pillinger, School of Manufacturing and Mechanical Engineering, University of Birmingham

Introduction

To study Mechanical Engineering at University, you will normally be expected to obtain high grades at A level/Higher/IB or equivalent in Mathematics, Physics and one other subject. If you have good grades, but have not studied both Mathematics and Physics, you may still be able study Mechanical Engineering by undertaking a preliminary Foundation Year. This year will be designed to bring you up to the required level in these subjects and so you would need to have good GCSE/SCE Standard Grade or equivalent passes in Mathematics and Physics.

Degree Courses

Accredited University degree programmes in Mechanical Engineering are now generally of four years' duration, at the end of which you obtain a Master of Engineering (MEng) degree. During the first two years, you study the fundamental subjects of Mechanics of Solids (how things deform under load), Statics and Dynamics of Structures (the behaviour of objects under balancing forces and when they are moving), Thermodynamics (the interaction between heat and movement) and Fluid Mechanics (the movement of gases and liquids in machinery).

Underpinning all these subjects will be Mathematics, and all the other subjects are drawn together by learning about design. You may take various other subjects that Mechanical Engineers need to know about, such as Electrical and Electronic Theory, Metrology, Computing and Information Technology and Manufacturing Processes. Some of the time you will be attending lectures, but you will also be carrying out laboratory work and computer exercises, and undertaking personal study researching a topic in the library. There will also be the opportunity to develop professional skills like report writing, making presentations, working through various mini-projects and assignments.

After your first two years, you may choose to take a year out to work in industry in order to gain some of the experience you need to become a Chartered Engineer. During the final years of your degree programme the core subjects you studied during your first two years are continued at a more advanced level, and in addition you will be able to choose from a range of specialised topics such as Automotive Engineering, Control of Machinery, Mechatronics (the integration of electrical and mechanical behaviour) and Thermal Power Systems. An important element of the final part of your degree studies will be the undertaking of a major project. The subject of this may well be related to the research your lecturers are doing, and you could find yourself working alongside a research team. Alternatively, it may be a topic you have brought back from a placement in industry.

There are many variations to this basic outline. For example, several Universities allow you to study a foreign language, materials science or business-related topics in addition to the Mechanical Engineering subjects. In some places; the mid-course year-out is compulsory, in others, it is optional. (Most universities would, however, be happy for you to work for a year in industry before starting your degree programme, and you would be encouraged to find industrial placements during the summer vacation.) Part-time study is also possible, generally by interspersing blocks of time (a term or a year) at university with similar periods in industry.

Career Opportunities

It is difficult to imagine a major industry that does not use the skills of mechanical engineers. Indeed, mechanical engineering usually plays a part in producing almost all the products and services we see around us. Mechanical engineers are likely to be recruited into the aerospace and automotive industries; the armed forces and the Defence Engineering and Science Group; energy utilities, including nuclear; engineering construction companies; engineering consultancies; manufacturing industries; medical engineering; oil and gas industries, including the petro-chemical sector; process industries, including pharmaceuticals, food and cosmetics; the public sector, including the Civil Service, local authorities, hospitals, and educational institutions; research establishments, both academic and commercial; and transport, including roads and railways.

Related Degrees

Automotive Engineering, Aerospace Engineering, Transportation Engineering, Agricultural Engineering, Marine Engineering, Motor Sport Engineering, Mechanical Electronic Systems, Manufacturing Engineering

Suggested Reading

The Engineer's Conscience
- Professor M W Thring, Thring Publishing, 1992

Foundations of Mechanical Engineering
- A. D. Johnson and Keith Sherwin, Taylor & Francis, 1996

Mechatronics Principles and Applications
- Dr Godfrey Onwubolu, Butterworth-Heinemann, 2005

Progression to Engineering and Mathematics 2011 entry
- UCAS, 2010

Further Information

Institution of Mechanical Engineers
www.imeche.org

Engineering Employer's Federation - EEF: The Manufacturers' Organisation
www.eef.org.uk

Engineering Council UK
www.engc.org.uk

Institute of Industrial Engineers Ireland
www.iie.ie

Engineers Ireland
www.engineersireland.ie

Medical Engineering/Technology

Clive Beggs, Professor of Medical Technology, University of Bradford

Introduction

Engineering plays as much a part in modern healthcare systems as pharmaceutical drugs, although few people are aware of it. Every year, millions of radiographs are taken of fractures bones; thousands of artificial hips are installed; and countless lives are saved through medical ventilation, and yet the massive contribution that engineering makes towards the diagnosis of disease and the treatment of patients goes largely unrecognised.

The fact is, however, that engineering in its various guises runs through the health service like writing through a stick of rock and engineering is responsible for many of the medical advances that we now take for granted. Prosthetic hip joints, pacemakers, magnetic resonance imaging (MRI), computed tomography (CT scanning) and image-guided surgery are just a few of the technologies that have revolutionised modern medicine and changed the lives of many for the better.

Advances such as those listed above are all examples of work pioneered by medical engineers, alternatively known as bioengineers or biomedical engineers. Such people combine their engineering expertise with biology to solve medical problems and improve the wellbeing of patients. Although lower in profile than the more traditional disciplines of civil, electrical and mechanical engineering, medical engineering is nonetheless a fast growing discipline, which is increasing in importance as more and more medical procedures rely on advanced technology.

Indeed, the US Department of Labor states that employment in biomedical engineering is expected to grow at a much faster rate than average (in excess of 27 per cent) in the foreseeable future[1], driven by the healthcare needs of an ageing population and increased demand for sophisticated medical equipment and procedures. Given that the healthcare industry is the world's largest sector, it is no surprise that opportunities for medical engineering graduates are huge. Indeed, it is one of the few areas in engineering that is predicted to continue to grow for many years to come.

Which Course?

Compared with civil, mechanical and electrical engineering, medical engineering is a new and emerging discipline - in every way it is a discipline for the 21st century. The UK is a world leader in medical engineering research and a number of universities now offer undergraduate programmes in this discipline. The broad range of activities covered by the subject means that the focus of medical engineering degrees can vary greatly from institution to institution. Some focus on mechanical engineering, while others are more electrical in their approach. Still others focus on materials science and the development of new biomaterials.

The medical engineering degree offered by the University of Bradford, while being mechanically based, has a very strong biological/clinical component, which means that students on this programme study cell biology, genomics and tissue engineering as well as more traditional subjects such as biomechanics, fluid dynamics and rehabilitation engineering. It is therefore wise when choosing a degree programme to look carefully at the course content, to check that it is what you want.

Given that medical engineering is very much a research-led discipline, it is also important to enquire about research activities of the various institutions. Lecturers tend

---

[1] US Department of Labor, Bureau of Labor Statistics. Engineers.
(http://www.bls.gov/oco/ocos027.htm)

to focus their teaching on their research interests - the best lectures are given by enthusiasts, and active researchers are great enthusiasts! Direct links with local hospitals are also important and are essential if the course is to have clinical relevance. Such links are an invaluable resource when it comes to final year projects and may prove useful when seeking employment after graduation.

Career Opportunities

Job prospects for qualified medical engineers are excellent - salaries are above average, with top engineers paid the same as hospital consultants[2]. Opportunities exist in a wide variety of roles. Many are employed in commercial organisations designing and developing medical devices, some specialise in sales and marketing, while others are employed by hospitals where they work with clinicians to provide care for patients.

Others may be employed in research facilities, pioneering the technologies which today might seem unrealistic but tomorrow may be commonplace. However, no matter the specific nature of the role, one factor remains consistent - that medical engineering is interesting, fast-moving and multi-disciplinary. Medical engineers therefore need to be people with advanced knowledge and skills, who have a good appreciation of developments in the clinical and biological fields.

Medical engineers may be employed on a wide variety of projects. For example, not only may they specialise in the development of superior artificial joints, they may also develop advanced surgical procedures, which enable surgeons to carry out hip replacement operations more effectively. Other engineers may specialise in medical imaging, developing better ways to see inside the human body without harming patients. Others may focus on the emerging field of tissue engineering, which involves culturing human cells to grow new body parts. Medical engineers therefore need to be flexible and willing to absorb new ideas. In medical engineering, nothing stays still for very long!

A Final Thought

People working in medical engineering have a great opportunity to influence the lives of many for the better. Hospital doctors can only treat individual patients, but engineers can develop technologies with the potential to save many millions of lives. This can be a great motivator and one tends to find that many medical engineers are extremely dedicated individuals who want their work to benefit mankind.

Suggested Reading

Medical Devices and Systems (Biomedical Engineering Handbook, Third Edition)
- Joseph D. Bronzino, CRC Press, 2006

Medical Physics and Biomedical Engineering (Medical Science)
- B.H. Brown, R.H. Smallwood, D. Hose et al, Taylor and Francis, 1999

Further Information

Institute of Physics and Engineering in Medicine
www.ipem.ac.uk

Association of Clinical Scientists
www.assclinsci.org

Engineers Ireland
www.engineersireland.ie

---

[2] Institute of Physics and Engineering in Medicine.
(http://www.ipem.ac.uk/ipem%5Fpublic/)

Medicinal Chemistry

Original article by James R. Hanson, University of Sussex

Introduction

Medicinal chemistry is the study of the chemistry of compounds that have a beneficial effect on disease states. The aim of the medicinal chemist is to enhance the therapeutic effect of a compound and to diminish unwanted side effects. The medicinal chemist is primarily concerned with the design and synthesis of new therapeutic agents but there must be an interaction with other disciplines such as medicine, biology, biochemistry, pharmacology and pharmacy. A medicinal chemistry course is not an alternative to a pharmacy course, and affords different career opportunities.

Before entering a course on medicinal chemistry, a student will require not only a firm grasp of chemistry, particularly organic chemistry, but also some biology and mathematics. The latter might be replaced by physics.

There are various ways of classifying the drugs that are the topic of medicinal chemistry. Firstly we may consider the chemistry of infectious diseases. Here the object is to design a compound that will target an invading organism without injury to the host. The compound must have an irreversible action on one cell in the presence of another. The development of antibiotics is an example of this. Secondly there is the chemistry of malignant disease in which drugs are designed to injure an aberrant, rapidly proliferating cell in the presence of a normal cell. The third area involves the chemistry of non-infectious diseases in which the compound has a selective action on one type of cell or organ within the host to modify its action. This class may be subdivided into substances which target the central or peripheral nervous system. Another sub-division includes compounds which affect the circulatory system, for example by dilation of blood vessels. A further sub-division involves agents which have a metabolic or endocrine function affecting the hormone balance within the body. Finally there are those agents which target the immune system.

Degree Courses

How are these reflected in a course? Firstly the medicinal chemist requires a knowledge of the organic chemistry of functional groups, stereochemistry, reaction mechanisms and synthesis. The physicochemical aspects of drug design involve a knowledge of bonding, of reaction kinetics and the nature of solutions whilst spectroscopy may shed light on structure. Areas of inorganic chemistry are involved in biological oxidative mechanisms, in the ionic balance in the body. A number of inorganic compounds are drugs in their own right. The first two years of a course must provide that breadth of knowledge without which a medicinal chemist can neither make compounds nor understand how they work In this period, some supporting biology teaching is provided. A good chemical base is constructed and the specialism follows with courses on medicinal targets in the cell, cell signalling and transduction processes, hormone and receptor targets including neurotransmission, antibiotics and antiviral agents, cancer chemotherapy, drug metabolism and the physicochemical aspects of drug design and molecular modelling. A useful aspect giving students an impression of the cutting edge of drug design would involve lectures from the pharmaceutical industry. A research project is an important feature of a medicinal chemistry course, giving the student the chance to make compounds for biological testing. Sometimes, a student spends a sandwich year in industry.

Career Opportunities

The pharmaceutical industry is one of the more buoyant parts of the chemical industry. Medicinal chemists are employed not just in the research laboratory: there are different and obviously challenging opportunities in the development laboratory, drug formulation and in analytical chemistry. Outside the laboratory, there are opportunities for medicinal chemists in drug registration, patent work, information retrieval, and in medical sales and marketing.

Related Degrees

Biological and Medicinal Chemistry, Medicinal Biochemistry, Chemistry, Life Systems and Pharmaceuticals

Suggested Reading

Introduction to Medicinal Chemistry
- Graham L Patrick, OUP, 2009

Fundamentals of Medicinal Chemistry
- Gareth Thomas, Wiley, 2003

Instant Notes in Medicinal Chemistry
- Graham L. Patrick, Springer-Verlag Telos, 2008

Medicinal Chemistry: a Molecular and Biochemical Approach
- Thomas Nogrady et al, OUP, 2005

Further Information

Medicinal Chemistry Research Group
www.staff.livjm.ac.uk/pacfisma

Royal Society of Chemistry
www.rsc.org

Institute of Chemistry of Ireland
www.chemistryireland.org

Medicine

Original article by Dr David Hughes, formerly Senior Lecturer in Medicine, London Hospital Medical College (now part of Queen Mary, University of London)
Additional material supplied by the British Medical Association

Introduction

Learning to be a doctor is one of the longest and most expensive courses of study for any degree (taking 5-6 years), so it is essential that those thinking of medicine as a career are absolutely sure this is what they want to do with their working lives, before taking the first step and applying to enter a medical school. These notes are merely a preliminary guide, and more detailed information can be obtained from the medical schools. Remember, the essential personal qualities for a doctor are compassion, resourcefulness, boundless energy and perseverance.

Degree Courses

There are generally three approaches to the training provided at medical school: the traditional pre-clinical and clinical course, an integrated course or the newer courses specialising in multi- or inter-professional learning. (See Medicine Dissected, page xxii)

For the traditional courses, students begin their training with two years of 'pre-clinical' work, involving study of the basic medical sciences. This is followed by the 'clinical' course, of approximately three years, during which they work in hospital wards under the supervision of consultants. Throughout the final three years they also attend lectures on all aspects of medical practice. Examples of universities who offer a traditional course include Oxford and Cambridge.

Integrated courses, which the majority of medical schools have now implemented, integrate what is usually learnt at the pre-clinical and clinical stages to provide a seamless course. Teaching methods can include problem-based learning and practical clinical skills. Examples of such universities are Liverpool and Imperial College.

Thirdly, there are now medical schools basing their teaching on or specialising in multi- or inter-professional learning, such as Peninsula and Southampton.

Each course is different and uses different methods of teaching, so it is important that you think carefully about the kind of course that would suit you. You can obtain a copy of the syllabus from each medical school.

Apart from the degree in medicine, most schools offer students the opportunity to take an extra year (sometimes two) in the middle of the medical degree to study a subject of interest, which will lead to an 'intercalated' BSc (Hons) or equivalent. At some schools this opportunity is only available to high achievers, whereas at other schools it is built into the curriculum. For full details on intercalated degrees, you should contact the medical schools directly.

In addition to exceptionally demanding academic entry standards, most schools have adopted the UK Clinical Aptitude Test (UKCAT) to help them select the best candidates. A much smaller group uses the Bio Medical Admissions Test (BMAT). Competition for places to read medicine is very intense. You would need to show that you have a genuine interest in the subject and if possible demonstrate relevant paid or voluntary work experience.

Career Opportunities

Newly qualified graduates from medical school receive provisional registration from the General Medical Council (GMC) and undertake foundation year 1 (F1), which is designed to build on the knowledge and skills gained during undergraduate training. On successful completion of F1, you receive full registration with the GMC and can continue to the second year of foundation training.

Foundation year 2 (F2) training continues the general training in medicine and involves a range of different specialties, which could include general practice. By the end of foundation training, you must demonstrate that you are competent in areas such as managing acutely ill patients, team working and communication skills, to continue training in your chosen specialist area or in general practice.

On successful completion of foundation training, doctors continue training in either a specialist area of medicine or in general practice. The area of medicine you choose will determine the length of training required before you can become a senior doctor. In general practice, the training is of three years' duration; while in general surgery, for example, the training is eight years in duration.

During postgraduate medical training, doctors learn and practise increasingly advanced areas of knowledge and skills in their chosen specialty or general practice in order for them to be able to undertake senior doctor roles once training is completed. Postgraduate training is overseen by the Postgraduate Medical Education and Training Board.

On successful completion of postgraduate training, doctors gain entry to either the GMC specialist register or general practitioner register and are able to apply for a senior post as a consultant or a GP principal. You should note that all doctors are expected to demonstrate continually their fitness to practise medicine, and so learning continues throughout your career as a doctor.

Related Degrees

Complementary Medicine Practice, Medicine (first year entry)

Suggested Reading

Becoming a Doctor: is Medicine really the career for you?
- Matt Green and Tom Nolan, Developmedica/Apply2Medicine, 2008

Learning Medicine
- Peter Richards et al, Cambridge University Press, 2007

The Essential Guide to Becoming a Doctor
- Adrian Blundell et al, Wiley-Blackwell, 2010

Becoming a Doctor
- downloadable from the BMA website below

Medical School Survival Guide
- Ashley McKimm, Trauma Publishing, 2004

Further Information

British Medical Association
www.bma.org.uk

Association for the Study of Medical Education
www.asme.org.uk

Irish Medical Organisation
www.imo.ie

Royal College of Physicians of Ireland
www.rcpi.ie

Biomedical Admissions Test
www.bmat.org.uk

UK Clinical Aptitude Test
www.ukcat.ac.uk

Microbiology

Original article by Professor F. G. Priest, Heriot-Watt University

Introduction

Microbiology concerns the study of micro-organisms (bacteria, mycelial fungi, yeast and viruses), which affect man in a number of ways, both beneficial and detrimental. Their metabolic activities are responsible for essential (or undesirable) processes which occur in the environment, or can be exploited for the production of compounds (including chemicals, hormones, antibiotics and enzymes) which are of use in the modern world. Micro-organisms are also the causative agents of disease in humans, animals and plants. The combined biochemical and genetic/molecular biological approaches to studying the functions of micro-organisms have led to an understanding of metabolic and disease mechanisms, with the real prospect of effective exploitation and control of microbial activities on a previously unimagined scale.

Degree Courses

Microbiology is a very broad discipline, incorporating aspects of biochemistry, molecular and cell biology, genetics and taxonomy (classification), and a microbiologist may specialise in areas such as food, industrial or clinical microbiology. Training is given in scientific methods and procedures to enable graduates to pursue careers in industry, research laboratories, or to continue with postgraduate training in microbiology or a related discipline. The learning experience involves use of tutorials, seminars, assignments, laboratory work, lectures, fieldwork, industrial visits, and literature and research projects. The particular flavour of a course will depend on the nature of the institution; for example, in a medical school environment there is likely to be more emphasis on clinical aspects of the subject.

At Heriot-Watt University, the Biological Sciences (Microbiology) course provides a thorough general training in the physiology, ecology and biotechnological applications of micro-organisms. It focuses particularly on microbes as producers, as spoilage agents of food, as components of the environment, and as agents of disease, with emphasis on new and emerging diseases. The course aims to provide knowledge and understanding of the microbiological sciences, and sufficient training in scientific methods and procedures to advance to a career in relevant industries, postgraduate training or other spheres of research.

The first and second years of the four-year Honours degree are the same as Biological Sciences. In the third year, the Microbiology course introduces detailed analysis of microbial systems, in particular: Microbiological Aspects of Food and Food Safety; Microbial Pathology and Infectious Diseases; and Molecular Biology, including Genetic Engineering.

Fourth Year students are introduced to advanced topics in microbiology through a choice of modules dealing with: Microbial Interactions with the Human Body During Disease; New and Emerging Diseases; Microbial Growth in the Environment and Molecular Biology; and Genomics. A laboratory-based research project introduces practical techniques at an advanced level.

Other specialisms are available elsewhere.

Career Opportunities

Many graduates enter industries concerned with drugs and agricultural chemicals, biotechnology, food processing, brewing, pest control, sewage and water. Hospitals use graduates in research and analytical diagnostic work. Work in government and private institutions can involve cancer research, entomology, timber technology, plant pathology and conservation. Others take higher degrees and can go on to university teaching. Many also enter the general graduate market for administrative, financial and managerial careers.

Related Degrees

Medical Microbiology, Virology, Environmental Microbiology, Biotechnology

Suggested Reading

Microbes and Man
- John Postgate, Cambridge University Press, 2008

Power Unseen: how microbes rule the world
- Bernard Dixon, PFD, 2008

Brock Biology of Microorganisms
- Michael Madigan, John Martinko, Paul Dunlap, David Clark and Thomas Brock, Pearson Education, 2008

Practical Skills in Biomolecular Sciences
- Rob Reed, Jonathan Weyers, Allan Jones, David Holmes, Benjamin Cummings, 2007

Further Information

Society for General Microbiology
www.sgm.ac.uk

Society for Applied Microbiology
www.sfam.org.uk

Federation of European Microbiological Societies
www.fems-microbiology.org

Microbiology Jobs Ireland
http://microbiology.ie

Modern Languages

Original article by Professor (Emeritus) Dennis Ager, Aston University

Introduction

Despite the title, no degree courses are limited to the study of a foreign language. They involve the student in learning one or more languages but also in covering a programme of literary studies or studies of linguistics, history, politics or social and economic structure of the relevant country. The reason for this is that learning a language at an advanced level is a matter also of learning to see the world the way foreigners see it, from within their own cultural and historical traditions. There is no point in being a graduate in Arabic if you don't understand Islam; and a graduate in German who has never heard of Goethe or Hitler is literally not able to understand what Germans are talking about. Ideally, of course, a graduate in languages would be an expert in the history of the relevant country; in its present-day political, social and economic problems and in its relations with other countries; in its cultural, literary, intellectual and artistic achievements; and be able to assess and compare these with a similar awareness of his own country. In practice, within a three- or four-year degree course, some selection has to be made and a lot of ground left to the initiative of the individual student.

It is possible to start a language course from scratch at most universities and colleges, although rarely in French or German. Success in language learning comes easily to some, who have an ear for the sound patterns of foreign tongues and are able to reproduce particular sounds accurately and to perceive and use the quirks of a foreign grammar very quickly. For those who are less fortunate, some effort is involved but, since the French and the Japanese are also human beings, this effort is almost certain to be crowned with success. There are few people who are unable to achieve something approaching perfection in the linguistic skills in a foreign language; the recipe is a mixture of high motivation, persistence, intelligence and, above all, practice. Modern learning aids can speed up the process, as can carefully designed teaching sequences; but there is no substitute for understanding that a language is a means of communication between human beings, and that the spoken language is more important than the written. In a degree course, however, one is often dealing with more written material than spoken; and the necessity for precision and often finicky accuracy which is a characteristic of some languages in their written form imposes a discipline which is not necessarily characteristic of the spoken language. It is possible, for example, to make oneself understood in general outline in speaking German without too much attention to the difference between 'n' and 'm' at the end of adjectives; in the written form, however, confusion of this sort is rightly seen as an indication of ignorance.

Degree Courses

At degree level, mastery of the skills of speaking, writing, reading and listening to the foreign language itself is often accompanied by practice in such skills as translating and interpreting. Departments vary in the importance they accord to the language skills: some delegate all the learning work to a language centre; others carry out all the work in the foreign language. Many courses now last for four years, with an integrated year abroad - an essential experience for the linguist.

The language may be studied in order to understand its literature. It is usual to provide general survey courses, showing the nature of the literary production of the relevant country over, say, the last 400 years, and in addition to ask students to examine an author, or sometimes even one noteworthy book, in considerable depth. Departments with literary interests may concentrate on one aspect, theme or period.

Alternatively, the 'content' may be oriented towards the foreign society - its institutions, politics, economy and international relations. There is usually some history; linguistics may be important. Students often research and write a mini-thesis in the last year.

Universities differ in orientation and course content: there are also differences of course structure to be aware of. You can study one language or two. It is often possible to study one language plus another subject e.g. French plus civil engineering, German plus architecture. A popular combination is a language plus business studies or economics. European Studies degrees are popular. Finally, languages often find a place within degrees in other subjects: historians find a knowledge of one or more invaluable, but their requirement is for reading ability; engineers need languages but their prime need is for enough to get the gist of specialist reports plus enough spoken foreign language to understand the main point of a conversation.

Career Opportunities

Modern languages currently enjoy one of the highest employment rates of all degree programmes. Language skills are in scarce supply and can be used in almost any job. Studying a language clearly makes you a communicator, both orally and in writing. Additional skills gained through a language degree include the ability to: gather information, assess and interpret it; lead and participate in discussions and groups; organise workload and work to deadlines; develop opinions and propose ideas; read pages of text and pick out the essential points. On top of this, a year spent abroad during your degree should give you insight into another culture, help you adapt to new and changing surroundings and give you the chance to work both in a team and independently. These skills have value in a job market which is becoming increasingly global and will be appreciated by employers, whatever career you go into.

Related Degrees

French, German, Italian, Spanish, Dutch, Modern Greek, Russian, Scandinavian Languages, Slavonic and Eastern European Languages, Oriental Studies, Chinese, Japanese, Asian Languages, African, Arabic, Persian, Turkish, Hebrew, Arabic/Middle Eastern/Islamic Studies, Latin American Studies

Suggested Reading

We suggest that, in preparation for a course in modern languages, you should visit a country in which your preferred language is spoken and immerse yourself in its culture and day-to-day life. You should also read novels, poetry, plays, newspapers and journals, listen to the radio and watch television, films, plays and so on.

Language and Power in the Modern World
- Mary Talbot, Karen Atkinson and David Atkinson, Edinburgh University Press, 2003

Languages and Careers Pack
- order via CILT website below

The Linguist
- magazine published six times a year by the Chartered Institute of Linguists. Subscribe via the website below

Further Information

Languages Work
www.languageswork.org.uk

CILT - National Centre for Languages
www.cilt.org.uk

Institute of Translation and Interpreting
www.iti.org.uk

Chartered Institute of Linguists
www.iol.org.uk

Irish Translators' and Interpreters' Association
www.translatorsassociation.ie

Music

Original article by Dr Christopher Mark, Department of Music, University of Surrey

Introduction

Music has undergone a considerable amount of change within the last 10 years or so, reflecting the diverse forms of contemporary music making and the pluralism of post-modern thinking about music and its place in society.

Whereas performance once seemed to be regarded as beneath the dignity of people engaged in lofty musical thought, such is the importance now given to it in university departments that many who intend to become professional performers choose a university rather than a music-college education. The range of subjects that can be studied is wider than ever, too. Western art music from ancient times to the present day still forms the backbone of the historical and analytical studies in most music degree courses, but an increasing number of departments offer units or modules in popular and non-western music. Tuition in composition, which has always been central to the university curriculum, is usually available (several of the country's finest composers hold senior positions in university departments), and performance of student compositions is strongly encouraged. Composition is one area in which computer-based technology has had a big impact, and many departments possess fine electronic-music studios.

Music can be studied either as a single-honours subject or, in some universities, in conjunction with another subject such as English or a European language. Combinations with science subjects are also possible.

Along with A levels or Higher Grades/equivalent, evidence of instrumental or vocal proficiency (Grade 7 or 8 in Associated Board exams) is required. Some departments call candidates to a selection interview, during which they may be auditioned and tested on general musical knowledge and harmony.

Degree Courses

The *first* year of courses is usually taught as a foundation year, consisting of overview history courses covering most of the Western art-music repertoire (sometimes with particular attention being paid to twentieth-century music), aural training, harmony and counterpoint, analysis, performance (individual and ensemble), and keyboard harmony. The subsequent years normally allow specialisation - typically in performance, composition, or musicology - with a good deal of choice of units/modules in historical, aesthetic, or analytical subjects. Teaching modes differ according to the level and the subject, but include lectures, seminars led by students, and one-to-one tutorials and instrumental lessons. Many departments have resident professional musicians who, in addition to performing and teaching individuals, coach instrumental ensembles. Types of assessment vary from department to department and from module to module, but you can expect a mixture of course work (ranging from short essays and harmony and counterpoint exercises to substantial projects) and examinations.

Opportunities for performance abound: orchestras, chamber orchestras, wind and jazz bands, choral societies, and chamber choirs are run either by departments or student societies. Some of these ensembles are run by student officers, allowing those interested in a career in arts administration to gain useful experience, and some are conducted by (usually more senior) students. But only part of the performing activity of a department is 'official': ad hoc ensembles of various sizes are the lifeblood of many lunchtime concert programmes.

It is important to research each prospectus with great care to ensure your interests and skills will flourish - and in addition to attend open days whenever possible.

Career Opportunities

Music related posts include music retailing, broadcasting, publishing, musical journalism, librarianship, information services and cathedral organist. Music graduates tend to show considerable resourcefulness in finding jobs in administration, finance, commerce, industry and government.

Competition for careers in music performance can be fierce and the pay is generally below that of other jobs requiring similar levels of skill, training and expertise. To succeed, you must have more than talent alone; you must also have absolute dedication and determination. To get work, you have to be known and this means taking every opportunity - concerts, auditions, awards, bursaries and competitions - to show that you are worth engaging. Even after becoming established, you would find that earning a living as a performer - out of recordings, broadcasts and concerts - is hard work. Many performers combine a performing career with teaching or other work in the community, perhaps as a music therapist. Job prospects for classroom teachers are good, since the demand for music teachers exceeds the supply.

Related Degrees

Music Technology, Music (Performing Arts), Music Production, Creative Music Technology, Electronic Engineering and Music, Popular Music, Jazz Studies, Electronic Music, Music Theatre, Musicianship (Band), Musicology, Music and Sound Recording

Suggested Reading

How Musical is Man?
- John Blacking, Faber, 1976

Performing Rites: Evaluating Popular Music
- Simon Frith, Oxford, 1998

Who needs Classical Music?: Cultural Choice and Musical Values
- Julian Johnson, OUP USA, 2002

All You Need to Know about the Music Business
- Donald S Passman, Penguin, 2008 (new edition due Jan 2011)

New Penguin Dictionary of Music
- Paul Griffiths, Penguin, 2006

Music: A Very Short Introduction
- Nicholas Cook, Oxford, 2000

Careers with Music
- downloadable from the Incorporated Society of Musicians website below

How to Make It in the Music Business
- Sian Pattenden, Virgin Books, 2007

Further Information

Incorporated Society of Musicians
www.ism.org

Musicians' Union
www.musiciansunion.org.uk

Conservatoires UK Admissions Service
www.cukas.ac.uk

Royal Irish Academy of Music
www.riam.ie

Neuroscience

Original article by Dr S Barasi, School of Biosciences, Cardiff University

Introduction

The human brain contains about 10^{12} neurones making multiple connections. Our understanding of how this extraordinarily complex arrangement of neurones functions is still rudimentary. Neuroscience is the study of how the nervous system responds to incoming sensory information and organises and executes its response. Study of the human nervous system is further complicated by the need to understand mood, memory and the ageing process, together with the response of the system to infection and accidental damage. Interest in neuroscience has expanded dramatically in the last two decades, and increases in our understanding of how the brain functions in health and disease have been translated into major advances in the treatment of many diseases of the nervous system.

Degree Courses

The discipline of neuroscience includes contributions from a wide range of traditional disciplines such as anatomy, biochemistry, physiology and psychology. Neuroscience courses will vary considerably in emphasis and content, so it is vital to study course contents and teaching/laboratory systems in their prospectuses and ideally via open day visits. Cardiff, for example, offers both a three- and a four-year course. The longer course offers students the opportunity to spend a year in a research setting, working on a neuroscience-based project. This professional training year may be based either in the UK or abroad.

In your first year at Cardiff, you would follow the School's common first year Biomedical Science programme. This provides you with a broad scientific base centred on biochemistry, biomolecular science and human biology that will give you a firm foundation for your subsequent years of study. The common first year also has the advantage of giving you flexibility of degree choice. At the end of the first year, you have a free choice of continuing with your original degree choice or changing to one of the other programmes served by the common first year.

In your second year, you take modules such as membrane biophysics, anatomy of the human brain, pharmacology, cellular signalling and neuro-endocrinology. In the final year, you take modules including molecular biology in neuroscience, neuronal development and plasticity and transmission and neural network theory. You would also study a module containing four optional topics chosen from a range of at least 15 taught by research leaders.

Students taking the four year sandwich programme spend their third year on placement in a research institute, hospital, or in the pharmaceutical industry, gaining first-hand experience of neuroscience research. Cardiff has links with partner institutions in the UK, EU and USA.

Career Opportunities

Graduates frequently continue to take higher degrees (PhD) with a view to becoming professional scientists. Others enter the pharmaceutical, pharmacological, industry, the NHS, medical research, teaching or enter the general graduate field for careers in administration, finance, managerial, etc.

Related Degrees

Cellular Pathology, Neuroscience with Study in Industry, Cognitive Science, Neuroscience with Psychology

Suggested Reading

Neuroscience - science of the brain: an introduction for young students
- Richard Morris and Marienne Fillenz, BNA, 2003, downloadable from the BNA website below. Available in English, Mandarin and Spanish

The Brain: A Very Short Introduction
- Michael O'Shea, OUP Oxford, 2005

Who wants to be a scientist? Choosing science as a career
- Nancy Rothwell, CUP, 2002

Further Information

British Neuroscience Association
www.bna.org.uk

Trinity College Institute of Neuroscience
www.tcd.ie/Neuroscience

Nursing

Original article by Ken Reynolds, specialist writer on careers and higher education

Introduction

Nurses work in a demanding profession, combining the art of caring with the science of health attainment, maintenance and restoration. To work as a nurse in the UK National Health Service (NHS), you must hold a degree or diploma in nursing (a 'pre-registration programme'), leading to registration with the Nursing and Midwifery Council (NMC). Nursing attracts people from all walks of life and so groups of student nurses are made up of a mixture of ages, sexes and cultures.

Degree and Diploma Courses

It is important to note that diploma courses will be phased out between September 2011 and early 2013, and new entrants to the nursing profession from September 2013 will have to take a degree. Some universities may only offer the new degree programme from September 2011.

The programmes are normally three years in length and are offered in four branches - adult, children (paediatric), learning disability and mental health. You normally need to decide before applying which of the four branches you wish to train for, although some HEIs offer you the flexibility to select your branch after having started the course. You should note that some degree programmes last four years, while there are accelerated programmes for graduates who already hold a health related degree. You are therefore strongly recommended to contact the HEI(s) that you are considering before making your application.

You would gain experience in a variety of care settings, including hospitals, nursing homes and the community.

The three-year course is divided into two distinct parts:

- the first year, the "Common Foundation Programme" or CFP, is undertaken by all students, regardless of branch choice. It includes core issues and topics, together with experience of a wide variety of care environments. The year focuses upon the concept of health through study of the biological and social sciences, professional studies and communication skills. Placements are based in both hospital and community settings. Depending on the range of courses offered by your chosen HEI, you may share a common foundation programme with, say, medical, physiotherapy, radiography and biomedical science students

- the second part, the branch programme, concentrates on specific branch subjects and practice placements. You will develop skills in, knowledge about and understanding of your chosen branch of nursing. If, for example, you choose to go into mental health nursing, the placements will be mainly concentrated in that environment, and will focus on patients with mental health problems. However, certain aspects of training will be common to all branches

Career Opportunities

Once you have successfully completed your pre-registration programme and registered with the NMC, you can apply for nursing posts.

In the adult branch of nursing, it is possible to work in hospitals or in the community - in patients' homes, attached to a health centre or in nursing homes. Once qualified, many nurses take extra courses to specialise in areas such as cancer care, women's health, accident and emergency, critical care, practice nursing, health visiting or school nursing.

In the children's branch of nursing, you would work with 0 to 18 year-olds in a variety of settings, from specialist baby care units to adolescent services. Children react to illness in a very different way from adults, which is why they need to be cared for and supported by specially trained nurses who understand their particular needs. Children's nurses also support, advise and educate parents and other close relatives. Once qualified, it is possible to specialise in hospital and community settings in areas such as burns and plastics, intensive care, child protection and cancer care.

In the learning disability branch, you would help your patients to live independent and fulfilling lives. This may involve working with people in supported accommodation - typically three to four people with learning disabilities live together in flats or houses with 24-hour support. Some nurses work with individuals who require more intensive support - in hospitals, for example, or in specialist secure units for offenders with learning disabilities. Others specialise in areas such as epilepsy management or working with people with sensory impairment.

Mental health nurses work with GPs, psychiatrists, social workers and others to co-ordinate the care of people suffering from mental illness. The vast majority of people with mental health problems live in the community. Nurses plan and deliver care for people living in their own home, in small residential units or specialist hospital services. Some are based in health centres. It is possible to develop expertise in areas such as rehabilitation, child and adolescent mental health, substance misuse and working with offenders.

Healthcare is constantly developing, the technology is improving, and the needs of the population are changing. Once qualified in any branch, you must keep yourself up to date with healthcare issues and practice. This will be required by the NMC and encouraged by your employer.

Related Degrees

Midwifery education is available at degree level. You will learn the theory and practical skills required to care for pregnant women, delivering babies, educating and supporting parents. The social, political and cultural issues affecting maternity care are also covered.

Suggested Reading

The Student Nurse Handbook: A Survival Guide
- Bethann Siviter and Denise Stevens, Bailliere Tindall, 2004

Careers Uncovered: Nursing and Midwifery
- Laurel Alexander, Trotman, 2010

Nursing Practice: Hospital and Home -- The Adult
- Margaret Alexander et al, Churchill Livingstone, 2006

Further Information

NHS Careers
www.nhscareers.nhs.uk

Nursing and Midwifery Council
www.nmc-uk.org

Royal College of Nursing
www.rcn.org.uk

Nursing Careers Centre, Ireland
www.nursingcareers.ie

Occupational Health and Safety

Original article by Dr Adrian Richardson, Faculty of Health and Environment, Leeds Metropolitan University

Introduction

Occupational health and safety is a subject rarely out of the news and there is great demand in industry, commerce and the public sector for individuals to work as health and safety advisers and managers. Courses at degree level are still rare at present but the number is growing. Look out for course providers enjoying strong relationships with employers and offering accreditation by the Institution of Occupational Safety and Health. These factors normally combine to mean that graduates are extremely successful at obtaining relevant employment.

Degree Courses

Here are examples of two current degree courses. At level one (the first year) in our first example - Safety, Health and Environmental Management - you would take core modules as follows: environmental health studies; law and constitution; investigating health; environmental sciences; the microbial world; introduction to health and health promotion; data analysis.

You would follow at level two with: health and safety legislation; research strategies; environmental protection; toxicology and health surveillance; enforcement strategies; safety technology; organisational and safety management. You can leave after successfully completing this level, in which case you will be awarded a diploma giving eligibility for Membership of the Institution of Occupational Safety & Health (MIOSH) after a period of practice.

To complete the degree, you would take these core modules in your final year: project; health economics and resource management; health promotion; global issues in health; professional and interdisciplinary intervention: health and safety, pollution and professional practice.

Our second example - Occupational Health, Safety and Environmental Management - follows a similar pattern, with the option to leave at the end of the second year with a Foundation Degree.

At level one, your studies include health and safety law, microbiology, information technology, statistics and communication, physics, human physiology, hazardous agents, health and safety management, chemistry and metallurgy/materials.

Level two takes you on to the areas of risk management, construction safety, fire safety, occupational hygiene/health organisations, psychology at work, ergonomics and transport and storage.

Progression to the honours degree at level three enables you to study the topics from level two in more detail and gives you the opportunity to research a topic of your choice.

Career Opportunities

Most graduates enter health-related careers. Recent graduates have obtained jobs in health education and health promotion, health-related research, health services administration, management and counselling. Most large commercial and public organisations and many consultancy companies employ professional practitioners in health and safety. Other opportunities are as inspectors with the Health and Safety Executive or local authorities.

Related Degrees

Environmental Health, Human Resource Management, Consumer and Trading Standards

Suggested Reading

Principles of Health and Safety at Work
- Allan St John Holt, IOSH Services, 2009

Essentials of Health and Safety at Work
- HSE, 2006

Health and Safety in Brief
- John Ridley, Butterworth-Heinemann, 2008

Further Information

British Safety Council
www.britsafe.org

Institution of Occupational Safety and Health
www.iosh.co.uk

Health and Safety Executive
www.hse.gov.uk

Safety and Health Practitioner
www.shponline.co.uk

Health and Safety Authority, Ireland
www.hsa.ie

Occupational Therapy

Original article adapted, with permission, from material supplied by the College of Occupational Therapists

Introduction

Think of the tasks that you do every day, from getting up in the morning, getting washed and dressed and preparing and eating a meal. How, when and where you do these things are unique to you. Think about your likes and dislikes, choosing and wearing your favourite clothes, preparing and eating your favourite meal and going out with friends. Think about how you would feel if you were no longer able to perform everyday activities for yourself. An occupational therapist would look at your lifestyle and help you to live as independently as possible.

As an occupational therapist, you would use your knowledge and skills with people of all ages - from small children to the very elderly - who, for many reasons, are unable to continue with their normal lives and routines. They may have physical or psychological problems. Even people whose difficulties are mostly physical may lack confidence and motivation or they may be depressed by their illness or injury. Occupational therapy covers an extremely wide range of work and career options, and therefore aims to attract a broad cross-section of applicants. The profession is recruiting a larger proportion of men and is currently building a workforce that better reflects Britain's wide cultural diversity.

Degree Courses

You can take a BSc (Hons) in occupational therapy with the following options:

-    3 years full-time (four years in Scotland)
-    2 years accelerated (if you already have a first degree)
-    4 years in-service or part-time for those who have the support of their employer in further training. For part-time programmes applicants do not need to be employed in health or social care

The accelerated postgraduate programmes are for students who already hold a degree, usually in a related field, and have some experience of working in health or social care settings.

The programmes combine both practical and academic study. Academic components include biological sciences (anatomy and physiology), behavioural sciences (psychology and sociology), occupational therapy knowledge and skills, creative and management skills, therapeutic interventions, environmental adaptations and research.

A minimum of 1,000 hours (approximately one third of the course) is spent on practice placements - gaining experience in the main areas of occupational therapy, usually in physical rehabilitation, learning disabilities, mental health or social care and increasingly in new and emerging areas. Students learn how to assess and treat people, normally under the guidance of an occupational therapist, and treat a small caseload of clients under supervision.

All programmes are approved by the Health Professions Council (HPC - the statutory regulatory body for occupational therapists) to meet their minimum standards for education, but most training providers also choose to be accredited by the College of Occupational Therapists, meeting its higher standards. Accreditation by the College brings with it automatic approval by the World Federation of Occupational Therapists You are strongly advised to check with your chosen university whether its occupational therapy programme is accredited by the College.

All the programmes are pre-registration, which means that upon successful completion of the programme, you will be able to apply to the HPC as a registrant to practise as an occupational therapist in the UK.

Career Opportunities

Traditionally, the majority of occupational therapists work in the National Health Service (NHS). Increasingly, however, qualified occupational therapists have found opportunities in other work settings, and this trend seems likely to continue. As a qualified occupational therapist, you can consider working in different job roles, as a practitioner, researcher, manager, lecturer or consultant. You can choose to work in different fields, such as social care, mental health, education, learning disabilities or physical rehabilitation. There are job opportunities in a number of settings including: charities and voluntary agencies; commercial and industrial organisations; disabled living centres; equipment companies; government agencies; housing departments; local community services; NHS and private hospitals; private practice; schools, colleges and universities; social services and social work departments; wheelchair services; hostels for the homeless; and residential care homes.

You also have a wide choice of practice specialisms to choose from, such as eating disorders, hand therapy and substance misuse. You may wish to specialise in working with children, adults or older people. You can also decide whether you want to work for someone else or for yourself, whether you want to work in the community, be based in a hospital, or work in a university educating future occupational therapists.

Related Degrees

Rehabilitation Studies

Suggested Reading

Occupational therapy: new perspectives
- J Creek Ed, WileyBlackwell, 1998

Theoretical basis of occupational therapy
- M A McColl et al, Slack, 2002

A Journey from Prescription to Self Health: a history of occupational therapy in the United Kingdom during the 20th century and a source book of archival material
- Ann Wilcock, COT, 2002

Occupational Therapy Careers Handbook 2011/12
- downloadable from the COT website below

Further Information

British Association of Occupational Therapists/College of Occupational Therapists
www.cot.co.uk

National Health Service Careers
www.nhscareers.nhs.uk

Health Professions Council
www.hpc-uk.org

Association of Occupational Therapists of Ireland
www.aoti.ie

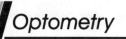

Optometry

Original article by Mark Dunne, Aston University

Introduction

Optometrists are primary health care specialists, trained to examine the eyes to detect defects in vision, signs of injury, ocular diseases or abnormality and problems with general health. A detailed examination of the eye can reveal conditions such as high blood pressure or diabetes. Optometrists make a diagnosis, offer advice and, when necessary, prescribe, fit and supply contact lenses or glasses. Referrals for specialist advice may be required, patients may require a corrective lens or no further treatment.

Degree Courses

To become an optometrist you will need to obtain a degree from one of the eight UK universities that run the course; Anglia Ruskin, Aston, Bradford, Cardiff, City, Glasgow Caledonian, Manchester and Ulster. Entry to these courses requires good A levels, higher grades or equivalent, of which at least two are in the sciences. One-year foundation courses are available for those lacking a science background. There is also one course in the Republic of Ireland, at the Dublin Institute of Technology.

Optometry courses are typically three years full time (four at Glasgow Caledonian), after which you are awarded a BSc (Hons) degree. Optometry requires a detailed understanding of the functions of the human eye, both as an anatomical structure and as an optical system. The course typically covers three elements: basic studies (such as biochemistry, microbiology, pharmacology, physiology, anatomy, perception and pure and visual optics), optometry and clinical practice. The former are predominant during the early years, with the emphasis moving towards clinical practice in later years.

In the first year you will cover basic studies such as clinical optometry, pure and visual optics, general and ocular anatomy and physiology, physiology of vision and perception, learning and key skills development, ophthalmic lenses and dispensing, and biochemistry.

In your second year you will study further modules in ophthalmic lenses and dispensing, and in physiology of vision and perception, as well as further modules including assessment of binocular vision, low vision and ageing, general and ocular pharmacology, contact lens practice, and clinical methodology and statistics.

The final year is focused towards clinical practice, preparing you for employment. Subjects covered in the final year include general clinical practice, binocular vision and orthoptics, visual ergonomics, abnormal ocular conditions, advanced clinical practice, contact lens practice, law and optometric management, and a research project.

After graduation, you complete a Pre-Registration period of training, including work based assessment and supervision by a registered optometrist, before taking a Final Assessment examination based on the General Optical Council Stage 2 core competencies for optometry. You can then register and practise optometry in your own right.

You may decide to continue your education towards obtaining a higher degree (Masters or Doctorate), which is traditionally research orientated. This, in turn, opens the door to careers in university or industrial research.

Career Opportunities

Once qualified, you have the opportunity to develop your interests in specialist aspects of practice such as paediatrics, contact lenses, low vision or sports vision. Optometrists can choose to practise in a number of settings, for example in independent or private practice, in a hospital eye department or in research or teaching.

Related Degrees

Ophthalmic Dispensing, Orthoptics

Suggested Reading

The Professional Qualifying Examinations: A Survival Guide for Optometrists
- Frank Eperjesi et al, Butterworth-Heinemann, 2004

Optometry A-Z
- Nathan Efron, Butterworth-Heinemann, 2006

See yourself as an optometrist?
- careers brochure, downloadable from the College of Optometrists website below

Further Information

Association of Optometrists
www.assoc-optometrists.org

General Optical Council
www.optical.org

College of Optometrists
www.college-optometrists.org

Association of Optometrists of Ireland
www.optometrists.ie

Pharmacology

Original article by Dr Susan Duty and the late Dr Robin Hoult, King's College London

Introduction

Pharmacology concerns the uses of drugs and the ways in which they and other biologically active chemicals affect the body. Particular emphasis is on the molecular mechanisms by which drugs alter biological processes at the cell and tissue level. Thus the subject is highly relevant to everyday life, not only because of the enormously important health benefits which derive from the intentional therapeutic uses of drugs, but also because it sheds light on topical problems such as drug misuse and addiction. Pharmacology is also very closely related to toxicology - the science of poisons - which seeks to understand how toxicants produce their effects and which is also concerned with drug safety, testing and legislation issues.

The pace of research has accelerated in response to the application of molecular biology techniques: for example, the cloning of many hitherto inaccessible regulatory biomolecules and the use of expression systems to synthesise macromolecules and bioactive proteins that were previously unobtainable. Pharmacology is right at the cutting edge of medical science, playing a very important role not only in new drug development and healthcare but also in the study of disease processes themselves.

Degree Courses

The ever-changing nature of pharmacology has prompted the British Pharmacological Society to develop guidance on core curricula for undergraduate courses that include the subject in the UK. The aims of a typical course will be develop your understanding of how medicines affect the body, how the body handles medicines and how new medicines are developed, as well as developing many practical and other key skills. The course would involve studying how the body works from the molecular level (e.g. how are genes switched on and off) to the whole body (e.g. what regulates blood pressure) and how diseases occur. You would study the actions of medicines in computer simulations, in cells and tissues from animals, possibly in whole animals, and in student volunteers. You need to understand how the whole body reacts to medicines from the point of view of effectiveness and safety. In addition, you would further your understanding of chemistry as you need to know the relationship between the structure of medicines and their actions.

The second and third years of most pharmacology degrees involve increasing specialisation within pharmacology as well as optional advanced courses in related disciplines. These advanced courses reflect the two different approaches to the study of pharmacology - the systematic one, which concerns the application of drugs to organ systems and disease treatment, and the analytical one, which is concerned with the way drugs work at the molecular level.

In some courses, you would have the valuable opportunity of an extra-mural year spent working in an industrial or academic research laboratory as part of a specialised research team. This is offered between the second and final years, and is an exciting and useful preparation for the final year's study as well as providing valuable perspectives for career opportunities. In many cases, you are placed in organisations abroad, including the EU, North America and the Far East, and language skills as well as technical benefits may accrue.

You can also combine a pharmacology degree with many other subjects, such as biochemistry, chemistry, foreign languages, immunology, management and physiology.

Do be aware that a BSc Pharmacology course is very different from a BSc Pharmacy course. A Pharmacy course aims to train someone so that they can work in a hospital pharmacy or chemist's shop or manufacture medicines in industry. This type of course would include pharmacology but also the formulation of medicines, chemical synthesis, microbiology and the social aspects of medicines.

Career Opportunities

Graduates often enter the pharmaceutical industry, where the degree is a good starting point for several positions such as marketing, medical information and product registration (none of which involve laboratory work) as well as research. Others enter alternative careers such as teaching, the civil service, business and publishing. A BSc in Pharmacology also enables students to gain a place for further study either towards a Masters or PhD (Doctorate) in a related research field, or for graduate entry to study Medicine or Dentistry.

Related Degrees

Pharmacology with Industrial Experience, Pharmacology with year abroad, Toxicology, Pharmacology with a Modern Language, Medical Chemistry

Suggested Reading

Pharmacology Condensed
- Maureen Dale and Dennis Haylett, Churchill Livingstone, 2008

Pharmacology
- Humphrey Rang et al, Churchill Livingstone, 2003

Careers in Pharmacology
- downloadable from the Careers in Pharmacology website below. Alternatively, email the BPS to request a Careers CD-ROM and/or relevant leaflets. *Careers in Pharmacology* is aimed at school students considering university, while *Careers in Pharmacology for Graduates* is aimed at university students.

Further Information

British Pharmacological Society
www.bps.ac.uk

Careers in Pharmacology
www.careersinpharmacology.org

Department of Pharmacology, University College Dublin
www.medicine.tcd.ie/pharmacology_therapeutics

European Association for Clinical Pharmacology and Therapeutics
www.eacpt.org

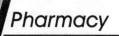

Pharmacy

Original article adapted with permission from material supplied by the Royal Pharmaceutical Society

Introduction

An expert in the field of drugs and medicines, the pharmacist may be involved in any aspect of their preparation and use, from the discovery and development of a medicine to its eventual supply to the patient and sometimes beyond, since she/he may well have a role in monitoring its effects.

Degree Courses

Pharmacy degree courses are currently offered at several universities in the United Kingdom and three in the Republic of Ireland. All UK courses last four years, are accredited by the Royal Pharmaceutical Society and lead to a Master of Pharmacy degree. To register and practise as a pharmacist after the degree, you must follow one year's pre-registration training in a community or hospital pharmacy and pass the Society's Registration Examination. University admissions tutors will be looking for evidence that you are equipped to gain from and succeed in such a demanding and highly focused degree course. The surest but not the only indication of this comes from achieved or expected academic qualifications. The course is geared to students who arrive with A level/Higher/IB or equivalent chemistry plus other A level/Higher/IB or equivalent, especially useful being biology and mathematics

The primary objective of the course is to provide the necessary theoretical knowledge, understanding and practical skills for the competent and successful practice of pharmacy. During the course, considerable emphasis is placed on the development of a professional attitude and responsibility through links with practising pharmacists.

There are four broad subject areas:

- Origin and chemistry of drugs. Emphasis is placed on the study of synthetic drugs, though drugs from natural sources are also studied

- Preparation of medicines. This includes pharmaceutics, which is the study of the formulation of drugs

- Action and uses of drugs and medicines. This covers physiology, biochemistry, microbiology, pathology and pharmacology

- Pharmacy practice. This covers the supply of medicines and provision of advice, including the laws and standards applying to pharmacy. It will include managing symptoms, promoting healthy lifestyles and advising on all aspects of drug therapy and medicines usage.

A typical course will cover the following subject areas in the first year *Pharmaceutical Chemistry, Physical Pharmacy, Molecular Biology, Mathematics, Information Technology, Pharmaceutical Microbiology, and the skills of compounding and dispensing medicines.*

In the later years *more advanced topics are studied. These might include Biopharmaceutics, Drug Metabolism, Medicines Design, Pharmacokinetics, Pharmacology, Medicinal and Analytical Chemistry and Dosage Form Design.*

In the last year, you will carry out a project under supervision, specialise in a selected area of the course and study integrated subjects such as Chemotherapy and Therapeutics.

Expect to make visits to a local hospital to study the work of hospital pharmacists and possibly have a spell with a Community Pharmacist.

Although the key areas of pharmacy are covered by all the degree courses, there may be a difference of emphasis depending on the school chosen and further information should be obtained from the schools themselves.

Career Opportunities

A pharmacist has a wide choice of career options. The principal ones are community pharmacy, hospital pharmacy, industrial pharmacy, research, agricultural and veterinary pharmacy.

Related Degrees

Pharmaceutical Science, Pharmaceutical Science with Year Abroad, Biopharmaceutical Science, Pharmaceutical Chemistry, Medicinal and Pharmaceutical Chemistry

Suggested Reading

Hospital Pre-registration Pharmacist Training
- Aamer Safdar and Shirley Ip, Pharmaceutical Press, 2009

The Pre-registration Interview
- Nadia Bukhari, Pharmaceutical Press, 2007

Careers with the Pharmaceutical Industry
- P D Stonier, Wiley, 2003

Interested in Pharmacy?
- careers leaflet downloadable from the RPS website below

Further Information

Royal Pharmaceutical Society
www.rpsgb.org.uk

National Pharmacy Association
www.npa.co.uk

Pharmaceutical Society of Ireland
www.pharmaceuticalsociety.ie

Irish Pharmacy Union
www.ipu.ie

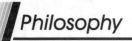

Philosophy

Original article by Antony Flew, formerly Professor of Philosophy, University of Reading

Introduction

It is difficult to explain to people who have never done any what, in this present sense, philosophy is. (Would you care to try to explain what mathematics would involve to someone who had been to a school in which no one had learnt any at all?) This difficulty is one of several good reasons why anyone considering this as a degree subject is well advised to try for one of the institutions - Keele, for instance, or Reading - giving students opportunities of sampling one or two new things before they have finally to commit themselves on what subject or subjects they will read for honours.

The distinguished Cambridge professor, G E Moore, always replied to the question, 'What is philosophy?' by pointing towards his bookshelves: 'It is what all those are about.' So let me too start by saying that philosophy is the main subject of most of the writings of Plato; of Aristotle's *Metaphysics* and *Nicomachean Ethics;* of large parts of the works of St Thomas Aquinas, Duns Scotus and William of Ockham; of the *Discourse* and *Meditations* of Descartes: of Berkeley's *Three Dialogues* and *Principles of Human Knowledge*; of Hume's *Inquiry concerning Human Understanding*; of Kant's *Critique of Pure Reason*; and finally, in more recent times, of Moore's own books, of Bertrand Russell's *Our Knowledge of the External World* and *Mysticism and Logic*, and of Wittgenstein's *Tractatus Logico-Philosophicus* and his posthumous *Philosophical Investigations*.

If you do decide to do philosophy you will certainly be introduced to many of these classics. However, unless and until you have been thus properly introduced, you had perhaps best stick to books written fairly recently, and books written as introductions. Try, for instance, Bertrand Russell The *Problems of Philosophy* (an OUP paperback); and/or either Anthony O'Hear *What Philosophy Is* or Brenda Almond *Exploring Philosophy* (Blackwell). And, whatever you do, don't set out for an interview without readying yourself to say something lively about some philosophy book which you have recently worked through. They probably want to sign you up. But you do need to give them some help!

You will not find many facts in any philosophy book, and those which you do find will be mainly facts about what particular philosophers have said. What you should find is arguments, and the more the better. So one good test for telling whether you are a person who could become fascinated by philosophy is to ask yourself whether you care about the validity or invalidity of arguments, and the sufficiency or insufficiency of evidence offered, as well as about the truth or falsity of conclusions reached, and the acceptability or otherwise of cases presented. If you do not, then certainly philosophy is not for you.

Consider, for example, the much disputed issues of 'free will or predestination' and 'free will or determinism'. The strictly philosophical questions here are not the questions of theological or scientific fact. They are not, that is, the questions: whether on the first day of creation God wrote what the last day of reckoning shall read; nor whether everything that happens, including everything which people do, could on the basis of a full knowledge of the laws of nature and the past condition of the whole universe, in principle be predicted. They are, rather, the questions: whether the idea of a creator God - not only all foreseeing, but also the sustaining cause of our every action and our very existence - is logically compatible with the ideas of human responsibility and human choice; and whether the sciences, and in particular the human sciences, logically presuppose or imply some form of determinism. If so, is this a sort of determinism logically compatible with our everyday talk and assumptions about human choice and action?

The philosophical questions about free will and determinism and predestination, therefore, like other philosophical questions, though they may arise out of suggestions or discoveries about what is as a matter-of-fact the case, are themselves not questions of this factual sort, but questions about what does or does not follow from what, and what is or is not logically incompatible with what else. It is this fact which makes philosophy excellent pure mental training. Certainly it is not career-linked in the way in which law, say, and medicine both are. Certainly too it is not, unlike the usual school subjects, something from which graduates can hope to earn their livings by teaching. But when you are competing for any of the other jobs done by arts graduates there is no call whatever to be shy about admitting that you read philosophy.

Career Opportunities

Philosophy graduates seem to do well in finding employment in a wide range of careers. Their intellectual training is greatly valued.

Related Degrees

European Philosophy and Literature, Mental Philosophy, Ethics, Moral and Religious Studies, History and Philosophy of Science, Philosophy, Politics and Economics, Intellectual Ideas

Suggested Reading

See paragraphs two and three above.

You might also consider:

Reading Philosophy: An Introductory Text with Readers
- Samuel Guttenplan et al, Blackwell, 2002

Philosophical Writing: An Introduction
- Aloysius P Martinich, WileyBlackwell, 2008

Think: A Compelling Introduction to Philosophy
- Simon Blackburn, Oxford Paperbacks, 2001

Philosophy in Practice: An Introduction to the Main Questions
- Adam Morton, Blackwell, 2003

Further Information

Philosophical Society of England
www.the-philosopher.co.uk/philsoc/philsocindex.htm

Philosophy by Topic
http://users.ox.ac.uk/~worc0337/phil_topics.html

Limerick Philosophical Society
http://sites.google.com/site/limerickphilosophy

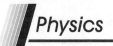

Physics

Original article by Dr Sarah Thompson, Department of Physics, University of York

Introduction

Physics is concerned with the fundamental laws which govern all natural phenomena. Because of this it pervades every part of the world of science, engineering and technology. Its methods and insights are widely applicable, and its practitioners widely sought. Physics has rarely been in such an exciting state as it is today. Physics aims to discover the ultimate structure of matter and the fundamental forces which determine the universe and the matter within it. Yet, even if these were achieved tomorrow, there is much which physics has to offer now and for the foreseeable future in improving the world in which we live.

Physicists deploy a mixture of experimental and analytical skills, and creative flair, but there is no norm. Some have a theoretical leaning, others excel as practical or computational investigators. Some are very analytical in their approach to the subject, others more intuitive. A few are highly gifted.

Degree Courses

Physics courses are broadly similar in content: electromagnetic waves, relativity, mechanics, matter, atomic physics, nuclear physics, quantum mechanics, thermodynamics, etc. However, the teaching methods and styles, the depth of core material and options, flexibility for changing course, the 'flavour' of the physics course (single or combined) do vary substantially between courses and universities. Many universities offer a three- or four-year BSc Honours course; some a four year M Phys Honours course. Often, you will not have to choose between them initially as there is a common entry code. Transferring from the M Phys to the BSc can often be left until the end of the second year. Transfers from the BSc to M Phys are usually possible in the first year, subject to suitable performance. The BSc and M Phys courses make compatible demands, and good results in either could let you enter scientific research; in some of the more competitive research areas the M Phys will be preferred.

The single Honours physics course will mostly include the basic physics material mentioned above, plus additional modules of which you may have a choice or it may be part of the core physics material. Example modules are acoustics, astrophysics, biophysics, electronics, plasma physics, particle physics, medical physics, cosmology, geophysics, group theory, spectroscopy, material science, optoelectronics, space physics, semiconductor physics. There may be choice throughout the degree course, or it may be restricted to later years. Laboratory work runs throughout the course. Usually, the final year will not have formal laboratory work but instead have project work which may be extended over two or three terms. Projects enable you to work more independently, and students widely agree that this is one of the most satisfying and rewarding parts of the course.

The range of physics courses combined with other subjects is extensive. They may take the form of physics being the minor, equal, or major component. Joint Physics courses are generally 50:50 split between physics and the other subject: for example, Physics and Maths, Physics and Astronomy, Physics and Electronics, Physics and Chemistry, Physics and a language. Major physics courses may be split two-thirds physics one-third other subject, e.g. Physics with Maths, Physics with Astrophysics, Physics with Business Management, Physics with Acoustics, Physics with Computing. In many cases some or all of these single and combined courses are offered with a Year in Europe option. This option is likely to extend your course to four years, with the year after your second year spent in Europe. You complete the 3rd year physics material in your fourth year. If you are on a 4-year M Phys course then the Year in Europe option will not extend the length of your degree. The year will be assessed as part of your overall degree result.

Career Opportunities

A high proportion of graduates go into careers in which they use their knowledge and skills in physics. However, physics is so central in the span of scientific subjects that physicists can be employed in areas involving peripheral disciplines such as electronics, computing, and mathematics. It can lead to careers in finance, management, teaching, patent agency, law and publishing.

Related Degrees

Theoretical Physics, Physics with Particle Physics, Experimental Physics, Biophysics, Physics with Overseas Studies, Physics with Photonics, Quantum Science and Lasers, Chemical Physics, Physics and Medical Physics, Mathematical Physics, Applied Physics, Physics with Acoustics, Engineering Physics, Atmospheric Physics, Technological Physics, Physics and Space Science, Computational Physics, Environmental Physics(Climate), Geophysics/Planetary Physics, Meteorology, Physics with Electronics, Physics with Instrumentation, Physics/Laser Optoelectronics, Mathematics and Theoretical Physics

Suggested Reading

Physics, Penguin Dictionary of
- Valerie Illingworth, Penguin, 2009

A Brief History of Time and the Universe in a Nutshell
- Stephen Hawking, Bantam Press, 2007

Degree Course Guide Physics and Chemistry
- Trotman, 2007

University Physics with Modern Physics (Pie) with mastering physics
- Hugh D. Young, Roger A. Freedman and Lewis Ford, Pearson Education, 2007

Further Information

Institute of Physics
www.iop.org

Institute of Physics and Engineering in Medicine
www.ipem.ac.uk

Institute of Physics in Ireland
www.iopireland.org

Physiology

Original article by Dr D J Begley, King's College London

Introduction

"General physiology is the basic biological science toward which all others converge. Its problem is to determine the elementary conditions of vital phenomena." (Claude Bernard, 1865)

Physiology is undoubtedly the most open-ended of the biological sciences and for this reason is also probably the most challenging. A physiologist is constantly attempting to explain, by a careful and critical analysis of well-planned research and experiment, how organisms work. A physiologist can work at any number of levels within the organisation of a species. At the cellular level they can study how cells function or move, or how the nervous impulse is transmitted and how messages are received and interpreted by the cell. Alternatively, they may focus on individual organs or tissues of the body (eg the brain or the liver) or on complete systems (eg the nervous or endocrine), studying how they control and regulate function. Or their interest can be in how several organs and systems interact (eg to maintain the constancy of the composition of the blood) or in the important area of developmental physiology (ie how the fertilised egg interprets and unfolds its genetic potential and develops into the mature adult). Or they may study the organism as a whole and its responses to external stimuli and environmental change.

In recent years, interest has been concentrated on cellular physiology as powerful new research tools have increasingly miniaturised the scales at which living systems can be experimentally manipulated. Of course, there is still much to be discovered in other areas but studies into these must be built on firm foundations at cellular levels. Recent advances in cellular physiology have revolutionised the ways in which we examine and interpret higher function (eg in the working of the brain).

Because physiology forms the meeting point for a number of biological sciences, the physiologist utilises experimental methods and tools derived from related disciplines - for example the electron microscope from anatomy, radioactively labelled molecules from biochemistry; x-ray analysis from biophysics and from pharmacology new substances which mimic or modify the action of natural molecules in the body. New applications of genetics such as transgenic animals are also becoming increasingly important. It also means that the physiologist's armoury of experimental techniques is constantly expanding.

Degree Courses

The content and structure of an undergraduate physiology or physiological science degree is very much dependent upon the university. The following outline gives an idea of typical course content and structure but you should look at individual university websites for more detailed information.

Physiology modules in the first year usually remain broad, ensuring that you gather a sound basic understanding of all aspects of the subject. Topics may include an introduction to the principles of cellular physiology and the functions of the major systems of the body (such as cardiovascular, respiratory, alimentary and the central nervous system).

In the second year, students begin to take a more in-depth look at specific areas of physiology, and consider recent advances within the field.

Physiology is very much a 'hands-on' subject, meaning that you would spend time in practical classes studying physiology in action. This might involve studying how the body reacts to different levels of exercise, measuring how quickly you can respond to a visual or auditory stimulus, or how your kidneys react when you drink different amounts and types of fluid.

During the first and second year of study, students are often required to choose from a selection of modules to study alongside and support their learning in physiology.

Modules may include anatomy, molecular biology, psychology and pharmacology, amongst others; this provides an opportunity for you to tailor your degree to your career aspirations.

The final year of study focuses entirely on physiology, with an emphasis on in-depth training in specialist modules. Topics covered in year three usually reflect the research interests of the university. There is greater opportunity for private study in year 3 and students are expected become familiar with reading and interpreting scientific literature; you would also be encouraged to attend seminars given by academics at the top of their field of physiology research.

A substantial research project usually forms a major component of the final year of study. At most universities this project is written up as a dissertation and presented orally to examiners.

In addition to the academic content, physiology courses develop IT knowledge and introduce students to new software packages. You should develop independent and team working skills, together with communication, analytical and time management skills.

A couple of universities now run a four-year programme in physiology, in which students can work towards gaining an MSci. In the third year, students undertake a one-year work placement. This placement would usually be paid employment in research (either in industry or another organisation).

Following successful completion of a three-year degree in physiology, students are awarded a single honours BSc. Students completing the four-year course gain the MSci qualification.

Career Opportunities

Physiology forms an excellent platform to gain a further qualification such as an MSc or PhD, and for postgraduate entry into many courses including Medicine.

There is great demand for graduates in the biomedical and biomolecular sciences within the health services and in industry, particularly leading or working as part of research teams, and many students choose this career path. Industries employ bioscientists for research and development into pharmaceuticals, biotechnology, chemicals, cosmetics and toiletries, food and drink.

Apart from laboratory work, some physiology graduates choose to enter legal careers, using their scientific knowledge to provide patenting advice, others opt for such areas as scientific journalism or teaching biology at school/college level.

There are also diverse career opportunities away from science, all of which will call on the broad analytical and scientific skills developed as an undergraduate; graduates might, for example, embark on careers in management, consultancy, investment banking, accountancy, political research or IT.

Related Degrees

Human Physiology, Clinical Physiology, Cancer Research, Physiological Health, Human Physiology with a Year Abroad, Animal Physiology, Sports Science, Psychology, Philosophy and Physiology

Suggested Reading

Understanding Life
- Physiological Society, details from the website below under Educational Resources
Principles of Anatomy and Physiology
- Gerald Tortora and Bryan Derrickson, Wiley, 2008

Further Information

Physiological Society
www.physoc.org
Federation of European Physiological Societies
www.feps.org

Physiotherapy

Original article written with the help of material supplied by the Chartered Society of Physiotherapy and the Admissions Tutor, School of Health Sciences, Faculty of Medicine and Dentistry, University of Birmingham

Introduction

Physiotherapists use physical means to help patients recover from injury or sickness, and assist them in rehabilitation after operations by restoring their muscle and other functions. Their main techniques involve therapeutic movement, electrotherapy, massage, manipulation, the use of vibration and certain types of radiation, e.g. infrared. They also frequently work with sports persons, e.g. footballers, cricketers, etc. to build up their strength, and thus avoid potential injury.

Physiotherapists are found almost everywhere in hospitals and the community. They are located in: *Outpatients*: treating spinal problems, arthritis, accidents, sports injuries; *Intensive care*: keeping limbs mobile, chests clear for unconscious patients; *Maternity*: ante-natal classes, exercise, posture.

Physiotherapy is a physically demanding profession. You will need to be generally fit and capable of moving and handling both equipment and patients. All offers made by universities are normally subject to your passing a health screening medical examination.

Degree Courses

Qualifying physiotherapy degree programmes now exist in over 30 schools/universities across the UK. The physiotherapy degree involves the study of clinical sciences such as anatomy, physiology and pathology while developing analytical and practical skills that will enable students to identify and resolve their clients' problems of movement and function following injury or disease. Most courses are of three and sometimes four years duration. Courses vary and it is essential to consult prospectuses to find out what each one covers.

A typical course is a three-year modular course (or four-year in Scotland) in which the emphasis is on small groups. The *First Year* is largely pre-clinical and includes studying anatomy and biomechanics in the human movement module, whilst physiology is studied with electrotherapy in the biomedical science module. A study of injury and disease is included alongside research method and behavioural science. (Later on, students are seconded to placements where they assess and treat patients under guidance.)

Students are later introduced to new areas of pathology, when disease processes are investigated and practical skills developed. The year is divided equally between the university and clinical work. In the *Third or Fourth Year* more specialist academic and practical work is introduced; students meet more complex clinical situations. This allows them to evaluate and modify treatment programmes in order to improve the standard of care. To develop research skills, each student completes a research dissertation.

Assessment for the final degree classification is by course work on both practical and theoretical components with occasional unseen examinations. Assessment of clinical work plays an important role in the final degree.

Career Opportunities

Physiotherapist numbers rose significantly last year, for the first time in recent years, according to government workforce statistics for England published in 2009. It is hoped that the increase in demand for physiotherapists after a period of negative or minimal growth indicates that the problems with NHS finances that brought about job freezes and very little graduate recruitment in 2006/7 have at last eased. There is still, however, some concern that the aftermath of the economic downturn of 2009 could affect employment prospects and bring about a reduction in the number of training places.

There are many employment opportunities beyond the NHS. For example, private practice - treating patients in independent clinics for a range of conditions similar to those seen in the NHS; occupational rehabilitation - getting people back to work after accidents or illness; working as a team physiotherapist at a sports club - helping athletes reach their full potential and aiding their recovery from injury. There are further opportunities in policy development and research, helping to develop the services that make physiotherapy an important part of modern healthcare.

Suggested Reading

Thinking of a career as a physiotherapist?
- downloadable from the CSP website below

Getting into Physiotherapy Courses
- James Barton, Trotman, 2010

Tidy's Physiotherapy
- Stuart Porter, Churchill Livingstone, 2008

The Physiotherapist's Pocketbook: Essential Facts at your Fingertips
- Karen Kenyon and Jonathan Kenyon, Churchill Livingstone, 2009

Further Information

Chartered Society of Physiotherapy
www.csp.org.uk

National Health Service Careers
www.nhscareers.nhs.uk

Health Professions Council
www.hpc-uk.org

Irish Society of Chartered Physiotherapists
www.iscp.ie

Podiatry (Chiropody)

Original article adapted with permission from material supplied by the Institute of Chiropodists and Podiatrists

Introduction

Podiatry is a healthcare profession involving the assessment, treatment and management of patients with foot and lower-limb abnormalities. Podiatrists give professional advice on the prevention of foot problems and proper care of the foot. As a podiatrist, you would become an autonomous professional with a caseload of patients from all walks of life and age groups and would become part of a highly skilled multidisciplinary team.

Graduate podiatrists are eligible for state registration in the UK, which means you can work within the NHS or privately. You will also learn the business skills needed to run your own clinic.

Degree Courses

You can choose from 13 accredited degree courses in the UK. Until recently, there was no relevant degree in the Republic of Ireland, so would-be podiatrists usually studied in UK - especially in Belfast - before returning home to develop their career. This remains an option but there is now a course offered by the National University of Ireland, Galway.

In the first year of a typical course you would study the key concepts and theories of podiatric practice, with topics including anatomy, biomechanics, physiology and podiatric medicine. You would also undertake shared learning to give you a broad perspective of multidisciplinary work and gain practice skills through supervised placements in local NHS Trusts.

The second year would see you increasing your podiatric knowledge and contributing to practice in the care of children/older people. You would take on more responsibility in placements, developing confidence and personal skills required to work in this field, and would learn about treating lower-limb disorders, applying physical/mechanical therapies, pharmacology and surgery.

In your final year, clinical practice and theory is patient-focused and addresses contemporary health issues. You would undertake an in-depth supervised project in an area of your choice and would learn essential management skills (including how to write a business plan) to prepare you for running your own practice.

Career Opportunities

Employment rates are very high for state registered podiatrists, providing opportunities to work in the public, voluntary or business sectors. You can gain employment with the NHS or with private health services, or after gaining experience, can opt to work as a self-employed podiatrist running your own clinic.

You may wish to set up a clinic or practice of your own specialising in particular areas of the discipline. Self-employment means that your career path and the hours you work can be extremely flexible.

One university reports that, in recent years, about 85% of qualifying students have been employed within 4 months of graduation and 100% within 9 months. This is excellent compared with many other graduate employment rates.

Suggested Reading

Clinical Skills in Treating the Foot
- Warren Turner and Linda M. Merriman, Churchill Livingstone, 2005

McMinn's Colour Atlas of Foot and Ankle Anatomy
- Bari M Logan et al, Mosby, 2004

Illustrated Dictionary of Podiatry and Foot Science
- Jean Mooney, Churchill Livingstone, 2009

Further Information

National Health Service Careers
www.nhscareers.nhs.uk

Institute of Chiropodists and Podiatrists
www.iocp.org.uk

Society of Chiropodists and Podiatrists
www.feetforlife.org

Society of Chiropodists and Podiatrists of Ireland
www.podiatryireland.com

Podiatry at NUI Galway
www.nuigalway.ie/podiatry

Politics and Government

Original article by Peter Dawson, London School of Economics

Introduction

Politics, political science, political theory and institutions, government - these are some of the names by which university departments teaching in this field are known and, although the specific subjects which they teach may differ, their broad concern is the same. The simplest way of describing this concern is to say that it is with the exercise of governmental power within and between nation states. Beyond that it is a concern with the processes by which power is acquired and used, and the restraints, both material and ethical, which may be placed upon it.

Degree Courses

The oldest and most persistent strand of political studies is political philosophy, with an ancestry going back at least as far as Aristotle and Plato. Political philosophy involves a concern - or 'engagement' - with the basic concepts of the discipline (eg politics, government, power, authority) and with the rights and obligations of both rulers and ruled, and much else. It cannot be assigned however to a separate and remote compartment. Philosophical considerations underlie all aspects of the study of politics and most enquiries tend to lead back to such concerns.

Some people distinguish political thought as a separate field from political philosophy. It entails an examination of the ideas of certain prominent thinkers and of their significance in their own and in subsequent times. Plato, Aquinas, Machiavelli, Rousseau and Marx would be just a few of the names which fall within this category.

Next there is a large area of empirical studies and theorising about them, which may, for convenience, be divided into three parts. The first is the study of individuals and their motivation and behaviour in different political roles (eg voters or leaders). The second is the study of groups from the organised and articulate (eg political parties or pressure groups) to those with a possibly more diffuse voice who are less organised (eg racial or religious groups). Third is the study of governmental institutions - parliamentary assemblies, courts, cabinets, civil services - and constitutionally defined offices of leadership or direction (eg those of presidents, prime ministers and ministers). Public administration as an academic study is principally concerned with this third part.

Comparative politics - the methodical and simultaneous study of several political systems -has been one of the major developments of political science in recent years. The study has been aided by an accompanying elaboration of the concept of political systems. A primary concern in comparative politics is to show by examination of a number of countries how apparently similar institutions and structures may perform different functions or, conversely, how the same function may be performed by different structures. It becomes possible, for example, to analyse in some detail how political parties or the mass media perform widely varying roles in different countries, or how the functions attributed in the UK to Members of Parliament may elsewhere be performed by civil servants or influential, non-elected intermediaries.

Another aspect of comparative politics is the attempt to classify political societies and order them in generic groups. It tends to lead to an examination of such terms as totalitarianism, pluralism and participation. Closely related to this approach is the examination of political ideas or bodies of widely held beliefs like nationalism, socialism or conservatism. But by now the circle is almost closed, since this sort of concern brings one into close proximity again with political philosophy.

A final area of concern is international politics or international relations, which in some universities is taught within a separate department but elsewhere is covered under politics or government. Essentially it is the study of politics between states and of such institutions as the United Nations and the European Union, which constitute forms of international government. The various approaches outlined above are equally appropriate in this field.

What are the principal methods of studying politics as an undergraduate? It remains above all a 'book' subject, pursued by reading the works of other scholars, but there also exist opportunities, which vary from topic to topic, to use primary sources such as official publications and newspapers both contemporary and historical. Novels, plays, poetry and other artistic works may have their relevance and there is an increasing use of survey data (eg public opinion samples), which in some instances is prepared by students themselves.

Career Opportunities

Graduates are often in demand for their understanding of the influences of government on industry, trade, export and import. Approximately 50% enter central and local government, Armed Services, rail, water, gas, electricity, banking, insurance, financial services and 25% enter Higher Education or train to be teachers, solicitors or barristers. Management, administration, sales and marketing are popular areas.

Related Degrees

International Politics, International Relations, European Politics, Parliamentary Studies, Public Administration, Public Sector Management, Government and European Politics, Politics, Philosophy and Economics, Political Science, Public and Social Policy

Suggested Reading

Plato to NATO: Studies in Political Thought
- Brian Redhead (intro), Penguin, 1995

Principles of Political Economy and Chapters on Socialism
- J.S. Mill, Oxford Paperbacks, 2008

The Politics
- Aristotle, introduction and notes by Richard Stalley, Oxford World Classics, 2009

Introducing International Politics
- Peter M Jones, Sheffield Hallam University Press, 2003

Introducing Modern Political Thought
- David Gregg, Perpetuity Press, 1998

Political Studies Journal
- free access to recent articles at: ***www.politicalstudies.org***

Political Studies UK
- free access to 90 departments offering relevant courses at: ***www.studypolitics.org***

Further Information

Home Office
www.homeoffice.gov.uk

Foreign and Commonwealth Office
www.fco.gov.uk

Political Studies Association
www.psa.ac.uk
Civil Service
www.civilservice.gov.uk

Political Studies Association of Ireland
www.psai.ie

Prosthetics and Orthotics

Original article by John Head, University of Salford

Introduction

Prosthetics is the science of body part replacement with artificial alternatives. Many people rely on prosthetic limbs to attain independence in their lives and work, and it is a tribute to the skill of prosthetists and their support staff, and a credit to today's technology, that many would appear to have no discernible loss of function or ability. Orthotics is similar to prosthetics, except that the body part is not replaced but is assisted by an artificial device. Such devices can be simple, such as an insole, or they can be intricate and complex, such as devices to assist in the walking of people who have total paralysis of both legs. The work of a prosthetist/orthotist is clinically based, usually within a hospital setting, and involves the prescription and assessment of the patient's needs, and ultimately the production of 3-D models of the body part or residual limb in what is known as the casting process. Traditionally, this is achieved using plaster of Paris, but more recently laser-pens and computer-aided design and manufacturing have been employed to complete the models required. It is from these that teams of technicians produce the prosthesis/orthosis to the specifications laid down by the clinician and which will then be fitted by the latter when it is complete.

Degree Courses

Training is centred at just two UK universities: Salford and Strathclyde. There are at present no degree courses in Prosthetics and Orthotics offered in Ireland. Prosthetic/orthotic education is currently a four-year honours degree course, which contains a final year of clinical experience. Although the courses vary, they both consist of three years of academic learning mixed with clinical tuition. The final year involves two six-month clinical placements, one orthotic and one prosthetic.

Subjects within the course include anatomy - the structure of the body, physiology - the functions of the body, pathology - causes and nature of disease, biomechanics - forces in/on the body, materials science - how materials perform, and orthotic/prosthetic science - practical solutions to problems.

For further information on courses, you should contact the universities directly.

The work is of a practical nature and is most suited to people who are keen on using their hands, looking after and dealing with people.   It is also important that the prosthetist/orthotist has an eye for problem solving and 'thinking on their feet'.

Career Opportunities

With an international shortage of prosthetists and orthotists, career prospects throughout the UK and the rest of the world, particularly the USA, are excellent. Most prosthetic and orthotic graduates start their careers working for commercial companies. However, an increasing number of opportunities are arising within the health service. As you develop skills and experience, you will be able to assume positions with increased responsibility. Eventually this may lead to a managerial role or you may become an acknowledged specialist in a particular area of clinical work. Teaching is another option and these posts offer opportunities for research. The UK training programme is recognised to be of an exceptionally high standard and many opportunities exist for graduates to work abroad. Prosthetic and orthotic work is especially important in areas of the world where development programmes are working with communities traumatised by war.

Suggested Reading

Prosthetics and Orthotics
- Donald Shurr and John Michael, Prentice-Hall, 2001

Orthotics: A Comprehensive Clinical Approach
- Joan Edelstein and Jan Bruckner, Slack Inc, 2002

Orthotics and Prosthetics in Rehabilitation
- Michelle M. Lusardi and Caroline C. Nielsen, Butterworth-Heinemann, 2006

Further Information

British Association of Prosthetists and Orthotists
www.bapo.com

University of Salford
www.healthcare.salford.ac.uk/prosthetic

University of Strathclyde
www.strath.ac.uk/prosthetics/index.html

NHS Careers
www.nhscareers.nhs.uk

Psychology

Original article by Dr Marie Falahee, Psychology Department, Aston University, with additional material supplied by the British Psychological Society

Introduction

Psychology is the scientific study of people: how they think; how they act, react and interact. Psychology is concerned with all aspects of behaviour and the thoughts feelings and motivations underlying such behaviour.

To study psychology you have to learn scientific methods - observing, measuring, testing, using statistics - to show that what you find is reliable evidence and not just down to chance. But psychologists do not simply collect evidence to explain people's behaviour; they use their understanding to help people with difficulties and bring about change for the better.

There are several main types of psychologists, depending on their specialist qualifications or training: Clinical, Counselling, Educational, Forensic, Health, Occupational, Neuropsychologist, and Teaching & Research.

Degree Courses

If you intend to pursue a career in psychology, it is important that you choose a degree course accredited by the British Psychological Society for the Graduate Basis for Chartered Membership (GBC, formerly known as GBR). University courses (whether single, joint or combined honours degrees) typically cover all of the main areas of psychological knowledge necessary to go into further training. However, more and more degrees are becoming modular and it is often necessary to choose particular modules to qualify for the GBC. Check with the individual course organisers the status of the course you are interested in and to ensure that you follow an accredited pathway of modules within your degree.

A typical course would cover all of the basic areas of psychology, such as cognitive, developmental, biological, social, and abnormal psychology. The first year modules would provide short introductions to these areas, while the second year modules would investigate them in greater depth. In the third year, you would choose options from modules which reflect the research interests of members of staff, and you would be given the opportunity to design empirical studies of your own There is usually considerable emphasis on practical work, and you would be given a thorough grounding in research methods (including methods of statistical data analysis).

For students on a four-year programme, the third year may sometimes be spent in work experience which can provide insight into the application of psychological principles in the outside world and allows students to see what a career in a particular branch of psychology or business might be like.

Career Opportunities

Psychology degrees develop many of the transferable skills which all graduate employers require, for example: communication; numeracy; information technology; independent learning; and the ability to work in teams.

Psychology courses accredited by the British Psychological Society contain substantial teaching on statistics and research methodology, as well as scientific methods. Because of these areas of study, psychology students are able to understand and manipulate both quantitative and qualitative data, use computers and problem solve effectively. Consequently, psychology graduates are well placed to move into research or numeracy-based careers such as market research, academia and accounting. Psychology students also develop many of the skills of humanities graduates, such as critical thinking and essay writing.

Only 15 to 20 per cent of psychology graduates progress to be chartered psychologists. If you want to move into this area of work, it is vital to undertake as much work experience as possible whilst on your undergraduate degree. Placements in clinical psychology can be notoriously difficult to access but any relevant paid or voluntary work can be beneficial, e.g. working with children or adults with learning difficulties; mentoring; befriending; working in care homes or with those who are mentally distressed.

Related Degrees

Psychology with Neuropsychology, Business Administration with Psychology, Applied Psychology, Sport and Exercise Psychology, Health Psychology, Social Psychology, Psychosocial Studies, Forensic Psychology, Human Psychology, Behavioural Science, Clinical Psychology, Psycholinguistics, Psychology, Philosophy and Physiology

Suggested Reading

The Psychologist
- official magazine of the British Psychological Society and an essential introduction to the main issues in psychology today

Aiming for Psychology and Psychology Career Opportunities
- two short films available at the British Psychological Society website below or on the BPS YouTube channel

Getting into Psychology Courses
- Maya Waterstone, Trotman, 2010

Atkinson and Hilgard's Introduction to Psychology
- Susan Nolen-Hoeksema et al, Cengage Learning, 2009

The Presentation of Self in Everyday Life
- Erving Goffman, Penguin, 1990

How to Think Straight about Psychology
- Keith Stanovich, Pearson Education, 2009

Psychology: The Science of Mind and Behaviour
- Richard Gross, Hodder Education, 2010

Further Information

British Psychological Society
www.bps.org.uk

Psychological Society of Ireland
www.psihq.org

European Federation of Psychologists' Associations
www.efpa.eu

Radiography

Original article adapted with permission from material supplied by the College of Radiographers

Introduction

To be a radiographer, you need an interest in science and you should be a caring and compassionate person, sufficiently level headed not to get upset when dealing with the sick. You should be calm when faced with people who may be frightened or difficult. Your health must be good and you have to be reasonably strong, because you may have to help lift people and move heavy equipment.

A **Diagnostic Radiographer** works with advanced technology to produce high quality images to help in diagnosis. Radiography equipment is becoming increasingly complex and much of it is computerised. For example, computerised tomography (CT) and magnetic resonance imaging (MRI) scanners can give information about the body not possible with conventional radiographs. The information obtained from this equipment can differentiate between the different organs without the need for the patient to undergo surgical procedures or injections. Radiographers who operate CT scanners have to be familiar with keyboards and computer language. As they learn to operate many different types of equipment, radiographers may specialise and train in different areas, including ultrasound.

Therapeutic Radiographers treat people with cancer and non-malignant diseases. The aim is to determine the correct dose of radiation, decide where the beam should enter and exit, and which structures should be treated and which avoided. The location of a tumour and its size are discovered with the aid of CT or magnetic resonance scans or other diagnostic procedures. Conventional X-ray and cobalt units are being phased out and being replaced by a new generation of treatment equipment. These include linear accelerators, which can treat either deep-seated or superficial tumours. Therapy radiographers are likely to work more regular hours than diagnostic radiographers, though it is necessary to have some out of hours cover for specific treatments.

Degree Courses

A typical **Diagnostic Radiography** course will be composed of time spent in the lecture theatre and tutorials and an approximately equal time spent working with patients in the actual department. Since radiography is a clinically orientated profession with a considerable degree of patient contact, students need a detailed knowledge of the human body - its structure, pathology and function. A diagnostic radiographer deals with potentially very dangerous equipment and has to acquire a knowledge of how to use this both confidently and safely.

In a typical course, you would study anatomy and physiology, physics, the science of imaging, pathology, pathophysiology, psychology and sociology. In your last year, you would extend your knowledge and experience of the practice and science of imaging, and probably also study sociology, ethics and management. In this year, and possibly earlier, you are likely to carry out some independent supervised research.

You would also, at some stage of the course, deal with the principles and practice of radiography and of complementary imaging, health and safety, principles of patient care and health education.

In a **Therapeutic Radiography** course, you will acquire the skills needed to be able to work in a department of clinical oncology. Modules might include health studies, radiation sciences, oncology, anatomy and physiology. There could be further modules such as psychosocial studies, oncology and radiotherapy, and radiation science, as well as further modules in anatomy and physiology. The final year would include further modules, often extensions of earlier ones and a research project.

Career Opportunities

There is currently a worldwide shortage of both diagnostic and therapy radiographers, which should mean excellent career prospects for anyone holding the highly regarded UK qualification. State registration is a key factor in developing your career, indicating that you meet the high ethical standards required, have achieved educational and professional excellence and are committed to duty of care.

Suggested Reading

Directory of Radiography Courses downloadable from the Society of Radiographers website at www.sor.org/public/careerinfo/careers.htm

Radiographic Techniques and Image Evaluation
- Amanda Royle and Elizabeth Unett, Nelson Thornes, 2004

Ball and Moore's Essential Physics for Radiographers
- John Ball and Adrian Moore, WileyBlackwell, 2008

A Guide to Radiological Procedures
- Frances Anne Aitchison, Saunders, 2009

Further Information

Radiography Careers
www.radiographycareers.co.uk

Society of Radiographers
www.sor.org

National Health Service Careers
www.nhscareers.nhs.uk

Health Professions Council
www.hpc-uk.org

Irish Institute of Radiography and Radiation Therapy
www.iirrt.ie

Religious Studies and Theology

Original article by Professor John R Hinnells, School of Oriental and African Studies, London

Introduction

Religion is a driving force both in contemporary society and in past history. It has inspired some of the most noble, creative and generous actions. Equally, it has been associated with the most savage cruelty, oppression and degradation. A balanced understanding of many major events commonly involves an appreciation of the religious factors at work. Whether it is in the Middle East, Latin America, Africa, Afghanistan or remote parts of China - religion and politics are commonly interwoven. Religion may inspire people, or it may be used by people, but it is commonly a significant dimension for the study of human life.

Many describe British society as secular and wrongly say that religion is declining. Membership of the established churches may be dropping, but that is not a measure of the state of religion in the country. This ignores the growth of new religious movements, the ecstatic movements, the 'cults', and the central importance of religion in Asian and Afro-Caribbean communities. People who have migrated, or feel victims of prejudice, commonly reassert their identity in and through religious traditions. Much of contemporary British law, custom, values etc., are the product of a particular religious tradition.

Religion is crucial not only in the understanding of politics and society but also of the arts. Until recently, the Church was the main patron of the arts - painting, music, architecture, and drama. The Church commissioned works of art and dictated the form, content and style of much of that art. The Church often repressed the artist - not only through the mass destruction following the Reformation, but also in more recent times when its stance on the depiction of the nude and the condemnation of some aspects of drama or literature has been narrow-minded. It is hardly possible to understand many of the art forms of other cultures without the religion of which they are an essential part - whether it is the great civilisations of China and India, or of the small-scale societies in Africa or the North American Indians. A failing of so many art histories is that they study the arts as though they were merely produced for the 'antiseptic' atmosphere of most art galleries, whereas often artefacts are produced to be used to inspire devotion or to teach the illiterate.

Degree Courses

Many students who are religious wish to study religion, and in Britain that often means Christian. But some people study religion in order to find a faith and some because they believe it will confirm or develop their faith. A few study religion because they want to enter the ministry. A university is a secular institution and not a priestly seminary. Within a department of religious studies there will be people of various faiths, and many of none. In theory, a student's own religious position should make no difference to their studies. That is an ideal situation - and neither students nor staff are ever ideal. It is a self-delusion for people to think they have no prejudices. The danger time is when we are not aware of them. At least one major benefit of the study of religion is that it compels people to recognise their prejudices and to analyse them.

How should one study religion? In some departments, religious studies means basically studying the Christian Bible. One argument for this is that it, more than any other document, has affected the course of western civilisation. The methods used to study that text are intellectually demanding and diverse (e.g. languages, archaeology, literary studies, Roman history etc.), but if you are interested in studying Asians in Britain then, frankly, it is not relevant. If you want both, make sure both are available.

I believe that religion has to be studied from many points of view. The study must necessarily bring together a range of disciplines - anthropology, sociology, languages, history, art, archaeology and philosophy. I accept the old dictum 'he who knows one knows none', i.e. that the study of any one religion is not the study of religion and such a focus precludes a balanced view of even that one phenomenon. It is only by a study of several that you see what is distinctive of each.

Religious studies more than any other subject wrestles with some of the ultimate issues: the concept of God; life after death; the nature of good and evil and ethical issues - what are the arguments for and against euthanasia, surrogate motherhood, nuclear power? If anyone thinks any of these are simple clear-cut issues they have evidently not thought them through.

Career Opportunities

Theology and religious studies graduates develop skills in communication, analysis, logic and argument, which can be valuable in many careers. A few theology graduates enter the ordained ministry but are often more attracted to 'caring' professions, such as social and community work, charity administration and nursing. Approximately 25% enter teacher training or train as solicitors, barristers, librarians, social workers etc. Others enter commerce, the Civil Service, careers in management services, computing, finance, sales and marketing.

Related Degrees

Religious Education, Divinity, Biblical Studies, Christian Ministry, Religion, Ethics and Western Society

Suggested Reading

The New Penguin Handbook of Living Religions
- John R Hinnells, Penguin, 2005

Religion Today: A Reader
- Susan Mumm, Ashgate, 2002

The Concise Oxford Dictionary of World Religions
- John Bowker, OUP, 2005

The World's Religions
- Ninian Smart, Cambridge University Press, 1998

Further Information

Religious Studies on the Web
www.rsweb.org.uk

Ethics Updates
http://ethics.sandiego.edu

Sociology of Religion Study Group
www.socrel.org.uk

Irish Theological Association
www.theology.ie

Retail Management

Original article by Jacqui Gush, Bournemouth University

Introduction

The definition of retailing is widening as more and more commercial activities participate in selling goods and services to the final consumer. This makes retailing an increasingly exciting area of study and employment. The retailing business is about people: our rapidly changing tastes and demand patterns; what influences us to buy and understanding where, how and when it happens. Some of the current challenges in retailing include the threat or opportunity of electronic shopping, the increasing merger between retailing and the leisure industry, meeting customer needs through the increasing use of technology and the internationalisation of retailing activities.

Students on a retail management degree course benefit from all the knowledge and skills gained as part of a more general business studies course. However, significant added value is gained by specialising in retailing, as the student develops a sound, in-depth knowledge of the sector. There is strong encouragement and support from leading retailers in the development, review and provision of specific courses.

Degree Courses

A typical course is a four-year sandwich, which includes a 40-week industrial placement.

Year one is a stimulating introduction to retailing at the sharp end, focusing on the role and responsibilities of the store manager.

Strong emphasis is placed on the development of commercial and personal skills. These are learnt from theory as well as practical retail work experience. Skills such as group working, writing business reports and making effective presentations are an important aspect of generic business skills learnt in year one.

In *year two*, retailing is studied from a head office perspective, concentrating on corporate functions and operations, e.g.. marketing, finance, buying and human resource management. At the beginning of this year, students are offered the opportunity to study on an exchange programme with a retailing school in mainland Europe.

The experience of the year out in industry during *year three* allows students to develop their personal skills and gives them the opportunity to put theory into practice by applying the knowledge and skills gained during their first two years on the degree programme. While on placement, students are able to qualify for the City and Guilds Licentiate award.

The *final year* concentrates on subjects which support top management decision-making for companies in an international as well as a national market. It reflects the dynamic nature of the retail industry and students analyse how companies seek to achieve advantage in an intensely competitive environment. The focus is strongly on student centred learning and includes two major group projects, which are commercially and academically challenging. Students work in the live business environment, and the project outcomes are presented to retailers and investment companies.

Career Opportunities

Opportunities are available in the major national retail organisations - but with competition from other graduate disciplines. The basic training, however, should open up many management, marketing, financial and commercial careers in business generally.

Related Degrees

Marketing, Retail and Distribution, Fashion Buying for Retail, Supply Chain Management, Food Management

Suggested Reading

Retailing: an Introduction
- Roger Cox and Paul Brittain, Financial Times/ Prentice Hall, 2004

Principles of Retailing
- John Fernie et al, Butterworth-Heinemann, 2003

Retail Desire: Design, Display and the Art of the Visual Merchandiser
- Johnny Tucker, RotoVision, 2004

Fashion Brands: Branding Style from Armani to Zara
- Mark Tungate, Kogan Page, 2008

Further Information

British Retail Consortium
www.brc.org.uk

Skillsmart Retail
www.skillsmartretail.com

Chartered Institute of Marketing
www.cim.co.uk

Retail on the Web
www.retailontheweb.co.uk

Chartered Institute of Purchasing and Supply
www.cips.org

Chartered Institute of Personnel and Development, Ireland
www.cipd.ie

Irish Management Institute
www.imi.ie

Enterprise Ireland
www.enterprise-ireland.com

Marketing Institute of Ireland
www.mii.ie

Rural Resource Management

Original article by Ken Reynolds, specialist writer on careers and higher education

Introduction

What is rural resource management? It is about using the rural environment for such purposes as:

- farming - crops and animals for food and fibres
- natural resources - timber, energy, water and minerals
- housing
- employment
- recreation and leisure

Rural resource management tries to balance all these demands to protect the long-term future of the rural environment. This means taking into account everything from animal welfare to environmental and socio-economic needs. Attitudes are changing and sustainable land use is becoming a key phrase.

Degree Courses

You will find that institutions offering degrees in rural resource management structure the course in different ways. At one university, for example, a common core for the first two years of study (Stages 1 and 2) is shared with all other agriculture programmes. This means that you could specialise in any of the Honours options (Agronomy; Farm Business Management; Animal Production Science; Organic Food Production) in your final year (Stage 3). In Stage 1 you would cover: soil and crop science; animal physiology, biochemistry, genetics and nutrition; economics and computing; current agricultural issues.

In Stage 2 you would apply these skills to both animal and crop production, and to farm management. The range of modules includes: agronomy and improvement of arable, grass and forage crops; farm management, agricultural economics and marketing; ruminant livestock, pigs and poultry; animal breeding, nutrition and health; agriculture and the environment.

You would not specialise in rural resource management until your final year, taking modules in: sustainable land management; rural enterprise diversification; estate management; countryside management; law and land use; options - including alternative agriculture, forage utilisation or land reclamation.

An important feature of the programme at another university is the wide range of visits to, and projects and exercises conducted with, rural enterprises and organisations. The visits programme enables you to explore management issues at first hand, and provides insights into a variety of career opportunities. You may elect to spend a year in between Parts 2 and 3 of the programme obtaining work experience and you can also spend one term studying in another European country.

In a third institution, a common first year lays the foundations for the sustainable management of the environmental, social and economic contexts of rural life and explores the interactions between these, conservation issues and future management policies.

All first year students have a timetabled opportunity to learn and hone practical countryside skills such as hedge laying and tractor driving.

Specialist areas of study or interest can be individually developed as part of the final year dissertation and consultancy modules.

It is clearly important to research course content and structure very carefully before you apply.

Career Opportunities

The realisation that wildlife and landscape conservation need to be considered to achieve the sustainable use of land for agricultural and forest production has created the need for rural resource managers who can work across traditional disciplinary boundaries.

People with such interdisciplinary skills are in demand as: managers of rural businesses, including farm and woodland enterprises which are diversifying to meet market needs; planners, who are increasingly required to integrate knowledge of the social and management sciences with an appreciation of the ecological problems and opportunities of the rural environment; ecological scientists and countryside managers, who are increasingly required to understand economic, social and cultural issues along with the scientific basis of conservation and sustainable land management.

Past rural resource graduates have found employment in sectors as diverse as local authorities, wildlife trusts, National Parks and forestry, as well as in educational and consultancy positions.

Related Degrees

You might also be interested in a degree in: *Agricultural Business Management, Agriculture, Animal Science, Countryside Management, Countryside Conservation, Landscape Management, Wildlife Management, Environmental Biology* or *Environmental Science.*

Suggested Reading

Visit the Earthscan website at: *www.earthscan.co.uk* for an extensive reading list

Further Information

Natural England
www.naturalengland.org.uk

Scottish Natural Heritage
www.snh.org.uk

Countryside Council for Wales
www.ccw.gov.uk

Northern Ireland Environment Agency
www.ni-environment.gov.uk

Heritage Council, Ireland
www.heritagecouncil.ie

Social Policy

Original article by Dr Tony Maltby, University of Birmingham

Introduction

Social policy is about the welfare of people. It is concerned with social needs and social problems. The study of social policy is largely concerned with those aspects of people's lives that are affected by government action or inaction. Recently, social policy has widened its scope to consider the family, the environment, penal policy and the role of the market in delivering welfare. We consider the contribution of non-government groups and agencies in the field of voluntary organisations, employer-provided services, self-help groups, family and neighbour support networks.

Degree Courses

In a typical **Social Policy** degree course (allow for an additional year in Scotland), through a series of lectures, classes and workshops, you would initially gain a broad understanding of the main disciplines involved: sociology, political science, social history, economics and research methods. You would also investigate and debate social policy issues (i.e. unemployment, poverty, the family, health, housing, education, citizenship and equal opportunities).

In the subsequent years, you would develop and refine what you have learned earlier. Thus students are able to choose combinations of specialist modules according to their particular interests. You would learn more of the ideas of different schools of political and social thought and about the way in which societies can be organised. You would consider different principles, such as those concerned with equity, citizenship, democracy and social justice. Students also begin to examine more closely the problems and issues involved in the removal of social, economic and political disadvantage in modern Britain.

Standing alongside the above example, the **Public and Social Policy Management** course is designed for people who feel they might be interested in pursuing a managerial career in the public or voluntary sectors - dealing with services such as education, health care, leisure and recreation, social services, consumer advice and housing. You would learn about government policies, and the institutions which currently provide services for the public. Within this context, the degree aims to give students an understanding of, and expertise in, areas of management which are relevant to the provision and delivery of services.

There are five streams, or sets of modules, which run in parallel through the programme.

- The *contextual stream* deals with the institutions and legislation which structure public and voluntary organisations.

- The *options stream* enables students to look in more depth at particular areas of social policy - such as education, housing, health care - and to examine the organisations which have been set up to produce these services

- The *management stream* focuses on the role and work of managers in the public and voluntary sectors. It analyses how organisations work, how co-operation between and within organisations can be hindered or achieved and what is meant by public accountability.

- The *techniques* and *economics streams* add to these skills by providing training in the information needs of managers, and the ways of analysing situations and problems.

Part of the degree requirement involves a part-time fieldwork placement within a public or voluntary organisation. This takes place during the third year and forms an important, and assessed, element of the degree programme. For, as well as providing relevant work experience, it gives you a glimpse of some of the real-world practicalities of public policy management.

Joint honours degrees are suitable for students who, while interested in studying Social Policy, also wish to pursue a companion subject in depth. The first year of all the degrees is very similar, while in the later years the equivalent of five single Social Policy modules and five single modules in the second discipline are studied.

Career Opportunities

Social policy graduates enter a wide range of careers, and national surveys show that there is a very good record of finding work in both the public and private sector. In general, a social policy degree is useful for any career that involves working with people. Typical careers for which social policy is particularly relevant include management or policy work in central or local government; human resource management; leisure and sports management; health service management and health education; law; the police; penal institutions; work in voluntary agencies.

In addition, social policy affords a good general grounding for those wishing to pursue careers in media or journalism, social research, nursing, librarianship, computing, retail management, marketing, teaching or work in developing countries.

These days, many careers require professional training as well as a first degree, and many social policy graduates continue their education either on postgraduate courses or when they begin employment.

Related Degrees

Public and Social Policy, Social Administration and Policy, Public Policy and Community, Housing Studies

Suggested Reading

Changing Welfare, Changing States: New Directions in Social Policy
- John Clarke, Sage, 2004

Critical Social Policy: A Reader
- David Taylor (ed.), Sage, 1996

The Classic Slum: Salford Life in the First Quarter of the Century
- Robert Roberts, Penguin, 2005

The Student's Companion to Social Policy
- Pete Alcock et al, WileyBlackwell, 2008

Social Policy
- John Baldock et al, OUP Oxford, 2007

Further Information

Social Policy and Social Work
www.swap.ac.uk

Institute of Public Administration, Ireland
www.ipa.ie

Social Work

Original article by Professor Ralph Firth, University of Northumbria

Introduction

A degree in Social Work will enable you to develop the skills for pursuing a career in social work by integrating academic study and professional practice. On successful graduation you will be eligible to register with the General Social Care Council (GSCC), which is responsible for regulating the workforce in England. There are equivalent bodies for the other countries of the United Kingdom.

You will be introduced to issues surrounding social welfare, social exclusion and models of intervention, together with the opportunity to explore specialist areas such as children and young people, adults and mental health.

The overall aim of the course is to equip you with the skills to become a competent social work practitioner. You will:

- Understand and promote social justice and challenge injustice
- Understand national/international issues in social work and values of diversity, equal opportunities and social work principles
- Work professionally with social workers and other professions, and understand the benefits of inter-professional collaboration
- Use skills to create change in individuals, families, communities and organisations and be able to evaluate their contributions to change
- Think critically and analytically in applying skills, and be able to transfer to a variety of environments over time
- Monitor and evaluate your own development and practice.

At some universities, you will study units alongside other students in health and social care, such as nurses, midwives, community workers, and occupational therapists. This inter-professional learning reflects the reality of the health care environment, where communication between professions is crucial to ensuring correct and appropriate care of clients.

Degree Courses

On a typical course, Year One units would include:

- Social Exclusion and Discrimination - exploring the nature and impact of possible causes of social exclusion and discrimination. You would also be introduced to sociological and anthropological enquiry
- Psycho-social Perspectives - learning the key theories and concepts of psycho-social development. This will enable you to appreciate that effective practice is grounded in knowledge and understanding of how people develop and change over time
- Models and Theories of Social and Community Work - introducing you to the underpinning methods, models and principles and values of social work and community work in contemporary society
- Law and Social Policy - developing an understanding of law and relevant social policy to meet social work demands
- Practice Learning in the Community - providing the work experience you require to meet the requirements of the regulatory body
- Communication and Group Working - developing communication skills and exploring group processes in both professional and partnership settings.

Year Two units would include:

- Mental Health and Working with Adults - developing an understanding of the social work role in relation to specific service user groups
- Safeguarding in Children's Services - developing your competence in assessment, intervention and evaluation in work with children, young people and their families/carers
- Globalisation and Marginalisation - considering the relationship between global processes, social policies and health and social care professions

- Practice Learning
- Exploring Evidence to Guide Practice.

Final year units would include:

- Safeguarding in Adult Social Services - giving an introduction to social work with adults
- Child Protection - developing your knowledge and understanding of child protection, including responsibilities, analytical skills and knowledge, practical skills and professional accountability
- Politics and Ideology
- Practice Learning
- Special Interest Study - requiring you to undertake a critical evaluation of a specific area of interest relating to your profession

Career Opportunities

The primary purpose of all programmes is to prepare students to be competent workers, working effectively and sensitively in a variety of statutory and voluntary agencies which provide social work and social care services. In all fields, job prospects are currently excellent and should continue to be, given the demographic trends.

As Social Work has a strong vocational element, you should check out if you actually enjoy working with people, and try getting involved in community and voluntary activities. The ability to work in a team, listen, see the other viewpoint, show care, concern and control are all key elements in social work practice, and you can test out your skills in these areas before applying

Related Degrees

Applied Social Work, Youth Studies, Community Studies, Counselling Studies and Society, Family and Child Care Studies, Women's Studies, Human/Community Care

Suggested Reading

Social Work Practice
- Veronica Coulshed and Joan Orme, Palgrave Macmillan, 2006
Effective Practice Learning in Social Work
- Jonathan Parker, Learning Matters, 2010
Modern Social Work Practice
- Steven Shardlow and Mark Doel, Ashgate, 2005
The Blackwell Companion to Social Work
- Martin Davies Ed, WileyBlackwell, 2007

Further Information

Social Work Careers (Site under review as we go to press)
www.socialworkcareers.co.uk
Social Policy and Social Work
www.swap.ac.uk
Student Social Workers
www.studentsocialworkers.co.uk
Skills for Care
www.skillsforcare.org.uk
General Social Care Council (functions transferring to Health Professions Council by 2012)
www.gscc.org.uk
Scottish Social Services Council
www.sssc.uk.com
Institute for Research and Innovation in Social Services, Scotland
www.iriss.ac.uk
Irish Association of Social Workers
www.iasw.ie

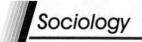

Sociology

Original article by Dr Jane Pilcher, University of Leicester

Introduction

A complex society surrounds us and shapes every aspect of our lives. In order to understand ourselves, we have to understand how that society works. Sociology attempts to do this through studying the relationship between people and social groups, the role of social institutions (like the family, paid employment, or education) and how all of these are related to the wider society. Students are encouraged to think and work in original and critical ways.

One way in which sociology tries to answer questions about contemporary society is through comparing it with earlier periods of history and with other societies around the world. Through encouraging students to think comparatively, sociology helps to increase our understanding of processes of social change and the distinctiveness or otherwise of current social arrangements. Sociological ideas or concepts and theories about how social groups, institutions and societies work are also tested through carrying out research, and in this way, we can see whether our ideas and theories match the way that society is organised.

Sociology isn't new. Most basic social theory, particularly the work of Karl Marx, Max Weber and Emile Durkheim has a pedigree dating from the nineteenth century. If you want a taste of timeless social theory, read the Communist Manifesto by Karl Marx and Frederick Engels (Bookmarks Publications).

You won't get much of a chance to research real live people actively and personally on a typical three-year course, although you will get a chance to study sociological analyses and descriptions of what life is like for other people. A brilliant example of what your and other people's life is like as seen through the eyes of a sociologist is Erving Goffman's The Presentation of Self in Everyday Life (Penguin).

A common but erroneous idea is that sociology analyses those bits of society which are left after economics, psychology and anthropology have carved off their bits. In fact the reverse is true. Sociology can be distinguished from all other disciplines through its ability not only to analyse society without the use of other disciplines (which is its chief function) but also to analyse competently the operations of all other disciplines. Natural science itself has become a target for some sociologists. They enquire: how do scientists make discoveries? Is it some sort of magical process? How is it that, occasionally, several scientists simultaneously but individually discover the same thing? Coincidence? If you want to know how it actually happens, take a look at Thomas Kuhn's The Structure of Scientific Revolutions (University of Chicago Press).

Degree Courses

Here is an example of sociology provision at one university. The BSc degree allows full-time study of sociology throughout three years, while the BA degree has a first year consisting of sociology and two supplementary social science subjects. Both courses, like most sociology degrees, are designed to introduce the subject, cover its central areas and enable considerable choice of specialised areas of study through optional modules.

All BA and BSc sociology students take modules in theory (Sociological Analysis modules, Sociological Texts modules), methods (Research Sources and Methods modules) and the comparative study of societies (Contemporary Societies modules). Although these modules are compulsory, a range of optional modules provides students with opportunities to construct large parts of their degree according to their own interests. Optional modules offered by the Sociology Department include Health, Illness and the Body, Popular Music and Society, Crime and the City, Research Project Option, Popular Culture and the Mass Media, Sociology of Education, Schools and Society, Childhood and Society, the Rise of Japan, Consumer Society, Race and Identity Politics and Football and Society.

Career Opportunities

Graduates enter administration, operational management, sales, marketing, buying, financial work, information, library, museum work and teaching/lecturing, in addition to employment in social work, the probation service and government, eg immigration, welfare advisory work, careers advisory services and so on. About 25% undertake further full-time study and training on graduation, leading into some of the above areas.

Related Degrees

Social Policy, Social Research, Social Sciences, Social Studies, Cultural Studies, Women's Studies

Suggested Reading

See suggestions in paragraphs 3, 4 and 5 above

The Student's Companion to Sociology
- Jon Gubbay, Chris Middleton & Chet Ballard (eds.), Blackwell, 1997

Thinking Sociologically
- Zygmunt Bauman and Tim May, Blackwell, 2001

Foundations of Sociology: Towards a Better Understanding of the Human World
- Richard Jenkins, Palgrave Macmillan, 2002

Further Information

British Sociological Association
www.britsoc.co.uk

Sociological Association of Ireland
www.sociology.ie

Speech Sciences

Original article by Dr Jane Maxim and Dr Janet A Wright
Department of Human Communication Science, University College, London

Introduction

When people talk to each other, a complex series of messages is sent out, received, understood and then responded to. The processes involved in human communication require the interaction of several brain functions, neuromuscular mechanisms, sight and hearing. Listening, for most people, involves paying attention to what is being said, to facial expression and body posture. Such complex processes may break down or not develop along normal patterns. Speech sciences is the study of these processes in both normal and abnormal human communication. There are several degree courses in this area, which usually appeal to students interested in speech therapy, audiology or the education of children with special needs. Not surprisingly, this science requires students to look at a range of widely differing subjects in order to acquire the integrated knowledge necessary to understand human communication. Speech sciences cross the boundaries between science and the arts, including anatomy, physiology, psychology, phonetics, linguistics, sociology, education, medical sciences and speech pathology and therapeutics.

It may seem incredible that we still know so little about human communication but it is certainly the most complex of human functions and, perhaps because of this complexity, we are still only at the start of solving this particular jigsaw puzzle. Let us consider how we understand just one word. We know that when it is heard, the acoustic and phonetic or speech sound properties have to be decoded. The brain then has to decide whether it has heard that particular word before. If it has then the word is processed to the semantic system, where its meaning is retrieved. But, even within this simple process, we still know very little about where words are stored in the brain and how they are stored in the semantic system.

For the student who is academically adventurous and sees research as a possible future goal, this field still holds many possibilities. For that same reason, this is not a field for those seeking ready-made solutions. Clients with communication disorders may have the same diagnosis but the severity of the problem and the way in which it affects that particular client mean that an individual programme of therapy has to be worked out for each client. Many students wishing to enter the field feel that they want to help such individuals but such a desire to help must be coupled with a real curiosity about human behaviour and what can motivate the individual to change that behaviour. The child with cerebral palsy or the adult with multiple sclerosis both have problems with neuromuscular co-ordination but the treatment needed may vary from a programme to help mildly unintelligible speech to the provision of a complex computer system through which the client may communicate.

In common with other science degrees, speech sciences require practical work. This component has two different strands: work in the laboratory concerned with speech and audiological sciences, and clinical work which takes place in a variety of settings. The practical work therefore has a dual purpose: to enable the student to understand normal and abnormal speech processes and to help the student apply that knowledge in a clinical setting. Knowledge used in a clinical environment also needs to be applied in a way which is appropriate for the client-therapist relationship; in other words, the student learns how to apply personal and communication skills in a professional and effective way. The application of these skills also has to be implemented with a compassionate understanding for that particular individual. In some client groups the cause of the disorder may be a psychological disturbance, manifesting as, for example, a voice disorder. In such a case, the student learns how to differentiate a voice disorder resulting from vocal abuse and poor vocal production from a voice disorder which requires counselling or referral to the psychiatric or psychology service.

Degree Courses

Most courses in speech sciences begin with study of foundation subjects, which usually include human anatomy and physiology, psychology, phonetics, linguistics and research design and statistics. In any science degree, the last subject is usually a basic component without which the student is unable to understand research methodology and critically evaluate research.

Students are introduced to clinical work first by structured observation of normal communication - observing the development of children as babies, in nursery schools and at primary schools; maybe also observing elderly people so as to gain perspective of development across the whole life span. Students then go on to acquire their clinical skills in a variety of settings, such as community clinics, mainstream and special schools, hospitals and rehabilitation centres. Some may have clinical placements in homes for the elderly, centres for adults with severe learning disabilities and psychiatric units. The timing and length of these clinical placements tends to vary between courses. Most courses mix weekly clinical placements with longer periods in a particular setting, while others use a sandwich course model.

Career Opportunities

The majority of openings occur in the NHS, where speech and language therapists use their clinical skills with a wide range of patients. However, although employed by the NHS, many work in schools with children.

Related Degrees

Human Communication Sciences, Speech Science, Speech Pathology and Therapy, Linguistics and Language Pathology, Clinical Language Sciences

Suggested Reading

These are not about speech sciences and speech and language therapy directly. Some are explorations of the issues of language development or of communication breakdown. But if you find them interesting and thought provoking, this may be the study area for you:

The Articulate Mammal: Introduction to Psycholinguistics
- Jean Aitchison, Routledge, 2007

How to Manage Communication Problems in Young Children
- Myra Kersner and Jannet Wright Eds, David Fulton, 2002

A Career in Speech and Language Therapy
- downloadable from the Royal College of Speech and Language Therapists website below

Further Information

Royal College of Speech and Language Therapists
www.rcslt.org

National Health Service Careers
www.nhscareers.nhs.uk

Irish Association of Speech and Language Therapists
www.iaslt.com

Sport and Exercise Science

British Association of Sport and Exercise Sciences (BASES), the recognised professional body for promoting sport and exercise sciences in the UK

Introduction

Sport and Exercise Science is the application of scientific principles to the promotion, maintenance and enhancement of sport and exercise related behaviour. It is fast becoming one of the most popular subjects to study at both undergraduate and postgraduate level.

Most undergraduate sport and exercise science degrees tend to be based around three aspects of science - physiology, biomechanics and psychology. A graduate would, therefore, be expected to have a broad knowledge base covering all three aspects, together with interdisciplinary approaches:

> **Biomechanics:** an examination of the causes and consequences of human movement and the interaction of the body with apparatus or equipment through the application of mechanical principles

> **Physiology:** the branch of the biological sciences concerned with the way the body responds to exercise and training

> **Psychology:** the branch of sport and exercise science that seeks to provide answers to questions about human behaviour and mental processes in sport and exercise settings

> **Interdisciplinary:** seeking to contribute to the body of knowledge or solve a real-world problem in sport or exercise using two or more disciplines in an integrated fashion from the outset

With so many courses available, it is important that you consider which would be the best for you. To help you with this decision, use the following questions as a guide to the key characteristics to look for in a sport and exercise science degree:

- Are all three aspects of science covered, as well as interdisciplinary approaches?
- Are there good laboratory facilities to which you will have access? Check that there is a strong practical skills element to the course.
- How many of the staff are accredited by BASES?
- What active research and community projects exist? Involvement in these projects will allow you the opportunity to gain experience and skills beyond the formal curriculum. Universities with high-ranking research groups will generally publicise this.
- Does the course provide you with information on the career pathways of its graduates? Look for institutions that are successful in placing graduates in sport and exercise related occupations.

It is important that you obtain detailed information about the actual content of the courses for which you are thinking of applying. Courses with the same name often have very different content; equally, courses with different names may in fact cover the same material.

Some universities offer discipline-specific programmes of study, for example in the psychology of sport and exercise. These courses tend to provide less breadth of study than traditional sport and exercise science courses, although they may appeal to applicants with a very clear idea of their disciplinary interests and potential career progression. Generally, however, a broad understanding of sport and exercise science is best achieved through multidisciplinary study at undergraduate level. A specialism can then be developed through relevant postgraduate study.

Career Opportunities

The career opportunities available to sport and exercise scientists are expanding all the time and this expansion appears likely to continue for the foreseeable future. Most sports now recognise sports science as an integral part of their sport's development and success, and most athletes consider the application of sport science as an important part of everyday training and competition. In relation to exercise, many hospitals and Primary Care Trusts are starting to appoint specialists with exercise backgrounds to work in areas such as cardiac rehabilitation and health promotion. The very fact that the National Health Service (NHS) plan has incorporated physical activity within its national service frameworks highlights both the job opportunities and the increasingly important role played by exercise in maintaining the nation's health.

Despite the increasing number of job opportunities in sport and exercise science, the number of sport and exercise science graduates is also growing, making competition for jobs intense. You should, therefore, take every opportunity to develop yourself whilst at university, by getting involved in activities that will enhance your career prospects.

Recent data suggest that 60% to 75% of sport and exercise science graduates find immediate employment after completing their first degree, while 15% to 20% go on to further study. Unemployment rates of sport and exercise science graduates 12 months after graduation are generally in the region of 5% to10% but this is often down to personal choice (e.g. a period spent travelling) rather than inability to find a job.

Around 50% to 60% of sport and exercise graduates enter jobs directly related to their area of study. The remainder use the skills and knowledge they have acquired during their degree to enter the wider job market as graduates with a strong and applied background in human science.

One increasingly popular option is to follow a taught Masters programme in sport and exercise science. Whilst the costs involved can be considerable, the long term returns in both financial and job satisfaction have been shown to be well worth this initial investment. The general expectation here is that applicants will be looking to develop an area of specialism based upon a more broad-based, undergraduate degree.

Related Degrees

Sports Studies, Sport and Management, Sport Development, Coaching Science, Physical Education, Sports Therapy, Fitness and Health.

Suggested Reading

Guide to careers in Sport and Exercise Sciences
- downloadable from the BASES website below
Sport and Exercise Science: an Introduction
- Dean Sewell, Murray Griffin, Philip Watkins and Ken Roberts, Hodder Arnold, 2005
Physiology of Sport and Exercise
- Jack H. Wilmore et al, Human Kinetics Europe Ltd, 2007

Further Information

British Association of Sport and Exercise Sciences
www.bases.org.uk
International Society of Biomechanics
www.isbweb.org
English Institute of Sport
www.eis2win.co.uk
National Strength and Conditioning Association
www.nsca-lift.org
Sport Scotland Institute of Sport
www.sisport.com
Sports Institute Northern Ireland:
www.sini.co.uk
Institute of Sport and Recreation Management
www.isrm.co.uk
UK Sport
www.uksport.gov.uk
Irish Sports Council
www.irishsportscouncil.ie

Town and Country Planning

Original article by Huw Thomas, Department of City and Regional Planning, University of Cardiff

Introduction

The Royal Town Planning Institute (RTPI) defines its basic discipline as 'spatial planning' and says that planning education should seek to "promote critical thinking about space and place as the basis for action or intervention." Spatial planning is regarded as much more than the operation of any statutory land-use system, or the broader historical concepts of town and country, or urban and regional planning, although it certainly embraces all of these.

Initial planning education is made up of three elements, two of which require academic study: 'spatial planning education' and 'specialist planning education.' The third element, known as the 'Assessment of Professional Competence' (APC), requires a period of structured experience in the workplace, culminating in a formal process of assessment.

Spatial planning education should be designed to provide a broad understanding of the main principles relevant to the making of place and the mediation of space, in particular sustainability, and of alternative ways in which such principles can be applied in practice. Emphasis should be placed on the integration of relevant knowledge, skills and values so as to produce rounded appreciation of how spatial planning can significantly enhance people's lives by improving the quality of place and organisation of space.

Specialist planning education should be designed to explore ideas, perspectives and debates to a considerable degree of depth in one distinct area of planning. The purpose of this is both to ensure that the breadth offered by a spatial planning programme is complemented by a period of in-depth study, and also to provide an opportunity to begin the process of specialisation. For some, this initial opportunity to specialise may subsequently be developed to a much higher level through professional experience, further in-depth study or lifelong learning. Although the RTPI does not seek to restrict what might qualify as a specialism, 'regeneration', 'environmental management', 'urban design', 'transport planning' and 'planning research' are examples of the scale expected.

Programmes that provide both the spatial and specialist element of planning education are now known as '**combined planning programmes**'. The RTPI believes that a healthy planning educational sector will be characterised over the next few years by a rich diversity of provision, with a range of spatial, specialist and combined programmes on offer to potential students.

Degree Courses

Students wishing to fulfil the RTPI's requirements for initial planning education must complete both its spatial and specialist elements. A four-year combined planning programme is required at undergraduate level to cover both these elements together. Students may alternatively choose to take an accredited three-year undergraduate programme covering only the spatial element of initial planning education but, in order to become Chartered Town Planners, they must subsequently complete an accredited specialist planning programme at graduate level which, if desired, could be taken at another planning school.

As an example, one school is now offering a brand new, restructured, fully accredited, four-year **BSc in City and Regional Planning**, which includes a placement in year three. The school also provides a choice of five areas of specialist study in the form of a one-year Masters Degree.

Career Opportunities

Planners work in a wide range of places and for a wide range of employers. Many follow careers in the private sector for consultancies; others choose the public sector, advising government or working for agencies providing specialist advice on the environment.

These are difficult times for all professionals connected with planning, surveying and construction, especially in the public sector. The economic climate has created uncertainty for employed planners, those who run their own practice and graduates looking to gain employment, leaving little doubt that the jobs market will remain challenging during 2010.

Planners have the opportunity to become involved in a wide range of disciplines, from traditional statutory planning through transport, regeneration, urban design and beyond. Planning's engagement with key national and international issues, such as climate change, housing supply and building sustainable communities, as well as development projects such as the 2012 Olympics, mean that planning's profile will become significant again when the economy strengthens.

Related Degrees

Urban Planning, City and Regional Planning, Urban Regeneration, Planning and Development, Design Development and Regeneration

Suggested Reading

Urban and Regional Planning
- Peter Hall and Mark Tewdwr-Jones, Routledge, 2010

Urban and Environmental Planning in the UK
- Yvonne Rydin, Palgrave Macmillan, 2003

Planning and Urban Change
- Stephen Ward, Sage Publications, 2004

Town & Country Planning in the UK
- Barry Cullingworth and Vincent Nadin, Routledge, 2006

Further Information

Royal Town Planning Institute
www.rtpi.org.uk

Irish Planning Institute
www.irishplanninginstitute.ie

Veterinary Medicine

Original article adapted from material supplied by the Royal College of Veterinary Surgeons

Introduction

There are seven universities in the United Kingdom and one in Ireland offering undergraduate Veterinary Medicine degree courses: Bristol, Cambridge, Edinburgh, Glasgow, Liverpool, London (Royal Veterinary College), Nottingham and University College Dublin. The length of the course is five years (six years at Cambridge).

The number of applications for entry to the Veterinary Schools far exceeds the number of places available. It is important to remember therefore that applicants who satisfy general entrance and course requirements are not necessarily guaranteed a place.

As well as the academic requirements, all of the university Veterinary Schools require candidates to show evidence of their interest and commitment by having gained experience of working in a veterinary practice and working with and handling animals, including livestock.

Degree Courses

The first two years are normally pre-clinical, involving lectures, practicals and tutorials, with a focus on the healthy animal. The newest course in the UK, at Nottingham, offers a clinically integrated programme throughout the five years. Although the title of the modules may vary, a typical university course will include anatomy, embryology, histology and physiology. You would also spend some time studying biochemistry, genetics, immunology and animal husbandry. You will learn about agriculture and will also study the nutrition and housing of animals.

Disease processes are studied in pathology, while courses on infectious disease and parasitology deal with the organisms that cause disease. You will become familiar with drugs used to combat disease and a course in pharmacology helps in this direction. Later in the degree course, in the clinical or final stage over your last two years, you will spend time on various aspects of veterinary clinical science

You are likely to be away from university, spending much of your time at the school's veterinary field station. When animals are diseased, their use for food is affected; you therefore study Veterinary Public Health (VPH), which encompasses issues relating to animals and the environment and food production methods as well as exposure to practical matters related to VPH e.g. community health.

In the earlier vacations during the course, you will normally be expected to spend time working on farms, in stables and in kennels, on what are known as extra-mural rotations. Later in the course, you will be expected to work in an abattoir and with veterinary surgeons in practice (possibly abroad).

The veterinary degree awarded by all the universities listed above confers on the holders the right to register and become a member of the Royal College of Veterinary Surgeons (MRCVS), and have your name listed within the RCVS Register of Members. Every veterinary surgeon has an obligation to deal with emergencies in any species at any time. Anyone contemplating a career in veterinary practice should remember this. A veterinary surgeon is a veterinary surgeon 24 hours a day, 365 days a year.

Career Opportunities

There are career opportunities in a number of areas including:

- **General Practice** - The veterinary surgeon is responsible for the maintenance of health and production of farm or domestic animals, for the prevention of disease and for the medical and surgical treatment of animals.

- **Veterinary Teaching and Research** - Teaching and research is undertaken at the Veterinary Schools and at research institutes, departments financed by the Government, in laboratories and by private enterprise. Many careers in research span the interface between human and veterinary medicine.

- **The Department for Environment, Food and Rural Affairs (DEFRA)** - A large staff, including veterinary surgeons, is maintained to control major epidemics. Other opportunities exist in commerce and industry, in the public health service and in countries overseas.

There is a growing trend towards specialisation in the veterinary profession within animal groups, such as farm animals, small animals and horses, or within disciplines, such as cardiology or anaesthesia. Any specialisation can only take place after first obtaining a veterinary science degree. There is a wide range of further postgraduate qualifications available, many of which can be taken by those working in practice.

Related Degrees
Bioveterinary Science, Equine Science, Veterinary Nursing, Animal Science, Veterinary Conservation Medicine, Pre-Veterinary Science, Animal Nutrition and Physiology, Animal Science, Care and Management

Suggested Reading
Getting into Veterinary School
- James Barton, Trotman, 2009 (new edition due February 2011)

Small Animal Surgery Secrets
- Joseph Harari, Hanley and Belfus, 2004

Veterinary Science...for all walks of life
- series of short films viewable on the VetCareers channel on YouTube

Further Information
Royal College of Veterinary Surgeons
www.rcvs.org.uk

VetCareers Channel on YouTube
www.youtube.com/vetcareers

Department for Environment, Food and Rural Affairs
www.defra.gov.uk

Veterinary Ireland
www.veterinary-ireland.org

Veterinary Council of Ireland
www.vci.ie

Zoology

Original article by Professor R McNeill Alexander, Leeds University

Introduction

Zoology is about animals, including the whole range from protozoans (although these are no longer formally included in the animal kingdom) to humans. It is about corals, beetles, dinosaurs, lions and all the rest. Zoology is also about all aspects of the structure and lives of animals. It includes the biochemistry of animals, not so much the universal processes of the tricarboxylic acid cycle and suchlike, which are studied mainly in biochemistry courses, but more special processes such as the metabolic tricks that enable tapeworms to live in the anaerobic environment of our guts. It includes the structure of animals, of their cells, their organs and their whole bodies, the amazing diversity of form in the animal kingdom and the ways in which structure is adapted to different ways of life. It is about how animal bodies work, dealing with all aspects of physiology but taking special notice of differences between animal groups. If you study physiology at university you will learn how 'typical' muscles (in practice that means frog muscles) work, but if you study zoology you will learn also about many other kinds of muscle: the muscles of insect wings with their built-in resonance, the special muscles that lock clams shut, and so on. Zoology includes the behaviour of animals, how their nervous systems control their behaviour and why particular behaviour patterns have evolved.

Zoology includes animal ecology, the study of the interactions of animal populations with each other, with plants and with the physical environment. Behavioural ecology asks what are the best ways to behave that will be favoured by natural selection. Should a redshank eat every worm it finds or just the big juicy ones, should a stag fight a rival and risk injury, and so on? Finally, zoology includes evolutionary theory, both the basic theory of how evolution works, and the evolutionary history of animals.

Degree Courses

Zoology is not all like the natural history programmes on television. It is about gorillas and whales and strange animals in exotic places, but there is a lot more to it than that. It involves painstaking work in laboratories with advanced, complex equipment. It involves difficult concepts, some of them mathematical. It involves muddy fieldwork and messy, sometimes smelly, dissections.

You should be prepared for dissection (that means cutting up dead animals). Some schools now do little or no dissection, and zoologists on degree courses do much less than in the past, but a limited amount of dissection is generally regarded as an essential (and very rewarding) part of a degree course in zoology. You cannot really appreciate how an animal is built until you yourself have taken it apart, and zoologists need dissecting skills for many kinds of research. Nearly all the zoologists I know have a profound respect for life and are careful not to cause pain to animals, but feel that it is justifiable to kill a few members of common species both for research and for teaching, and also of course to use animals that have died naturally. If you feel otherwise you probably ought to avoid zoology (and most other biological subjects).

Zoology is not an easy option for students who have trouble with physics and mathematics. Zoologists use physics to explain how nerves, muscles and cilia work; to sort out the osmotic problems of life in fresh water; to understand the heat balance of desert animals; and for many other purposes. The mathematics we use is not just statistics (though that is important). We use mechanics to explain how people and other animals run, how fish swim and how birds fly; we use computer models to develop ecological theories; and we use calculus to work out optimum strategies for behaviour and reproduction. We also use chemistry, as is well known. Most zoology lecturers assume that their students have a good basic knowledge of biology but may know less about some of the other sciences and teach accordingly.

Many people study zoology simply because they are interested in animals (an excellent reason). Others have more practical motives. Zoology is the essential basis for conservation work, and for understanding the effects of pollution. It deals with agricultural pests, with parasites that cause disease in humans and farm animals and with vectors (such as mosquitoes) that transmit diseases. It is important for commercial fisheries and for aquaculture. Finally, much of our understanding of humans comes from research done by zoologists on other species.

Career Opportunities

Graduates enter posts in the medical/veterinary industries and professions, the Civil Service, agricultural industries, pharmacy, teaching and also financial and general administrative/management careers

Related Degrees

Animal Biology, Applied Zoology, Zoology with Industrial Experience, Parasitology, Marine Zoology, Biological Sciences (Zoology), Animal Ecology

Suggested Reading

How Animals Work
- Knut Schmidt-Nielsen, Cambridge University Press, 2008

The Blind Watchmaker
- Richard Dawkins, Penguin, 2006

Oxford Dictionary of Zoology
- Michael Allaby, OUP Oxford, 2009

Integrated Principles of Zoology
- Cleveland P Hickman et al, McGraw-Hill Higher Education, 2010

The Naked Ape
- Desmond Morris, Vintage, 2005

Further Information

Zoological Society of London
www.zsl.org

Edinburgh Zoo
www.edinburghzoo.org.uk

Dublin Zoo
www.dublinzoo.ie